The United States and the Future of Europe

Michael Kaeding · Johannes Pollak ·
Paul Schmidt
Editors

The United States and the Future of Europe

Views from the Capitals

Springer

Editors
Michael Kaeding
Institut für Politikwissenschaft
University of Duisburg-Essen
Duisburg, Nordrhein-Westfalen, Germany

Johannes Pollak
Webster Vienna Private University
Wien, Austria

Paul Schmidt
Austrian Society for European Politics
Wien, Austria

ISBN 978-3-031-83349-6   ISBN 978-3-031-83350-2 (eBook)
https://doi.org/10.1007/978-3-031-83350-2

© The Editor(s) (if applicable) and The Author(s), under exclusive license to Springer Nature Switzerland AG 2025

This work is subject to copyright. All rights are solely and exclusively licensed by the Publisher, whether the whole or part of the material is concerned, specifically the rights of translation, reprinting, reuse of illustrations, recitation, broadcasting, reproduction on microfilms or in any other physical way, and transmission or information storage and retrieval, electronic adaptation, computer software, or by similar or dissimilar methodology now known or hereafter developed.
The use of general descriptive names, registered names, trademarks, service marks, etc. in this publication does not imply, even in the absence of a specific statement, that such names are exempt from the relevant protective laws and regulations and therefore free for general use.
The publisher, the authors and the editors are safe to assume that the advice and information in this book are believed to be true and accurate at the date of publication. Neither the publisher nor the authors or the editors give a warranty, expressed or implied, with respect to the material contained herein or for any errors or omissions that may have been made. The publisher remains neutral with regard to jurisdictional claims in published maps and institutional affiliations.

This Springer imprint is published by the registered company Springer Nature Switzerland AG
The registered company address is: Gewerbestrasse 11, 6330 Cham, Switzerland

If disposing of this product, please recycle the paper.

The European Commission's support for the production of this publication does not constitute an endorsement of the contents, which reflect the views only of the authors, and the Commission cannot be held responsible for any use which may be made of the information contained herein

Foreword

The aftermath of a United States (U.S.) presidential election seems like the perfect point at which to take stock of transatlantic relations. Out with the old, in with the new. Or, in the case of President Donald Trump, it is a case of old and new. While the term 'transatlantic relations' suggests a singular, cohesive relationship, the truth is of course much more complex. Each European country brings its own interests and priorities to the table, which frequently diverge considerably, as this collection of chapters makes abundantly clear.

Still, there is an overarching theme in the transatlantic relationship: How do Europe and the U.S., broadly speaking, view each other? How much do they need each other? To what extent might they even depend on each other?

Richard Haas, the former President of the Council on Foreign Relations and Director of policy planning in the U.S. Department of State, arrived at a sober conclusion in 2011: 'Europe no longer matters'. For Haas, the facts were straightforward: Europe is no longer the region where the twenty-first century will be forged. The 'old continent' is increasingly irrelevant in world affairs and the era when transatlantic relations dominated U.S. foreign policy has thus come to an end.

Others have expressed similar sentiments in less diplomatic terms. During the Obama administration, frustration with European hesitancy over Ukraine's pro-democracy protests led Victoria Nuland, then U.S. Assistant Secretary of State, famously to exclaim in a leaked phone call, 'Well, f*** the EU'.

So, when even seasoned diplomats such as Richard Haas and Victoria Nuland over a decade ago had already reached the conclusion that Europe matters less and less for the U.S., one can only imagine how the incoming Trump 2.0 administration will be looking at Europe. Is Europe a valued partner or a continent that elicits fondness? Not really, it is a rather quaint destination for holidays and not much more.

The truth is that the gap between the U.S. and Europe has steadily grown. Between 2010 and 2023 alone, the cumulative growth rate of gross domestic product (GDP) reached 34% in the U.S., compared with 21% in the European Union (EU). Over the same period, labour productivity grew by 22% in the U.S., while the Eurozone managed just 5%. Those are just two indicators, but there are plenty more. Which are the largest global tech companies by market capitalisation? Here are the names: NVIDIA, Apple, Microsoft, Alphabet/Google, Meta/Facebook, Tesla and others. The list goes on and all are from the U.S. Indeed, there is not a single European company in the top 10—or top 20.

On environmental issues too, the gap between the U.S. and Europe will grow considerably during the next Trump presidency. Because whenever Donald Trump talks about climate change, he calls it 'the big hoax'. The Inflation Reduction Act (IRA), introduced by President Joe Biden and containing a historic commitment to build a new clean energy economy, is in the eyes of Donald Trump a 'green new scam'. The world can thus expect, in the words of Rachel Cleetus, the Policy Director at the Union of Concerned Scientists, 'that the incoming U.S. administration will take a wrecking ball to global climate diplomacy'. Leaving the Paris Climate Agreement yet again upon taking office will only be the first of many steps. Europe, on the other hand, will most likely continue to push ahead with its own domestic decarbonisation agenda, trying to lead by example at global level. Only time will tell whether or not Europe will unite around the objective of pursuing decarbonisation, while boosting industrial competitiveness, or whether it will fracture and falter. The coming years will clearly be a challenge for Europe's climate policy, but of course it is often said that every crisis can be turned into an opportunity.

Does this mean that the transatlantic relationship is doomed to fade, with Europe and the U.S. inevitably drifting apart, turning their backs on each other? The change may not be quick, but nevertheless it is a good starting point from which to accept the fact that those transatlantic heydays of the 1990s are over and they are not coming back.

Yet, strange as it may seem, the Russian war of aggression against Ukraine has strengthened the cohesion within the North Atlantic Treaty Organisation (NATO) (and enlarged the alliance!) and led altogether to a more passionate reengagement between the U.S. and Europe than we have seen for many decades. Defence spending in Europe has grown considerably, with even Germany having passed the 2% GDP threshold for military spending and is on its way to 3% or even 3.5% with the explicit support of the German public!

On energy, Europe is step by step reducing its reliance on Russian gas. At the same time, it has increased its liquefied natural gas (LNG) imports, much of which has been supplied by the U.S.

Economically, the volume of transatlantic trade in goods and services is still huge and going up year on year. An annual value of EUR 1 trillion makes it the world's largest economic relationship by far. Make no mistake, we are still each other's best customers.

When it comes to defence issues, 'strategic autonomy' for Europe is still not much more than a buzz phrase. However, the realisation grows all over Europe that it is not the greatest of all strategies to leave Europe's security in the hands of 'the voters of Wisconsin every four years', as stated by French Minister Delegate for European Affairs Benjamin Haddad.

Furthermore, the mood in the U.S. might slowly be changing. In the past, the U.S. was less than enthusiastic about Europe trying to develop its own defence capabilities. As one U.S. defence official once put it: 'I told my wife this morning that I wanted some more strategic autonomy. Tonight, I was sleeping alone in a hotel room...'. An incoming Trump administration, though, might look somewhat differently at the emergence of new European defence capabilities. 'You want to grow up and do more for yourselves? Be our guests'.

Finally, there's the shared challenge of China. If the U.S. hopes to confront China effectively, it will need all the allies it can gather together. An enhanced cooperation with Europe will be essential if the goal is to forge a common front. Because after all, if one is truly interested in securing a stable, peaceful and fundamentally liberal world order the U.S. and Europe must lock arms and find all the allies we can find in this endeavour. Turning away from this simple reality would mean inviting defeat in the struggles that lie ahead.

By contrast, a Europe that is alienated by an uncompromising 'America First' agenda will be much more tempted to cut its own deals and try to escape the tit-for-tat cycle of escalating trade retaliations with China and beyond. After all, Europe is far less inclined to view China as a threat than the U.S. is.

When all is said and done, one can surely turn one's back on the 'aged transatlantic alliance' in disdain. However, that would have serious consequences on both sides of the Atlantic—simple as that!

Martin Weiss
President and Chief Executive Officer
of the Salzburg Global Seminar,
Salzburg, Austria

Why This Book?

The U.S. election results of the 5 November 2024 sent shockwaves around the globe. An impressive victory made Donald J. Trump the 47th President of the U.S. Most Europeans watched anxiously as swing-state after swing-state fell to a convicted perpetrator of sexual violence, providing him with a comfortable majority in both houses. Backed by a six-justice majority of conservative and originalist Republican appointees on the current Supreme Court and the first popular vote win for the Republicans since 2004, Trump did not waste any time appointing cabinet members. Usually, appointments are understood to give some clues about the broad future direction of an administration. If this is the case, the overwhelming conclusion is that these recess appointments will serve as a major disruption for U.S. politics, both domestic and foreign. While Europe and the world still look on with a mixture of shock and amazement, the usual and repetitive calls for a 'European awakening' can be heard. Yet, words are not enough.

Trade

The relationship between the U.S. and Europe has been one of sturdy support for almost 100 years. Despite all the different interests, they have worked together as partners to secure a liberal world order. The U.S. did so with the backing of a force capable of being projected anywhere around the globe, while the Europeans tried to convince with the power of democracy and the EU single market. Today, the U.S. and Europe account for 25% of world trade. Their bilateral trade has picked up pace, reaching an all-time high of EUR 1.2 trillion in 2023, surpassing pre-pandemic levels by more than 10%. The U.S. (EUR 1.483 trillion, 9.6%) alone was the third largest exporter in the world, preceded by China (EUR 2.844 trillion, 18.4%) and the EU (EUR 2.181 trillion, 14.1%). It was the largest importer in the world (EUR 2.482 trillion, 15.8%), followed by China (EUR 2.273 trillion, 14.4%) and the EU (EUR 2.126 trillion, 13.5%). In 2022, the U.S. was the largest partner for EU exports of goods (19.8%) and the second largest partner for EU imports of goods (11.9%). Following Russia's invasion of Ukraine and the imposition of bans on many Russian products, the U.S. has to some extent replaced Russia as partner particularly for some energy products.

However, Trump's intention to protect U.S. economic interests by introducing huge tariffs are not only testament to a lack of understanding and interest in how international economic relations work, but ultimately it could also make the average U.S. household poorer, and potentially not just U.S. households. Such measures could potentially disrupt the European economy, given such strong trading ties.

Security

While trade relations historically have been a story of success, albeit with occasional friction, for instance over the proposed Transatlantic Trade and Investment Partnership (TTIP), this was not only to do with protection of agricultural goods on both sides, but also steel safeguards measures, biotech products (such as genetically modified organisms), beef hormones and foreign sales corporations. Hitherto, the first cracks in security cooperation appeared in 2003 with part of Europe, especially Germany and France, rejecting the U.S. reason given for disarming and invading Iraq. Indeed, according to public polls in 2003, 82% of respondents disagreed with this action. This triggered the Secretary of State Donald Rumsfeld's biting comment dividing Europe into old and new. Ever since, sometimes more tactfully, sometimes less, U.S. presidents have urged Europe to step up its defence efforts. The NATO countries have largely lived up to their defence spending commitment.

However, in the context of Russia's continuing aggression against Ukraine and new European security architecture on the horizon, the 2% ceiling will not be adequate by a long shot. Amidst Trump's outlandish statements about ending the Ukraine war 'within 24 hours' Europe needs to be ready for a higher degree of involvement and coordinate its contingency planning for possible new and large waves of refugees from war-torn Ukraine. Should the new U.S. administration really decide to reduce or stop support for Ukraine, it remains highly doubtful if Europe can master the will and resources to step up its efforts sufficiently. This is all against the background of a weakened French Presidency, a Germany that has largely been rudderless for the better part of 2024, and an emboldened Hungarian prime minister looking for allies to join his calls for an end or a loosening of sanctions against Russia.

A Glass Half Full

Yes, one could also look at the glass half full. In the political arena, a new European Commission is up and running and pressure will be on for the next German government to show European leadership. Meanwhile, Poland is filling the gap by increasing its European and international weight, in particular in the area of security and defence. Moreover, when reality catches up, it may not be Hungary, but Italy or Poland who might become the pragmatic transatlantic bridge-builders that political strategists are looking for.

Since 2014, the EU has been developing guidelines for its foreign policy (EU Global Strategy of 2016) and a number of strategies aimed at controlling air, territories, sea areas, cyber domains and space through, for example, a cybersecurity strategy, a space strategy and a maritime strategy. The EU Maritime Strategy was the first of these adopted in 2014 and experiencing constant updating ever since. Today, European Coordinated Maritime Presence focuses on the Mediterranean, the West Indian Sea (notably the Horn of Africa) and the Gulf of Guinea. Moreover, terms for the Strategic Compass of 2023 were agreed, which basically formulates two tasks: the need to invest more in defence capabilities and the 'ability to work with partners to safeguard' European interests and values. In addition, the concept of strategic autonomy, namely the capacity to enhance Europe's self-sufficiency and independence in critical areas while staying open to global trade and cooperation, was again at the centre of the European Council's Versailles Declaration of 11 March 2022. Furthermore, the war in Ukraine has prompted an unprecedented 18% increase in defence spending for 2024 among NATO allies across Europe and Canada. In addition, its enlargement to include Finland and Sweden signifies not only the importance of this alliance, but also a considerable strengthening of NATO's northern flank.

Moreover, Europe has shown resilience in the face of Russian fossil fuel cuts. Within a very short time-span, Europe banned the import of Russian oil and cut its imports of Russian gas considerably, the costs of which to European economies were certainly not marginal. Moreover, Russia's action also provided the basis for massive investments in the renewable sector and a surge in U.S. LNG imports.

Most importantly, since the start of Russia's full-scale invasion of Ukraine on 24 February 2022, the EU and the U.S. have imposed unprecedented sanctions against Russia by freezing assets on most Russian banks and strategic industries, banning travel and restricting trade. At the end of 2024, the EU was readying its 15th package of sanctions against Russia, in close cooperation with the U.S. to align the implementation of sanctions, promote compliance, strengthen enforcement and address shared foreign policy challenges. Implementation and enforcement of EU sanctions are primarily the responsibility of EU Member States and circumvention is still a major challenge.

United by Diversity?

This book is essentially a political travel guide through Europe. It covers perspectives from 41 European countries, which give evidence of the importance and diversity of transatlantic relations, with different views and public perceptions, and provides a perspective from the U.S. in its epilogue. The collected chapters offer snapshots, first assessments from countries, and indeed the EU, of a changing environment and the possible impact of the second Trump presidency. Each contribution ends with recommendations of what Europe should do to weather the storm. They range from cries for more independence, strategic autonomy, investments in Europe's security architecture (e.g. France) and industrial infrastructure to a careful crafting of relations with China so as not to be drawn into a looming trade war (e.g. Germany). Other recommendations include a strengthening of cooperation in the area of technological advancement and climate change (e.g. Hungary); promoting the EU pillar within NATO, especially in view of hybrid warfare; and raising funds to invest in the European defence industry through Eurobonds (Estonia) as well as pushing for further NATO enlargement (Kosovo, Bosnia Herzegovina).

Trump and his team are not known for their interest in multilateral organisations and supranational institutions, but rather for defending strict national and transactional interests together with their preference for a 'divide and conquer approach'. Europe, by contrast, would be well advised to pool its power and negotiating leverage when dealing with the U.S. and, in many areas of cooperation, coordinate well and speak with one voice. However, judging by the chapters here, many countries seem to rely on perceived special, but likely deceitful, bilateral relationships. Trump's election and economic competition is likely to strengthen nationalistic tendencies in Europe, which would impact the various elections and formations of European governments, thus complicating European cooperation and exploiting the full potential of European integration.

When it comes to the respective public and party-political perception of the U.S. we find an overwhelmingly positive attitude (see Georgia, Italy, Kosovo, Poland, Lithuania, Latvia, Estonia) with a few, albeit notable, exceptions (see Bosnian Serbs, Bulgaria, Greece, Turkey). Moreover, there are those who clearly differentiate between the U.S. and Trump (see Iceland, Netherlands, United Kingdom, Germany). The Italian chapter, for example, posits whether Trump's victory is likely to embolden European far-right parties to promote the vision of a white, Christian and illiberal West of sovereign nationals. However, overall, we see a European political landscape clinging to the transatlantic relationship, even though such a preference might not be reciprocated from across the Atlantic.

For most countries, the U.S. is the largest trade and investment partner outside the EU. The EU-U.S. trade and investment relationship remains strong despite economic challenges related to the COVID-19 pandemic. The U.S. remains the EU's number one trading partner in services, which is matched by their mutual investments, which are the biggest in the world: total U.S. investment in the EU is four times higher than in the Asia-Pacific region; and EU foreign direct investment in the U.S. is around 10 times the total amount of EU investment in India and China. These are substantial drivers of the transatlantic relationship.

The vast majority of authors also emphasise the U.S.' pivotal and existential security involvement in Europe, with NATO demonstrating its vital role, despite the French president mistakenly having called it 'brain-dead'. Although there have been unprecedented increases in defence spending among NATO allies across Europe, certain EU Member States are still lagging behind the 2% of GDP commitment, namely Spain, Slovenia, Luxembourg, Belgium, Italy, Portugal and Croatia.

Consequently, the prospects for European political and security architecture hinge on U.S. policy towards Ukraine.

Yet, the U.S. partnership is also relevant for further shaping post-communist transitions across the European continent, including U.S. financial aid and the establishment of American Universities, strengthening democracy and the rule of law across the European continent, paving some countries' paths towards EU accession (Moldova, Georgia).

It is safe to say that Europe's efforts to uphold a rule-based liberal order will be tested to the full. Continuing to implement the Paris Climate Agreements, safeguarding World Trade Organisation (WTO) principles and the massive transformation of industrial and energy policies are areas of mutual interest where cooperation is a necessity. Notwithstanding, it might well turn out that Trump's 'America first' policies will shake the international system to the core. Instead of standing by and wondering how this could possibly have happened, Europeans need to seize this opportunity to implement reforms urgently. The Draghi, Letta and Niinistö Reports are available as guidebooks for reforming the European economic model and increasing resilience by deepening the Single Market, in addition to enlarging the Union and redesigning Europe's security architecture with a strong democratic anchor in EU values and the rule of law.

This book is not a scientific textbook, but rather a European journey as part of our 'Views from the capitals' series. Readers will travel through a tremendously complex, but dynamic and exciting political landscape elaborating on a breathtaking diversity that sometimes defines and divides, but ultimately unites this continent.

We would like to thank Allegra Wirmer, Project Manager at the Trans European Policy Studies Association (TEPSA), for the book's editorial processing and her tireless efforts in making this timely project become a reality.

November 2024

Michael Kaeding
Johannes Pollak
Paul Schmidt

Contents

EU Member States

From the Danube to D.C.: The Enduring Legacy of Austrian-U.S. Relations 3
Franz Eder and Martin Senn

In Good Times and in Bad: Cementing Belgo-U.S. Relations in an Age of Turmoil 7
Alexander Mattelaer

Mission (Im)possible: Big U.S. Brother Helps the Development of Bulgarian Democracy 11
Ivan Nachev and Hristo Panchugov

Croatia: Irreplaceable Strategic Partnership in Need of Additional Content 15
Hrvoje Butković

The U.S. And the Republic of Cyprus: Newfound Partners Amid Geopolitical Shifts 19
Zenonas Tziarras

Czechia and the United States: A Victim of Increased Global Instability? 25
Zdeněk Sychra and Petr Kratochvíl

Atlanticism in Times of Change: A View from Copenhagen 31
Mikkel Runge Olesen and Jakob Linnet Schmidt

Distant but Important Partner: Estonia and the U.S. 35
Merili Arjakas

Finland: From Partner to Ally in a World of Crises 39
Ville Sinkkonen and Niklas Helwig

**France, the U.S.' Oldest and Most Complicated Ally: A Stubborn
Defender of a Truly European Industrial and Defence Policy** 43
Marie Krpata

**A Tested Friendship: Ensuring the Resilience of U.S.-German
Relations in a Changing World** 49
Tobias Hofelich, Klara Stecker, and Funda Tekin

**From Myth to Reality: The Odyssey of U.S.-Greek Relations
Finding Safe Harbour** 55
Dimitris Tsaknis and Athina Fatsea

**The U.S. and the Future of Europe: Is There a Quest for Plan B
in Budapest?** 61
Ádám Kerényi

Ireland: An Unusual Transatlantic Partner 65
Andrew Cottey

Italy, the EU and the U.S.: A Multifaceted Bond 69
Riccardo Alcaro

A Friend in Need Is a Friend Indeed: Latvia and the U.S. 73
Karlis Bukovskis and Aleksandra Palkova

**Lithuania's Transatlantic Dilemma: How to Maintain U.S. Interest
in Baltic Security?** 77
Ramūnas Vilpišauskas

**Malta and the United States: A Common Interest in Mediterranean
Security** 83
Mark Harwood

Dutch-U.S. Relations: Navigating Atlanticism under Pressure 87
Giselle Bosse, Lion Lehmbecker, and Lia Spornraft

Devoted Atlanticists in Warsaw, Irrespective of Circumstances? 93
Magdalena Góra

**Portugal and Transatlantic Relations: A Bridge between the U.S.
and Europe** 99
José Gomes André and Alice Cunha

**The U.S.-Romania Relationship is Set to Stand the Test of Time
in a Volatile Global Context** 105
Mihai Sebe and Eliza Vaș

Slovak-U.S. Relations: Balancing Strategic Partnership 111
Kateryna Kasatkina and Lucia Mokrá

Slovenes Like the U.S., but not its Politics 115
Boštjan Udovič and Maja Bučar

Spain and the U.S.: Friends, Partners and Allies 119
Carlota García Encina

Sweden–U.S. Security Cooperation in a Changing World Order 125
August Danielson and Ulla Reinfeldt

EU Neighbours

From Staunch Enemy to Strategic Partner: Albanian-American
Relations in Transition 131
Albert Rakipi

The U.S. and Bosnia and Herzegovina—Ties that Do (not) Break? 137
Vedran Džihić

Changing Times, Changing Priorities: Will the U.S.-Georgian
Partnership Weather the Storm? 143
Irakli Sirbiladze and Giorgi Khishtovani

The Icelandic-U.S. Relations: Back on Track 149
Baldur Thorhallsson

The U.S. Impact on the Future of Europe: Views from Kosovo,
the Newest State in Europe 153
Labinot Greiçevci

The U.S. and Liechtenstein: Intensifying Relations Between
Unequal Partners 157
Sieglinde Gstöhl

Moldova-U.S. Partnership: Towards a More Ambitious
and Strategic Engagement 161
Iulian Groza and Mihai Mogildea

NATO's Reality to Montenegro; It Marks Real Progress 165
Danijela Jaćimović and Dženana Đurković

North Macedonia—U.S. Relations: Dominated by Politics
and Diplomacy 169
Irena Rajchinovska Pandeva

Norway and Transatlantic Relations: From Predictability
to Uncertainty 175
Pernille Rieker

Serbian-American Relations: Navigating Historical Alliances,
Open Conflicts and Strategic Partnerships 179
Sava Mitrović and Milena Mihajlović Denić

Switzerland: Sister Republics and Their Squabbles 185
Frank Schimmelfennig

U.S.-Turkey Relations and the EU: Managing Cooperation in an Era of Strategic Autonomy 189
Megan Gisclon

The Price and Weight of the Washington-Kyiv Strategic Partnership ... 193
Yuriy Yakymenko and Mykhailo Pashkov

Will the UK Choose America or Europe? 199
Brendan Donnelly

The Future of Transatlantic Relations 203

Contributors

Riccardo Alcaro Istituto Affari Internazionali, Rome, Italy

José Gomes André Practical Philosophy Research Group, Lisbon, Portugal

Merili Arjakas International Centre for Defence and Security, Tallinn, Estonia

Giselle Bosse Maastricht University, Maastricht, Netherlands

Karlis Bukovskis Latvian Institute of International Affairs, Riga, Latvia

Hrvoje Butković Institute for Development and International Relations, Zagreb, Croatia

Maja Bučar University of Ljubljana, Ljubljana, Slovenia

Andrew Cottey University College Cork, Cork, Ireland

Alice Cunha Portuguese Institute of International Relations, Lisbon, Portugal

August Danielson Swedish Institute of International Affairs, Stockholm, Sweden

Brendan Donnelly Federal Trust, London, England

Dženana Đurković University of Montenegro, Podgorica, Montenegro

Vedran Džihić Austrian Institute for International Affairs, Vienna, Austria

Franz Eder Foreign Policy Lab, Department of Political Science, University of Innsbruck, Innsbruck, Austria

Carlota García Encina Elcano Royal Institute, Madrid, Spain

Athina Fatsea ELIAMEP, Athens, Greece

Megan Gisclon Istanbul Policy Center, Istanbul, Turkey

Labinot Greiçevci Research Institute of Development and European Affairs, Pristina, Kosovo

Iulian Groza Institute for European Policies and Reforms, Chișinău, Moldova

Sieglinde Gstöhl College of Europe, Bruges, Belgium

Magdalena Góra Institute of European Studies, Jagiellonian University, Kraków, Poland

Mark Harwood Institute for European Studies, University of Malta, Msida, Malta

Niklas Helwig Finnish Institute of International Affairs, Helsinki, Finland

Tobias Hofelich Institut für Europäische Politik, Berlin, Germany

Danijela Jaćimović University of Montenegro, Podgorica, Montenegro

Kateryna Kasatkina Comenius University in Bratislava, Bratislava, Slovakia

Ádám Kerényi Institute of World Economics of HUN-REN CERS, Budapest, Hungary;
University of Szeged, Szeged, Hungary

Giorgi Khishtovani PMC Research Centre, Tbilisi, Georgia

Petr Kratochvíl Institute of International Relations Prague, Prague, Czechia

Marie Krpata French Institute of International Relations, Paris, France

Lion Lehmbecker Maastricht University, Maastricht, Netherlands

Alexander Mattelaer Centre for Security, Diplomacy and Strategy, VUB Brussels School of Governance, Ixelles, Belgium;
Egmont Institute, Brussels, Belgium

Milena Mihajlović Denić European Policy Centre (CEP), Belgrade, Serbia

Sava Mitrović European Policy Centre (CEP), Belgrade, Serbia

Mihai Mogildea Institute for European Policies and Reforms, Chișinău, Moldova

Lucia Mokrá Comenius University in Bratislava, Bratislava, Slovakia

Ivan Nachev New Bulgarian University, Sofia, Bulgaria

Mikkel Runge Olesen Danish Institute for International Studies, Copenhagen, Denmark

Aleksandra Palkova Latvian Institute of International Affairs, Riga, Latvia

Hristo Panchugov New Bulgarian University, Sofia, Bulgaria

Mykhailo Pashkov Razumkov Centre, Kyiv, Ukraine

Irena Rajchinovska Pandeva Iustinianus Primus Law Faculty, Ss. Cyril and Methodius University in Skopje, Skopje, North Macedonia

Albert Rakipi Albanian Institute for International Studies, Tirana, Albania

Ulla Reinfeldt Sweden's Youth Atlantic Treaty Association, Stockholm, Sweden

Pernille Rieker ARENA, Center for European Studies, Norwegian Institute of International Affairs, University of Oslo, Oslo, Norway

Frank Schimmelfennig Centre for Comparative and International Studies, ETH Zurich and University of Zurich, Zurich, Switzerland

Jakob Linnet Schmidt Danish Institute for International Studies, Copenhagen, Denmark

Mihai Sebe European Institute of Romania, Bucharest, Romania

Martin Senn Foreign Policy Lab, Department of Political Science, University of Innsbruck, Innsbruck, Austria

Ville Sinkkonen Finnish Institute of International Affairs, Helsinki, Finland

Irakli Sirbiladze PMC Research Centre, Tbilisi, Georgia

Lia Spornraft Maastricht University, Maastricht, Netherlands

Klara Stecker Institut für Europäische Politik, Berlin, Germany

Zdeněk Sychra University of West Bohemia, Pilsen, Czechia

Funda Tekin Institut für Europäische Politik, Berlin, Germany

Baldur Thorhallsson Institute of International Affairs, University of Iceland, Reykjavík, Iceland

Dimitris Tsaknis EPLO, Athens, Greece

Zenonas Tziarras University of Cyprus, Nicosia, Cyprus

Boštjan Udovič University of Ljubljana, Ljubljana, Slovenia

Eliza Vaş European Institute of Romania, Bucharest, Romania

Ramūnas Vilpišauskas Institute of International Relations and Political Science, Vilnius University, Vilnius, Lithuania

Yuriy Yakymenko Razumkov Centre, Kyiv, Ukraine

Abbreviations

CFSP	Common Foreign and Security Policy
CSDP	Common Security and Defence Policy
ECFR	European Council on Foreign Relations
EDTIB	European Defence Technological and Industrial Base
EEA	European Economic Area
EU	European Union
FDI	Foreign Direct Investment
GDP	Gross Domestic Product
IMF	International Monetary Fund
IRA	Inflation Reduction Act
IRI	International Republican Institute
LNG	Liquefied Natural Gas
MP	Member of Parliament
NATO	North Atlantic Treaty Organisation
NGO	Non-Governmental Organisation
OSCE	Organisation for Security and Co-operation in Europe
PESCO	Permanent Structured Cooperation
RoC	Republic of Cyprus
TTIP	Transatlantic Trade and Investment Partnership
UK	United Kingdom
UN	United Nations
U.S.	United States
WTO	World Trade Organisation

EU Member States

From the Danube to D.C.: The Enduring Legacy of Austrian-U.S. Relations

Franz Eder and Martin Senn

The U.S. is still one of Austria's most important political and economic partners. Most political parties and a solid majority of the population are in favour of good relations. Although Austria is moving closer to NATO, joining the alliance has little to no political backing.

Neutral and Western-Oriented

Ever since the U.S. liberated Austria from Nazi rule in 1945, relations between both countries have been close and friendly. Initially as an occupational force and then as a global hegemon with vested interests in establishing a liberal world order, the U.S. has been keen to ensure that Austria is independent and West-oriented. Despite taking on the status of permanently neutral state from 1955, Austria has always considered itself a part of the Western hemisphere, sharing its political (liberal democracy) and economic (free market) pillars. Accordingly, the U.S. acted as a guarantor of Austrian independence, while Austria contributed to U.S. hegemony with its unwavering support of U.S. interests (demonstrated, for example, by Austria's voting behaviour in the United Nations [UN], siding overwhelmingly with the U.S. or abstaining from votes critical to U.S. concerns).

This close and mutually beneficial relationship is underlined by the economic relations of both countries. Foreign direct investments (FDI) of the U.S. to Austria

---

F. Eder (✉) · M. Senn
Foreign Policy Lab, Department of Political Science, University of Innsbruck, Innsbruck, Austria
e-mail: Franz.Eder@uibk.ac.at

M. Senn
e-mail: Martin.Senn@uibk.ac.at

© The Author(s), under exclusive license to Springer Nature Switzerland AG 2025
M. Kaeding et al. (eds.), *The United States and the Future of Europe*,
https://doi.org/10.1007/978-3-031-83350-2_1

in 2023 accounted for up to EUR 14.5 billion (according to the National Bank of Austria), whereas Austrian FDI to the U.S. accounted for EUR 17.4 billion. In the same year, Austria imported goods and services from the U.S. worth EUR 7.9 billion and exported goods and services worth EUR 14.7 billion (according to the Statistical Office), resulting in a trade surplus of EUR 6.5 billion. According to the Austrian Federal Ministry for Labour and Economy, the U.S. "ranked second (behind Germany and before Italy) among Austrian export destinations. At a share of 7.4% of Austria's total exports, the USA remain by far the most important sales market both outside the EU and outside Europe (the share is three times higher than that of China)".

This close economic relationship is also reflected in the positive view of the U.S. by government institutions and most political parties. The Austrian Ministry of European and International Affairs is traditionally in favour of good transatlantic relations and its current minister is a particularly strong advocate. Beyond that, U.S. culture massively influences Austrian society when it comes to fashion, sports, music, TV and food.

Party Positions and Population Views

Most political parties, especially the Austrian People's Party (ÖVP), the Greens, the Liberals (NEOS) and with some restrictions the Social Democratic Party (SPÖ), have a positive view of the U.S. Only the Austrian Freedom Party (FPÖ), with its populist-right policy ideology, is increasingly becoming anti-American and more sympathetic to revisionist powers such as Russia. In addition, the Freedom Party conceives neutrality as a form of isolationism and political neutralism. This is due to its ideological orientation and its adverse stance towards concepts such as globalisation and liberal values. This also explains why the FPÖ is the only party that favours Donald Trump despite its inherent anti-Americanism. But the FPÖ's stance is also the result of electoral considerations. A decisive and slowly growing part of Austrian society is sceptical when it comes to economic globalisation and favours a more Austria/European-centred economic system ('Austria First').

Nevertheless, media (newspapers, TV and radio stations) have a positive view of the U.S., which also reflects public opinion. As data from the Austrian Foreign Policy Panel Project from 2023 show, almost half of the Austrian population is in favour of good relations with the U.S., compared to 43% for the UK and 37% for China (Germany is leading the list with 68.95%, followed by Italy and France with just over 50% in favour).

Moving Closer to but not into NATO

Austrian security profits massively from U.S. involvement in European affairs. As a neutral state with small armed forces and limited intelligence capabilities, Austria has been largely dependent on other countries and NATO to secure a stable Europe and to profit from intelligence exchange. Since the illegal and unprovoked Russian invasion of Ukraine, though, Austria has made steps towards a closer partnership with NATO and already trains its troops according to NATO standards. Although a membership is still unrealistic, given the population's support for neutrality and its critical stance towards NATO (68% are against joining NATO according to an Austrian Foreign Policy Panel Project survey from 2024), Austria is increasing its defence expenditures and starting to cooperate with NATO members on the European Sky Shield Initiative. When it comes to climate change, Austria has a more pronounced approach and is therefore critical of U.S. reluctance to take a more dominant position. This is also one of the major issues that influence Austrian scepticism towards (or even rejection of) the Trump administration. Austria also questions international trade relations—despite its rejection of the TTIP—and a possible retreat of the U.S. from European security affairs.

A Pro-U.S. Member State of the EU

Within the EU, Austria belongs to those Member States that are more U.S. friendly. Although not as close as countries such as the Netherlands or the Baltic states, Vienna articulates its pro-U.S. (and Israel) stance and hence influences the EU's position towards Washington in various international fora. Austria is especially interested in close trade relations with the U.S. and argues in favour of less trade restrictions. Hence, Austria overwhelmingly (except for the FPÖ) rejected the election of President Donald Trump, fearing that the U.S. could decouple itself from its trade and security relations with Europe.

Recommendations

Austria and the EU should increase their contributions to European security, thereby signalling to the U.S. that Europe is willing and capable of securing a stable European security architecture and hence worthy of American assistance. Within Europe, Austria should exert more pressure on the U.S. to increase its efforts in climate change mitigation.

Austria and the EU should take more responsibility in upholding the liberal world order, which serves their needs and interests most. The election of President Trump may contribute to the accelerated erosion of this order, the introduction of trade barriers and the rise of an illiberal order pushed by countries like China and Russia. Hence, only a strong Europe with a single voice in international affairs can counter this erosion and make it harder for a Trump administration to lay the transatlantic partnership to rest.

Franz Eder is an Associate Professor for International Relations in the Department of Political Science, University of Innsbruck, and Deputy Director of its Foreign Policy Lab. He is co-editor of the Handbook of Austrian Foreign Policy and an initiator of the Austrian Foreign Policy Panel Project.

Martin Senn is Professor of Political Science and Director of the Foreign Policy Lab in the Department of Political Science, University of Innsbruck, as well as a Lecturer at the Diplomatic Academy Vienna. He is co-editor of the Handbook of Austrian Foreign Policy and an initiator of the Austrian Foreign Policy Panel Project.

The Department of Political Science at the University of Innsbruck is home of the Foreign Policy Lab. This lab seeks to advance our understanding of Austrian foreign policy, promote public awareness and knowledge of Austrian foreign policy and world politics, stimulate public debate, strengthen the research community and foster the exchange between scholars and practitioners.

In Good Times and in Bad: Cementing Belgo-U.S. Relations in an Age of Turmoil

Alexander Mattelaer

For Belgium, a deeply rooted Atlanticism goes hand in hand with strong support for a federal approach to European integration. The key challenges ahead relate to maintaining Euro-Atlantic cohesion on strategic issues and resisting the siren song of economic protectionism on both sides of the Atlantic.

The Belgo-U.S. Relationship

Few foreign relations are as important to Belgium as that with the U.S. This multifaceted relationship is grounded in shared historical experience, most notably, the liberation of Belgian territory from Nazi occupation in 1944 and post-war reconstruction enabled by the Marshall Plan.

Today, the relationship continues to thrive in different domains. In economic terms, the U.S. is the fourth most important partner, after Germany, France and the Netherlands, for both imports and exports valued at around EUR 45 billion. This trade relationship encompasses goods and services and has remained broadly balanced over time (unlike the trade balance with China).

Furthermore, Belgium's NATO membership constitutes the cornerstone of its national security. In this framework, it maintains a deep bilateral security relationship with the U.S., ranging from cooperation in counterterrorism to nuclear

A. Mattelaer (✉)
Centre for Security, Diplomacy and Strategy, VUB Brussels School of Governance, Ixelles, Belgium
e-mail: a.mattelaer@egmontinstitute.be

Egmont Institute, Brussels, Belgium

deterrence. All of this underpins a political relationship that is rich in substance, nuanced in detail and overwhelmingly cooperative—notwithstanding the occasional policy disagreements.

Belgian Public Perceptions of the U.S.

Based on this multifaceted relationship, Belgians have largely maintained a positive public perception of the U.S.—especially in the more Anglophile northern part of the country. This can be strongly felt in terms of the influence that the U.S. wields regarding popular culture and political ideals. English has increasingly become the second language for all Belgian linguistic groups—turning it into an unofficial fourth *lingua franca* (alongside Dutch, French and German). This does not mean that all Belgians automatically subscribe to U.S. policy preferences. Especially in progressive circles, palpable unease exists over U.S. policy towards the Middle East (most notably its strong support for Israel) and the perceived influence exercised by the defence industrial complex.

Within the Belgian business community, widespread admiration of U.S. entrepreneurship and innovation combines with concern over the rise of economic protectionism—and the impact thereof on Belgian exports. As many Belgian businesses are part of the U.S. supply chain and significant investors in the U.S. economy (some EUR 73 billion in 2023), strong incentives are in place to maintain close economic relations. The ongoing diversification of Belgian society due to immigration is watering down as well as increasing cultural affinity with the U.S. Many new Belgians may lack the historical attachment to the transatlantic link, but their growing number—close to 200,000 immigrants every year—implies that Belgian society has increasingly more in common with the American melting pot than before. Whilst opinion polls indicate that high levels of migration do fuel the extreme right's electoral rise, this does not translate into major discontinuity in how foreign relations are perceived more generally—including that with the U.S.

Atlanticism and Europeanism as Twin Pillars of Belgian Foreign Policy

Successive Belgian governments have taken a voluntarist approach towards European integration. Strong Belgian support for the European project—including its federalist aspirations—is rooted in the country's geopolitical position on the map of the European continent and the country's fractious internal politics. As such, Belgium's position within the EU is conceptually separate from its relationship with the U.S.: Atlanticism and Europeanism are complementary reflexes in Belgian diplomacy (even if the latter has greater traction on the left and the former on the right of the political spectrum). Palpable concern exists over the potential for transatlantic trade rifts that result from protectionism on both sides of the Atlantic. This would force Belgian authorities and businesses into choices they do not want to make. When such choices become unavoidable, the trend is that economic policy will align itself with the European single market on which Belgian businesses critically depend, whilst security policy will remain more Atlantic in its preference.

Strategic Issues for Belgium: Deterrence, Allied Enablement and Euro-Atlantic Cohesion

As host nation to the principal NATO headquarters and founding member of the alliance, Belgium is acutely aware of how central the role of the U.S. is in underpinning deterrence and defence. First and foremost, this relates to extended nuclear deterrence. Belgium participates in NATO nuclear sharing by making personnel, equipment and infrastructure available to the nuclear mission. Notwithstanding the long-standing political contestation thereof by some parliamentarians (mostly on the left of the political spectrum), this continues to provide the foundation for all conventional defence plans. This is especially the case today when the Russian Federation is aggressively exploring the coercive value of its daunting nuclear arsenal.

In addition, the presence of major North Sea ports endows Belgium with a special responsibility for enabling the reception and onward movement of U.S. forces reinforcing the eastern flank. Finally, Belgium also counts on the U.S. as the ultimate backstop for meeting unexpected security contingencies. After the Brussels terrorist attacks in 2016, for instance, U.S. support was critical in addressing urgent operational requirements. In case of NATO Article 5 scenarios, the Belgian government also relies on the U.S. for providing leadership and buttressing alliance cohesion—by giving European countries greater confidence to stand and fight together rather than to fend for themselves.

Recommendations

Following the election of Donald Trump, outgoing Belgian Prime Minister Alexander De Croo immediately highlighted the need to strengthen the transatlantic bond. The increased uncertainty about U.S. security assistance in case of crisis is confronting the Belgian government with its own national responsibilities. The new Belgian coalition government led by Prime Minister Bart De Wever can be expected to look to maintain a healthy dose of continuity in its relationship with the U.S. It will do so by means of bilateral diplomatic engagement as well as Belgian positioning in the EU and NATO. Within the EU framework, Belgium should continue making the case for transatlantic economic interdependence. An important point of emphasis concerns the synchronisation of policy responses on the safeguarding and diversification of high-tech supply chains via the EU-U.S. Trade and Technology Council.

In considering the deteriorating security environment, Belgium should team up with the other European allies engaging in NATO nuclear sharing (and those keen to join the system) to propose necessary adaptions of the NATO nuclear deterrence policy (on which the most vulnerable allies in Eastern Europe critically depend). Finally, Belgium should urgently ensure that its national level of defence investment catches up with the European NATO average to shake its reputation as a free-rider—something that Donald Trump has been notoriously critical about. In this regard, the European Semester should incentivise Belgian defence investment as well as structural reforms in Belgium's public finances. In turn, this will allow for building stronger conventional defences as well as civil resilience mechanisms.

Dr Alexander Mattelaer is Professor of European Politics and International Security at the VUB Brussels School of Governance and a Senior Research Fellow at Egmont—the Belgian Royal Institute for International Relations. Within the VUB Brussels School of Governance, he is affiliated to the Centre for Security, Diplomacy and Strategy.

The Centre for Security, Diplomacy and Strategy seeks to contribute to a better understanding of key contemporary security and diplomatic challenges of the twenty-first century—and their impact on Europe—whilst reaching out to the policy community that will ultimately need to handle such challenges.

Mission (Im)possible: Big U.S. Brother Helps the Development of Bulgarian Democracy

Ivan Nachev and Hristo Panchugov

This chapter reviews the evolution of U.S.-Bulgarian relations, emphasising the U.S.'s role in Bulgaria's post-communist transition. The analysis highlights both positive and negative aspects, including U.S. cultural influence, defence cooperation and energy partnerships, while addressing the rise of anti-American sentiment driven by pro-Russian propaganda and media oligarch control. Also discussed here are challenges that hinder EU and U.S. support for Bulgaria's democracy.

Historical Background

Diplomatic relations between Bulgaria and the U.S. were established on 19 September 1903, but then interrupted in 1950, due to the Bulgarian government accusing a U.S. minister of espionage. They were subsequently restored a decade later. Caught between Soviet and American influence, bilateral relations with the U.S. significantly improved after the fall of communism. The U.S. played a critical role in Bulgaria's transition to democracy, supporting the development of a multi-party system and a market economy. By 1996, the U.S. had provided substantial financial assistance under the 1989 Support for Eastern European Democracies Act. Between 1990 and 2007, Bulgaria received USD 600 million in aid. In 1994, the Bilateral Investment Treaty granted Bulgaria most-favoured-nation trade status, thereby strengthening economic ties.

I. Nachev · H. Panchugov (✉)
New Bulgarian University, Sofia, Bulgaria
e-mail: h.panchugov@gmail.com

I. Nachev
e-mail: ivannachevbg@gmail.com

U.S. investments in Bulgaria for 2023 amounted to USD 514 million, with Bulgarian investments in the U.S. reaching USD 102 million. While trade between the two countries is growing, it still represents a small share of Bulgaria's overall trade, accounting for only 1.4% of imports and 2.3% of exports.

The 1990s saw a surge in Bulgarian-U.S. relations, especially after Bulgaria's 1997 NATO membership plan was secured, signalling a shift towards Euro-Atlantic integration. However, following Bulgaria's NATO accession and focus on EU membership, U.S. interest waned. Security and defence cooperation became the focal points of bilateral relations, driven by counterterrorism efforts and NATO operations. In 2020, a Strategic Dialogue was established, focusing on security, energy and Bulgaria's inclusion in the U.S. Visa Waiver Program and the Organisation for Economic Cooperation and Development.

Bulgaria hosts the American University, which was founded during 1991 in Blagoevgrad and continues to play a key role in promoting liberal democratic values across Southeastern Europe. The U.S. also maintains strong ties with Bulgaria's diaspora, particularly in cities such as Chicago and Los Angeles, where a combined of 300,000 Bulgarians live.

Public Perception: A Mixed Image

During the 1990s, Bulgarians largely viewed the U.S. positively, seeing it as a symbol of the Western world and democracy. The U.S. had a significant influence on Bulgarian society, especially in pop culture and the non-governmental organisation (NGO) sector. However, anti-U.S. sentiment began to rise during NATO-related crises, such as Bulgaria's decision to allow NATO air corridors during the 1997 Kosovo crisis. This opened the door to anti-U.S. rhetoric, fuelled by pro-Russian propaganda and disinformation.

Today, public opinion on the U.S. is mixed. With no real evidence of U.S. interference in Bulgarian politics or U.S. interests clashing with those of Bulgaria, citizens' views of the relationship are currently 35% positive, 30% negative and 35% undecided. Pro-Russian narratives, fake news and media manipulation play a significant role in shaping these attitudes, citing the U.S. as an imperialist power, willing to sacrifice Bulgarian interests for the sake of their own goals. The Bulgarian media landscape has deteriorated over recent years, with oligarchs controlling major outlets, leading to journalistic self-censorship and corporate pressure. The U.S. State Department has highlighted media manipulation as one of Bulgaria's most pressing human rights issues.

Anti-U.S. sentiment has further been exploited by populist parties such as Revival (*Vazrazhdane*) accusing American foundations, such as America for Bulgaria, of influencing key sectors such as media, education and politics, framing them as tools of U.S. interests. Revival even proposed a law resembling the U.S. Foreign Agents Registration Act, targeting foreign influence in Bulgaria's politics and NGOs.

Mainstream political parties such as Citizens for European Development of Bulgaria (GERB) and We Continue the Change (PP) seek U.S. support for foreign policy but do little to protect democratic values. This leaves space for Russian narratives to penetrate Bulgarian politics. The Bulgarian Socialist Party (BSP) does not regard the U.S. as a strategic partner, while the Movement for Rights and Freedom (DPS) faces internal division after one of its leaders was sanctioned under the Global Magnitsky Act.

Is Bulgaria on the Periphery of U.S. Interests?

Bulgaria initially held a peripheral place in U.S. strategic interests but gained prominence after 11 September 2001 and its inclusion in the global war on terrorism. The 2006 U.S.-Bulgaria Defence Cooperation Agreement gave the U.S. access to various Bulgarian military sites. In 2009, a double taxation agreement was signed.

The war in Ukraine and deteriorating U.S.-Turkey relations have renewed Bulgaria's strategic importance. Its position in the Black Sea region and role in maintaining regional security have put it back on the U.S. radar. Bulgaria has already increased military spending and modernised its armed forces, with U.S. support aimed at enhancing NATO interoperability. In this context, Bulgaria and the U.S. are developing a 10-year roadmap for bilateral defence cooperation.

Energy cooperation also holds promise, particularly in nuclear energy. In 2019, Bulgaria began exploring the licensing of American nuclear fuel to diversify its energy supplies. Despite uncertainty about future U.S. foreign policy following Trump's success in the 2024 presidential elections, Bulgaria remains a key partner in this sector.

EU or U.S.: Is There a Choice?

Bulgaria remains largely a free-rider within EU policy-making, benefiting from EU financial instruments without fully committing to reforms. The EU is Bulgaria's largest investor, but both the EU and U.S. have limited capacity to influence democratic processes in the country. Corruption and oligarchic control of resources, highlighted by U.S. sanctions imposed over a number of Bulgarian politicians under the Magnitsky Act, demonstrate that neither power has the leverage to push for meaningful reforms.

The outcome of recent U.S. elections is unlikely to have a significant impact on bilateral relations between Bulgaria and the U.S. While Trump's election brings a little more unpredictability to transatlantic relations, Bulgaria will remain on the periphery of new strategic challenges for the U.S. Trump will probably submit to the functional and strategic needs of U.S. foreign policy, leaving bilateral relations on the inert side of politics. However, his election as president will strengthen GERB's positions.

Bulgaria continues to navigate between the interests of the EU, the U.S. and Russia. Despite declaring allegiance to Euro-Atlantic values, Bulgaria's government often appeases pro-Russian interests, making future reform agendas challenging. The mainstream political establishment's reluctance to confront corruption or challenge oligarchs weakens Bulgaria's democratic development.

Recommendations for the EU

For democracy to flourish in Bulgaria, the EU must increase political pressure on Bulgarian governments to implement reforms and combat corruption. Bulgaria plays a minimal role in EU-U.S. relations, weakening the pro-European and pro-American factions within the country. Without external pressure on Bulgarian political leaders tied to both U.S. and EU interests, populist and anti-Western rhetoric will continue to thrive and the democratisation process will stall.

In conclusion, while Bulgaria's democracy remains fragile, external powers such as the EU and the U.S. must carefully balance their strategic interests with a genuine commitment to democratic reform. The mission, though difficult, is not entirely (im)possible.

Ivan Nachev is a Bulgarian political scientist at the New Bulgarian University and an expert on the EU's political integration. His interests are in the fields of political theory and practice, European values, European integration theories, strategies and political practices. He is a member of the Bulgarian Association for Political Sciences, the Institute for Public Policies and Partnership, the European Community Studies Association (ECSA) and Team Europe at the European Commission. Currently, he is a Director of Bulgarian School of Politics.

Hristo Panchugov is a Bulgarian political scientist, Assistant Professor in the Department of Political Science at the New Bulgarian University and a graduate from the Central European University (Hungary). He is an expert in the field of political parties, European integration and international relations, as well as political organisations and civic education.

The New Bulgarian University (NBU) was established on 18 September 1991 as the first private university in Bulgaria. It is an autonomous liberal education institution dedicated to the advancement of university education, cultivation of critical and creative thinking, sensitivity to cultural difference and problem-solving. NBU has received maximum accreditation scores in three consecutive accreditations. Since 2004, NBU is an accredited partner of the Open University UK.

Croatia: Irreplaceable Strategic Partnership in Need of Additional Content

Hrvoje Butković

Relations with the U.S. have been crucial for Croatia since its independence in the 1990s. Three important areas where these relations are reflected are economy, politics and security. In the area of security, there could hardly be any objection to Croatia's current policy direction. However, concerning its economic and political relations with the U.S., Croatia could benefit from a certain intensification, namely reformulation of its current policy patterns in the EU framework.

Historical Background

Upon the dissolution of Yugoslavia, the U.S. recognised Croatia as an independent state on 7 April 1992. In 1994, the U.S. played a pivotal role in brokering and signing the Washington Agreement, which effectively stopped hostilities between Croats and Bosniaks in the neighbouring war-torn Bosnia and Herzegovina. One year later, in 1995, the U.S. brokered the Dayton Agreement, co-signed by Bosnia and Hercegovina, Croatia and Serbia, which put an end to the three-and-a-half-year-long Bosnian War. In 1996, the U.S. proclaimed that Croatia was its most crucial political connection in Southeast Europe. The Croatian diaspora in the U.S. is estimated to be around 500,000, which to some extent informs Croatia's foreign policy. From 23 October 2021, Croatian citizens can travel to the U.S. without a visa.

H. Butković (✉)
Institute for Development and International Relations, Zagreb, Croatia
e-mail: butkovic@irmo.hr

Limited Economic Relations

The U.S. and Croatia have good but not extensive trade relations, with bilateral investment and trade totalling EUR 1.5 billion annually. Croatia has a trade surplus with the U.S., as almost three-quarters of the total relate to exports from Croatia, while only one-quarter refers to imports from the U.S. However, given that the total value of Croatian exports in 2023 was EUR 22.9 billion, exported merchandise to the U.S. represents only a tiny proportion. Croatia mostly exports medicines, electrical transformers and weapons to the U.S., while imports from the U.S. largely comprise petroleum gases and other gaseous hydrocarbons. The floating LNG import terminal off Krk Island commenced operations on 1 January 2021, positioning Croatia as a regional energy leader and contributing to Europe's energy supply diversification. In December 2022, Croatia and the U.S. signed the Double Taxation Avoidance Agreement, which enables Croatian companies operating in the U.S. and U.S. companies operating in Croatia to do business more easily.

Politically Blind Following of the U.S.

Croatia considers the U.S. to be its strategic partner and hence acts as a loyal U.S. ally in international relations. Regarding foreign policy matters, Croatia often sides with the U.S. when the EU does not have a unified position. For example, in the 2012 UN Assembly vote on the position of Palestine in that organisation, the Croatian delegation abstained and thus sided with the U.S. and a minority of other countries. Similarly, in 2017, Croatia was one of the six EU Member States that did not vote for the UN General Assembly resolution calling for the U.S. to withdraw its recognition of Jerusalem as the capital of Israel. This example bears particular importance because it happened under Trump's first presidency, demonstrating that Croatia follows the U.S. foreign policy lead regardless of the political and ideological orientation of the current U.S. administration. Finally, in 2023, Croatia was among 14 countries that, in the UN General Assembly under U.S. lead, voted against the resolution calling for an immediate ceasefire between Israeli forces and Hamas militants in Gaza. The listed chronology shows that both the current centre-right and the previous centre-left (2011–2015) governments blindly followed the U.S. lead concerning the conflict in the Middle East, taking a different stance from the great majority of other EU Member States. In the Croatian parliament, currently and historically, no political parties or independent members of parliament (MPs) question U.S.-Croatia relations, which, according to the current U.S. ambassador to Croatia, H.E. Nathalie Rayes, are "at the highest level". Such excellent relations imply joint active work on the affirmation of the Euro-Atlantic integration process in Southeast Europe as well as strong support for a defensive war of Ukraine. Nevertheless, Croatia's president, Zoran Milanović, recently expressed some scepticism about closely following U.S. foreign policy on Ukraine, noting that, in his opinion, Croatia should be involved in the conflict as little as possible.

Security and Defence Issues

The U.S. Department of Defence has a robust military-to-military relationship with Croatia and provides military assistance through training, equipment, equipment loans and education in U.S. military schools. So far, the total U.S. military and defence aid to Croatia amounts to slightly more than USD 800 million. On 1 April 2009, Croatia became a member of NATO, a military alliance in which the U.S. plays a crucial role. As a member of NATO, the country has participated in the International Security Assistance Force and, subsequently, the Resolute Security Force in Afghanistan, the Kosovo Force and Operation Unified Protector in Libya. At the beginning of the Russian aggression against Ukraine, an unidentified drone flying from the direction of Ukraine crashed in the capital city of Zagreb. Fortunately, the incident passed without casualties, although it caused fear and resentment among the citizens. As a sign of support, the NATO command sent two U.S. F-16 fighter jets to Croatia to strengthen its national air defence forces.

What to Expect from the Trump Administration?

For the EU and Croatia as a Member State, Donald Trump's victory could mean the introduction of new U.S. customs and tariffs. This would lead to increased costs for EU and Croatian exporters, potentially reducing their competitiveness in the U.S. market. On the foreign policy front, the U.S. could become even more confrontational with China. For Croatia and the EU, this could also be problematic because if the principal EU ally decides to embark on a trade war with China, extensive economic relations between the EU and China could be put into jeopardy. Finally, with Donald Trump in office, membership in NATO may become more expensive in a situation where, due to Russian aggression against Ukraine, it has become completely indispensable.

Recommendations

To further economic relations between Croatia and the U.S., Croatian businesspeople should study the U.S. economy's structure in order to find trade opportunities and niches. Moreover, the EU should support these efforts by providing adequate financing opportunities from its funds. Such efforts would particularly be welcomed in the IT and technology sector, which holds the greatest potential for cooperation.

Concerning future international relations, Croatia might profit from rethinking its current blind following of the U.S. based purely on its political strength and replace it with a more principled approach, which would also be better coordinated with other EU Member States. Such a change would allow Croatia to continue supporting just causes such as the war in Ukraine, while simultaneously permitting it not to take clear sides in more controversial conflicts such as that in the Middle

East. In the area of security, Croatia should continue its active role in the NATO alliance, which remains the best guarantee of its sovereignty in the difficult security circumstances in Europe. At EU level, this implies advocating for more and better coordination between the EU and NATO.

Hrvoje Butković works as Research Advisor at the Institute for Development and International Relations (IRMO), Zagreb. The topics of his primary scientific interest are democracy at the national and supranational level together with industrial relations in an internationally comparative perspective.

The Institute for Development and International Relations (IRMO), Zagreb, is a public, non-profit, scientific research organisation engaged in multidisciplinary research. It provides strategic decision support and analysis to decision makers and ensures dissemination of research results and information through publishing activities.

The U.S. And the Republic of Cyprus: Newfound Partners Amid Geopolitical Shifts

Zenonas Tziarras

During the twenty-first century, the Republic of Cyprus (RoC) has deepened its relationship with the U.S. Enhanced security cooperation, economic ties and shared strategic interests highlight this evolution.

Background and Relations

The U.S. established diplomatic relations with the RoC in 1960 following its independence from the United Kingdom (UK). However, the island has been divided since 1974, following a Greek junta-backed *coup d'état* and the subsequent Turkish military invasion and occupation of the island's north which remains to this day under Turkish-Cypriot administration. The U.S. maintains that the division of Cyprus is unacceptable and continues its support of efforts to reunify the island.

For years, the relationship was rather weak, affected by historical narratives about the negative role that the U.S. and NATO played in the Cyprus conflict, as well as the RoC's traditionally close ties with the Soviet Union and later Russia. This gradually changed in the twenty-first century, partly after the RoC's accession to the EU in 2004, but mostly after the mid-2010s for various reasons. Firstly, the financial crisis that hit Cyprus and the EU imposed bail-in started to sever the RoC's financial dependencies on Russia. Soon after, Turkey made a significant shift towards Russia, developing strong bilateral ties on different levels including trade, energy, security and defence. The RoC saw its traditional partner, Russia, aligning with Turkey and hence feared potential repercussions. Thus, the RoC's

Z. Tziarras (✉)
University of Cyprus, Nicosia, Cyprus
e-mail: tziarras.zenonas@ucy.ac.cy

gradual shift towards the U.S. was born out of pragmatism, driven by structural changes which were further assisted by a right-wing, pro-Western government domestically alongside the U.S.'s growing interest in the Eastern Mediterranean and Middle East—as seen for instance through the adoption of the EastMed Act (2019) and the Abraham Accords (2020).

Between 2014 and 2023, RoC-U.S. economic relations showed distinct upward trends in trade and FDI. According to the U.S. Bureau of Economic Analysis, U.S. exports to Cyprus included services, capital goods and industrial supplies, while imports from Cyprus mainly comprised transport services and various goods. Cyprus exports to the U.S. increased from USD 353 million in 2014 to USD 2.2 billion in 2023, while imports grew from USD 472 million to USD 1.7 billion, resulting in a 2023 trade deficit of USD 508 million, compared to a surplus of USD 119 million in 2014. In terms of FDI, U.S. investments in Cyprus rose significantly, from USD 2.7 billion in 2014 to around USD 15 billion in 2023. Conversely, Cypriot FDI in the U.S. declined from USD 2.5 billion in 2014 to USD 215 million in 2023. This latter decline was mainly due to the imposition of stricter American screening on Cypriot FDIs as the country was in a process 'de-Russianising' its economy. However, Cypriot FDIs to the U.S. are now expected to increase against a background of improved relations. For the moment, though, despite Russia's financial influence waning in the 2010s, according to the International Monetary Fund (IMF), it still remains the strongest partner for both inward and outward FDIs.

Public Perceptions

Although public perceptions in Cyprus have traditionally been pro-Russian and anti-Western, there has been a shift in recent years. This is partly because of Russia's relationship with Turkey, the Russian invasion of Ukraine and the more significant U.S. engagement in RoC initiatives or networks of cooperation in the Eastern Mediterranean. Although there is lack of adequate data, information provided by a 2010 survey conducted in the context of an EU-funded project 'Reconciliation and Peace Economics in Cyprus' (EuropeAid Cypriot Civil Society in Action II Programme) is nevertheless indicative.

This survey queried Greek Cypriot opinions regarding the influence of various countries and organisations in solving the Cyprus problem. Perceptions of the EU and Russia stood out in contrast to opinions about the UN, UK and U.S. Most Greek Cypriots had negative views of the UK (76%) and U.S. (68%), while around 33% viewed the UN negatively. Positive views of Russia (35%) were lower than the EU (46%) but much higher than the UN (20%). Russia, the EU and the UN were similarly regarded as neutral mediators, with around 40% seeing them as potential unbiased brokers. The UK (12%) and U.S. (18%) did not share this status. Overall, Greece, Russia and the EU were seen as having a positive impact on resolving the Cyprus problem, while Turkey, the UK and the U.S. were viewed negatively.

Contrarily, in a survey conducted in 2019 by Kappa Research, Russia is listed third as a desired ally after the U.S. and France. In this context, the media in Cyprus generally portrays the U.S. in a positive light, emphasising the benefits of bilateral cooperation in security and economic sectors. However, there are nuanced views, with some political factions, particularly certain centrist and left-wing parties, expressing caution about over-reliance on the U.S. According to the government, and the biggest party, right-wing Democratic Rally (DISY), Cyprus is becoming a strategic partner of the U.S. and that comes with many benefits. On the other hand, the left-wing Progressive Party of Working People (AKEL)—the second biggest party—made the case that 'the country's submission to the U.S. does not render it a pillar of security but the opposite'.

Security Cooperation

Within the framework of recent improvements, the U.S.-RoC relationship has *inter alia* been marked by significant security cooperation, including the 2018 Statement of Intent on bilateral security cooperation, accreditation of the RoC's first defence attaché in Washington and the establishment of the Cyprus Centre for Land Open Seas and Port Security (CYCLOPS) that aims to strengthen security capacity-building in Cyprus, the EU and the Eastern Mediterranean through international partnerships. These offer training in non-military security areas such as customs and export controls, port and maritime security, chemical, biological, radiological and nuclear substances and explosives material management as well as cybersecurity. Other significant developments included the lifting of the U.S. arms embargo from the RoC, joint military exercises and a Defence Cooperation Agreement signed in 2024. The bilateral relationship culminated in a meeting between U.S. President Joe Biden and Cypriot President Nikos Christodoulides at the White House in October 2024. Further, in the context of the Eastern Mediterranean Security and Energy Partnership Act of 2019, the RoC has acquired a place in the U.S. regional security architecture which includes the countering of Russian influence.

Being rather new, the RoC-U.S. partnership has to date had enough time to develop only in the more traditional security sectors. The deals made so far encompass mostly cooperation in military security, training, intelligence exchange, search and rescue operations, research and innovation, as well as the prospect of energy collaboration. Lastly, there is some expectation that the U.S. could meaningfully contribute to resolution of the Cyprus conflict by leveraging Turkey. However, given the complex geopolitical landscape and the U.S.-Turkey relationship, it is not certain that Washington will be able to play such a role or that Turkey considers it to be an 'honest broker'.

Policy Implications for the EU

The RoC's partnership with the U.S. certainly enhances its role within the EU and positions Nicosia as a crucial intermediary, promoting EU policies that align with U.S. interests in the region. The RoC leverages its U.S. ties to advocate for a more integrated EU approach to security and energy policies, emphasising the need for collective measures to address regional challenges. What is more, the partnership has been contributing substantially to the RoC's capacity-building, rendering it a more capable EU Member State. Nicosia's proactive stance in regional diplomacy highlights the constructive role that it can have on the EU's most southeastern edge, not least in areas such as security, conflict resolution, development and energy security.

The election of Donald Trump is not expected to change U.S. foreign policy towards Cyprus or the Eastern Mediterranean substantially, even if his approach towards Turkey is more lenient than that of his predecessor. Indeed, one could argue that at its core the U.S. approach to these issues—based on the logic of offshore balancing—has not significantly changed since the administration of Barack Obama. However, when it comes to U.S.-EU relations, the Trump administration is likely to follow a more unilateral and divisive approach, including a possible effort to mitigate the U.S.' engagement in the Ukrainian conflict, thereby creating more challenges for the U.S.-EU-RoC triangle and perhaps even presenting Cyprus with dilemmas. Also unknown is whether the U.S. under Trump will shift away from its principled stance on the Cyprus Problem, towards a more pragmatic and transactional approach in the context of U.S.-Turkey relations.

Recommendations

In terms of how to move forward in the EU-RoC-U.S. relationship, there are a few possible suggestions.

Firstly, the EU and RoC should deepen defence cooperation with the U.S. to bolster regional security. This includes joint military exercises, intelligence sharing and collaborative defence projects. Such integration ensures robust preparedness against common threats and strengthens the Western bloc's strategic depth in the Eastern Mediterranean, not least based on the RoC's growing capacities and activities.

Secondly, cooperation with the U.S. in the energy sector should be extended, focusing on the development of renewable energy sources and regional energy infrastructure. The EU and RoC can leverage American technological advancements and investments to diversify energy sources, reduce dependence on external actors and enhance overall energy security.

Thirdly, economic ties should be expanded by facilitating greater trade and investment opportunities between the EU, RoC and the U.S. This includes promoting bilateral business exchanges, supporting start-ups and small and medium-sized enterprises as well as collaborating on technological innovation and digital transformation. Enhanced economic relations will drive growth, create jobs and foster sustainable development.

Lastly, while deepening ties with the U.S., the RoC should also advocate for a more autonomous EU. This includes developing independent EU defence capabilities, coherent and comprehensive foreign policies on issues such as the Middle East peace process and crafting tailored economic sanctions and trade agreements. Strategic autonomy will enable the EU to act decisively in its own interests while maintaining a strong transatlantic partnership.

Zenonas Tziarras is a Lecturer in the Department of Turkish and Middle East Studies at the University of Cyprus. He authored *Turkish Foreign Policy: The Lausanne Syndrome in the Middle East and Eastern Mediterranean* (Springer, 2022), and edited *The Foreign Policy of the Republic of Cyprus* (Palgrave Macmillan, 2022).

The University of Cyprus, established in 1989, is the largest and most prestigious public university in Cyprus. Located in Nicosia, it offers a wide range of undergraduate and postgraduate programmes across disciplines.

Czechia and the United States: A Victim of Increased Global Instability?

Zdeněk Sychra and Petr Kratochvíl

Czech-U.S. relations underwent three phases in the post-Cold War era: from a honeymoon in the 1990s, to a significant cooling during the Presidency of Miloš Zeman, to the current renewed cooperation. However, the intensity of mutual ties is accompanied by increasingly polarised domestic political debates in Czechia, the growing unpredictability of future Czech policy towards the U.S. and the U.S. administration towards Europe, and the transatlantic nexus.

Relations with the U.S. as a Flagship of Pro-Western Orientation

Development of Czech-American relations over the last 35 years is certainly not linear, but rather firmly linked to key post-Cold War geopolitical changes: the fall of the communist regime in 1989; the country subsequently joining NATO in 1999; and membership of the EU in 2004. Any turbulence in the relationship should thus be seen as a mixture of attempts by some Czech governments to come as close to the U.S. as possible whilst others subsequently rejected this policy.

The honeymoon period covers the time from 1990 to 2006. Symbolically, it began with President Václav Havel's famous address to the U.S. Congress in

---

Z. Sychra (✉)
University of West Bohemia, Pilsen, Czechia
e-mail: sychra@ff.zcu.cz

P. Kratochvíl
Institute of International Relations Prague, Prague, Czechia
e-mail: kratochvil@iir.cz

February 1990. Most importantly, the U.S. played an important role in supporting Czechia's entry into NATO (1999). The accession of Czechia to the EU in 2004 then opened another chapter in relations with the U.S., as U.S. administrations, despite some internal differences, typically saw EU enlargement as a crucial factor for the stabilisation of the Central and Eastern Europe region. Subsequently, within the framework of transatlantic relations, Czechia has often tried to serve as a mediator between the EU and the U.S., for instance concerning disagreements over the 2003 invasion of Iraq. As a consequence, but also due to the political elites' growing Euroscepticism, (right-wing) successive Czech governments have been sensitive to any weakening of transatlantic cooperation.

From 2006 onwards, though, relations started to sour. A turning point here was the debate about placement of a U.S. military radar unit in the Brdy Mountains, southwest of Prague. This was to be part of the U.S. missile defence system in Europe. Over two years of politically heated debate polarised society, with most Czechs rejecting America's military presence. Negotiations ended in 2009 with Obama's decision not to pursue the project further. This decision was highly symbolic: it was the first time when Czechia challenged the country's erstwhile seemingly unshakable pro-Atlantic course. A further significant cooling of relations followed after the election of Miloš Zeman as Czech president in 2013, who openly sought rapprochement with Russia and China in direct conflict with American interests.

However, the current period is again defined by stronger ties with the U.S., for three key reasons. Firstly, the dreams of some Czech politicians about closer ties to Russia have dissipated. An explosion at the Vrbětice ammunition depot, staged by the Russian secret services, was a major contributing factor here, followed by the shock from Russia's full-scale invasion of Ukraine. Increased cooperation with the U.S. in security quickly followed, with its culmination being the Defence Cooperation Agreement between Czechia and the U.S., which entered into force in August 2023. Secondly, the U.S.-China rivalry has started to affect Czech-U.S. relations directly. A consequence of this is the increasingly critical attitude of the Czech state towards Chinese technology companies. Thirdly, modernisation of the Czech military is now going ahead with the purchase of U.S. weapons, heavily supported by the right-wing government of Petr Fiala, including not only F-35 fighter jets, which will replace Gripen aircraft, but also attack helicopters and missiles. However, the questioning of the close transatlantic relationship after the arrival of the second Trump administration has introduced considerable uncertainty into the mutual cooperation.

From an economic point of view, the U.S. is one of Czechia's traditional trading partners. Although it does not belong within the top 10 in terms of volume, the U.S. is the second largest non-EU export market (after the UK). In 2023, total bilateral trade volume reached approximately USD 12.3 billion. The main export items are machinery, transport equipment and industrial goods, whilst imports include aircraft and components, chemical and pharmaceutical products as well as IT technology. Similarly, mutual investment activity (FDI) is rather low compared to major investor countries (the U.S. ranked 11th in 2022). The dominance of right-wing views in Czech politics led to the government supporting the (Trump-postponed) TTIP agreement, arguing that as an export economy, Czechia would benefit from a more open access to U.S. markets, both directly and indirectly (due to the country's links with Germany's automotive industry).

Internal Political Cleavages and Public Attitudes

Significant for Czechia's foreign policy debate is competition between the EU's increased role and continued reliance on the U.S. The strongly pro-Atlantic right-wing parties (especially the conservative and soft Eurosceptic Civic Democratic Party [ODS]) are extremely wary of European strategic autonomy and thus of strengthening the Common Foreign and Security Policy (CFSP) (or also the Common Security and Defence Policy [CSDP]). The left, albeit now seriously weakened, is more critical of the U.S., but the Social Democrats (and the governments of which they were part) did not question the basic axiom that the U.S. should constitute the main guarantor of European security. However, some repositioning has been underway resulting in a new axis starting to emerge: on the one hand, the firmly pro-American liberal/conservative right; and on the other hand, Eurosceptic populists with varied, but generally critical attitudes to the U.S.: the Freedom and Direct Democracy party (SPD), the new Motorists for Themselves party (AUTO) and parts of the ANO movement.

Furthermore, the positions of political parties reflect Czech public opinion, which is also rather varied. The election of Petr Pavel (former chairman of NATO's military committee) as Czech president in January 2023, who openly advocates for strong transatlantic relations, helped stabilise positive public attitudes though. According to a 2023 Pew Research poll, around 55% of Czechs expressed positive attitudes towards the U.S., compared to 30% with negative attitudes. Most Czechs see the U.S. as an important strategic partner. Critical attitudes, on the other side, are particularly evident in the context of U.S. military interventions. According to surveys, perceptions of the U.S. are often linked to generational and ideological differences. Younger people and supporters of pro-Western parties generally have a more positive view of the U.S., whilst older people and voters of populist or left-wing parties tend to be more critical.

The U.S. as an Important Factor in Czech European Politics

Czechia continues to be one of the strongest supporters of transatlantic ties in the EU. Russia's invasion of Ukraine, rearmament of the Czech army and the purchase of U.S. weapons have further strengthened the Czech emphasis on promoting EU-U.S. cooperation. In economic terms, Czechia is a strong proponent of liberalising mutual trade to the greatest possible extent. On the foreign policy level, Czechia usually supports a tougher stance towards Russia and China, with a conspicuously lenient stance towards Israeli actions in its occupied territories, often echoing the U.S. position.

The victory of Donald Trump in the U.S. presidential election in 2024 will also have an impact on Czech European politics. Obviously, Kamala Harris would have been more comfortable for Czech-U.S. relations in many ways: stability, supporting Ukraine, not attempting to drive wedges among EU Member States, not questioning the role of NATO, energy (including securing energy supplies) and economic cooperation. However, not so surprisingly for those who follow Czech politics, there are influential politicians who do not complain about the outcome, such as former presidents Václav Klaus and Miloš Zeman, as well as far-right leader Tomio Okamura. Others share Trump's hostility towards liberal democracy (this includes the main opposition leader Andrej Babiš and many members of parliament [MPs] of his ANO movement) or appreciate some aspects of Trump's foreign policy during his first term (Alexandr Vondra, Member of the European Parliament and Vice-Chairman of the ODS). In general, Trump's views tend to attract Eurosceptic, populist and conservative politicians who often share his views on the Middle East and China, as well as his anti-liberal political style. The major points of contention will thus be the approach to Ukraine, U.S.-EU trade relations and the future of an increasingly shaky trans-Atlantic security. So far, it seems that the fears of a threat to all these pillars after Trump's second inauguration are beginning to come true.

Recommendations

To serve Czech interests, the EU should strive for an autonomous trade policy that is not too dependent on the U.S. or China. This will help diversify export markets, create new contractual links and ensure stable conditions for European (and therefore Czech) companies globally.

The EU must strive for greater energy autonomy, regardless of the U.S. presidency. This includes the promotion of renewable energy sources, but also joint energy purchases that can increase energy security for the whole Union. Together with the U.S., it can create an energy alliance that will enable affordable energy supplies, including joint investment in green infrastructure and energy research.

Strengthening the EU's technological autonomy and reducing dependence on U.S. technology companies is essential. The EU should invest in research and development in industry 4.0, cybersecurity and digital technologies to increase Europe's innovation potential and global competitiveness. As a world leader, the U.S. will serve as both an inspiration and a competitor.

The still evident distrust towards the EU and a wariness of EU strategic autonomy signify more a reflex reaction in parts of some Czech political parties than a result of a strategic analysis. This rigidity should be overcome, irrespective of which U.S. president is in office.

Zdeněk Sychra works in the Department of Political Science and International Relations, University of West Bohemia, and as an external associate at the Institute of International Relations Prague. His academic interests focus on the politics of the EU, specifically the Economic and Monetary Union and political governance in the EU. As an author and co-author, he has published numerous articles and book chapters on European politics.

The University of West Bohemia is one of the most visible public educational institutions in Czechia. The Department of Politics and International Relations of the Faculty of Arts is an academic institution offering a broad range of undergraduate, graduate and postgraduate study programmes, conducting research in political science, international relations and territorial studies.

Petr Kratochvíl is Full Professor and Senior Researcher of the Institute of International Relations Prague and a member of the TEPSA Board. He has written dozens of monographs, book chapters and journal articles. His research interests cover theories of international relations, European studies and the religion-politics nexus.

The Institute of International Relations Prague (IIR) is an independent public research institution which has been conducting scholarly research in the area of international relations since 1957. As an institution originally founded by the Ministry of Foreign Affairs of the Czech Republic, the IIR also provides policy analysis and recommendations. It tries to form a link between the academic world, the public and international political practice.

Atlanticism in Times of Change: A View from Copenhagen

Mikkel Runge Olesen and Jakob Linnet Schmidt

Denmark has been among the most pro-Atlantic EU countries following the Cold War. Despite Donald Trump's widespread unpopularity in Denmark, this approach is likely to remain in place barring any drastic U.S. foreign policy reversals.

America's Friend

Denmark and the U.S. have a long-lasting relationship. Denmark recognised the U.S. in 1792, and diplomatic relations were established in 1801. However, prior to the Second World War, the U.S. was seen merely as a distant country known for its impressive industrial capacity. This changed during the Cold War, when U.S. culture gradually made its entrance. By the end of the Cold War, Denmark had become a U.S.-friendly country and increasingly continued to be so over the following decades. Denmark and the U.S. share values and interests, albeit their relationship is not equal. In terms of security, the U.S. has been Denmark's most important ally, while Denmark is, at best, a premium small ally to the U.S. and one of many. In recent years, the U.S. has gained a more prominent position in Denmark's economy, being its single largest export market since 2019, though the EU combined export markets remain significantly larger. Regarding imports, the U.S. is currently the second largest country surpassed only by Germany. Denmark's security policy and, to a lesser extent, its economy is linked to the U.S. and

M. R. Olesen (✉) · J. L. Schmidt
Danish Institute for International Studies, Copenhagen, Denmark
e-mail: mro@diis.dk

J. L. Schmidt
e-mail: jals@diis.dk

maintaining that alliance and friendship will remain a top priority for Denmark regardless of who holds office in both countries.

Public Perception

As mentioned, Denmark has traditionally been one of the most pro-American countries in Europe. In broad terms, most members of the Danish Parliament are positively inclined towards the U.S., with only the far-left wing sometimes characterising U.S. actions on the world stage as "imperial". Denmark's policies, though, are traditionally seen more in line with the Democratic Party, becoming even more pronounced with recent years' policy shift in the Republican Party under Donald Trump. The same tendency is true for Danish media coverage, which has been significantly more positive towards Joe Biden's administration than towards that of Trump. This is also reflected by public opinion. In 2021 a poll commissioned by the European Council on Foreign Relations (ECFR) found that 65% of Danes surveyed either agreed or strongly agreed with the statement that "the world is in a worse place because of Donald Trump's presidency". Additionally important for public perception today is the war in Ukraine, because it underscores the transatlantic bond's value. In two ECFR surveys of twelve European countries conducted in April 2021 and April 2023, the proportion of Danes considering the U.S. as an ally in sharing Denmark' values and interests grew from 35% to 55%, while the proportion that considered the U.S. a rival or an enemy fell from 13% to 4%. Whether this positive turn will persist during the second Trump presidency remains to be seen, but a certain downturn is to be expected.

The U.S. as a Security Provider

Since the formation of NATO, Denmark being a founding member, the U.S. has been at the forefront of Danish security policy. Throughout the Cold War, Denmark pursued a dual policy reassuring the U.S. and NATO of its loyalty while striving to avoid unnecessary tensions with the Soviet Union. However, this dynamic changed following the Cold War, when Denmark realigned its foreign and security policy in order to become a core U.S. ally in NATO. Accordingly, to demonstrate its value Denmark actively supported and participated in U.S.- and NATO-led international stabilisation missions, while simultaneously seeking to keep defence spending relatively low.

In recent years, though, U.S. demands for contributions for international stabilisation missions have been replaced by a clear focus on defence spending. This development has been underscored by the withdrawal from Afghanistan in 2021 and Russia's invasion of Ukraine in 2022. Consequently, Denmark's military contributions to international missions outside Europe, including those in Iraq and the Sahel, are now small. A broad consensus has now emerged in Parliament on the need to focus on territorial defence—as well as military aid for Ukraine—and on meeting (and currently even exceeding) NATO's guideline of 2% of GDP minimum on defence expenditure. In addition, the more than 70-year-old policy of not allowing the stationing of allied troops in Denmark in peacetime was abolished with the signing of a bilateral U.S.-Danish Defence Cooperation Agreement in 2023 set to be ratified in Parliament in 2025. Denmark's persistent Atlanticist line regarding security matters, now being pursued in new ways, is likely to remain intact under the second Trump presidency, the security guarantee from the U.S. forming the cornerstone of Danish security policy, for as long as the U.S. remains willing to reciprocate. However, should the Trump administration take steps towards seriously undermining the security guarantee under NATO's Article 5, EU defence cooperation is likely to emerge as Denmark's plan B, albeit this worst-case scenario is not openly addressed by decision-makers.

Reluctance of European Defence Cooperation at the Cost of Transatlantic Relations

Denmark's relationship with the EU has traditionally been focused on economic dimensions. Even though the U.S. market has grown, the combined EU market remains far more important to Denmark. Similarly, Danish policies on climate and energy are much more closely entwined with EU policies than with those of the U.S., especially in times of Republican presidencies. When it comes to defence and security, though, Denmark has always prioritised transatlantic relations over the EU. Concern for potentially weakening the U.S. security commitment to Europe has traditionally been a strong argument against Danish support for increased European defence cooperation. Indeed, when Russia's invasion of Ukraine triggered a referendum on the abolition of the Danish opt-out on EU defence cooperation in 2022, a broad majority in the Danish Parliament recommended voting in favour of abolishing the opt-out, because it was also welcomed by the U.S. (and NATO). With 66.9% in favour, the referendum was a resounding "yes". However, barring drastic changes, Denmark is likely to keep prioritising the U.S. over the EU in matters of security.

Recommendations

The EU institutions should seek to minimise the damage to transatlantic relations following the return of Donald Trump, by: seeking to work with him on issues where common ground can be found; striving to prevent a trade war with the U.S., which could have severe negative consequences for Denmark and the EU; seeking to preserve institutional bonds for as long as possible; and trying to restrain his worst impulses. They should build an independent capacity for the EU to do more on defence—especially concerning Russia, but also with an eye to China—while constantly reassuring the U.S. that European defence cooperation is a means for Europe to do more and not meant to undermine NATO or the U.S.' commitment to Europe. Given its staunch Atlanticist credentials, Denmark could play a role as mediator in this regard. Finally, the danger of a serious breakdown in transatlantic relations is real and the EU institutions should prepare for this by taking steps to accelerate European defence integration. Similarly, Europe may need to consider shouldering aid for Ukraine without U.S. assistance.

Mikkel Runge Olesen is Senior Researcher at the Danish Institute for International Studies researching Danish foreign and security policy, NATO and transatlantic relations as well as security in the Arctic and Nordic regions.

Jakob Linnet Schmidt is PhD Fellow at the Danish Institute for International Studies researching Danish security and defence policy, transatlantic relations as well as Nordic security and defence cooperation.

The Danish Institute for International Studies is an independent public research institution for foreign, security and development studies.

Distant but Important Partner: Estonia and the U.S.

Merili Arjakas

Bilateral relations between Estonia and the U.S. have a strong focus on defence and security. Estonia wishes to see a sustained U.S. presence in Europe, but also urges European allies to contribute more to their defence.

Atlantic Allies

The U.S. first recognised the Republic of Estonia in 1922 and maintained its acknowledgement of Estonia's legal continuity throughout the Soviet occupation, which was keenly appreciated by the Estonian government after the restoration of independence in 1991. Estonia's relations with its EU neighbours are close due to their relatively equal standing, whereas in global affairs, the U.S. remains Estonia's most important partner and ally, especially in security cooperation.

According to Statistics Estonia, the U.S. was Estonia's 11th largest export partner in 2023, with goods exported to the U.S. totalling EUR 501 million, down from EUR 1.16 billion in 2022 and EUR 1.67 billion in 2021. Over half of these exports comprised: machinery and mechanical appliances; followed by optical, measuring and precision instruments; wood products; mineral products; and furniture. Estonia imports significantly less from the U.S., with imports valued at EUR 315 million in 2023, ranking the U.S. as Estonia's 14th largest import partner. Machinery and mechanical appliances were also the largest category of imports. In 2023, Estonia's trade surplus with the U.S. was EUR 186 million.

M. Arjakas (✉)
International Centre for Defence and Security, Tallinn, Estonia
e-mail: merili.arjakas@icds.ee

U.S. companies have invested EUR 536 million in Estonia, accounting for 1.6% of all FDIs, primarily in the information and telecommunications sectors, followed by real estate activities and manufacturing. Meanwhile, Estonia has invested EUR 449 million directly in the U.S., representing 3.8% of its total foreign investments, mainly in the manufacturing sector.

Estonian cultural influence in the U.S. is most visible in music, particularly within symphonic orchestras and choral works, though its overall impact remains modest. By contrast, the U.S. is the most important foreign influence on Estonia's pop culture and public discourse.

Keener on the U.S. than Americans

All Estonian political parties are committed to maintaining strong ties with the U.S., an alliance which is seen as the strongest external deterrent against Russian aggression, hence a guarantor of Estonian security and support for its sovereignty. Estonian governments have worked and will continue to work closely with all U.S. administrations. Any official criticism of the U.S. is subdued.

Public debate is more vibrant and includes a wider range of perspectives, from pro-American to anti-American views, though the latter constitutes merely a fringe stance. Only the most far-right or far-left politicians and pundits question Estonian or European alliance with the U.S. Unlike official positions, public discourse also allows for open commentary on U.S. parties, politicians and policies. In broad terms, the conservative public in Estonia tends to favour the Republicans and the progressive public leans towards the Democrats. This preference is reflected in the tone of the media and carries over to debate topics imported from the U.S. to Estonia (such as discussions over the Black Lives Matter movement). Yet it does not become a point of division, because no Estonian government would publicly choose a side in American politics.

In discussions on Estonia's security and international relations, the prevailing sentiment is to sustain a close alliance with the U.S. For example, if the Estonian government diverges from U.S. positions, such as on resolutions regarding Israel and Palestine, the very fact of not following the U.S. as a crucial ally can be used by the opposition and media as grounds for criticism.

When U.S. policies are subject to criticism, it is often framed within the context of urging greater American involvement in European security. For instance, the conventional wisdom in Estonia holds that the U.S. should contribute more to Ukraine's war efforts by military aid, lifting the restrictions on the use of American weapons and supporting Ukraine's accession to NATO, seeing Ukraine's victory against Russia as a necessity for safeguarding the rules-based international order.

Primacy of Security

NATO membership is vital to Estonia's security policy. This has made the preservation of transatlantic ties a top priority, but also narrows any public perception of security to military matters. Estonia has undertaken security commitments by participating in the U.S.-led operations within Afghanistan and Iraq to contribute to its security partnership with the U.S.

The U.S. is an important weapons provider for Estonia, exemplified by the 2022 agreement for the Baltic states to acquire the HIMARS rocket system—Estonia's largest-ever weapons procurement. The U.S. has also deployed around 600 troops in Estonia to ensure that the U.S. can and will be engaged at the first sign of Russian provocation.

Estonia would welcome all U.S. initiatives to strengthen security in the Nordic-Baltic region and in Europe, regardless of who holds the presidency. Additionally, Estonia not only continues to vouch for policies that embed the U.S. presence in European security but is also strongly against any initiatives that could lead to a reduction in U.S. involvement on the continent.

Thus, Estonia has been sceptical in discussions on European strategic autonomy, prioritising instead the goal of strengthening the European pillar within NATO. Nevertheless, in recent years the country has emerged as a vocal advocate for EU defence cooperation, viewing it now as a means of reinforcing rather than weakening the transatlantic relationship. This focus on security and defence will continue to play a central role in Estonia's relationship with the U.S. and shape its objectives for related EU policies.

Estonia wishes to see all NATO countries raise their defence expenditures to at least 2.5% of GDP, with a bigger priority on weapons procurement. To convey their contributions to the alliance, during the second Trump presidency Estonia will place emphasis on its defence commitments, including high spending on its own armed forces (3.5% due in 2025) and its troop contributions to U.S.-led operations. A potential point of contention for Estonia and the U.S. might emerge if a future U.S. administration were to reduce its support to Ukraine and seek to pressure Kyiv into accepting a perilous ceasefire agreement. Hence, the aim of Estonian diplomacy is to ensure that such a scenario is never presented.

Recommendations

With the war of attrition in Ukraine and U.S. priorities shifting to the Indo-Pacific, it is crucial for European allies to contribute more to their own security. One approach could be to issue joint Eurobonds so that countries could raise funds rapidly for investment in their own and Ukraine's defence industries, thereby scaling up production. Within the EU and NATO connect defence planning processes and enhance information sharing between the two organisations, including classified intelligence. By strengthening the European pillar within NATO, Europe could become more autonomous in setting its strategy and defence policies, thus making it less vulnerable to Russian belligerence and shifts in U.S. policy.

Merili Arjakas is a Research Fellow at the International Centre for Defence and Security in the Foreign Policy Programme since December 2021 and Editor-in-Chief of *Diplomaatia* since 2022. Her research focuses on EU affairs. She is most interested in the interplay between domestic and international politics and how various dynamics affect societies in Europe and the Middle East.

The International Centre for Defence and Security (ICDS) is the leading think tank in Estonia specialising in foreign policy, security and defence issues. ICDS was founded in 2006. In 2018, the Estonian Foreign Policy Institute merged with the ICDS. ICDS' mission is not only to strengthen Estonia's security and defence sector, but also sharpen strategic thinking in NATO and the EU on security issues that affect the Nordic-Baltic region.

Finland: From Partner to Ally in a World of Crises

Ville Sinkkonen and Niklas Helwig

Finland's NATO accession presents not only a profound shift in the country's foreign policy, but also the culmination of its long road from neutrality and military non-alignment to alliance membership. In the process, the Finland-U.S. relationship has been upgraded to a new level, especially in the security domain. Paradoxically, this has occurred at a time when U.S. commitment to Europe is increasingly uncertain, necessitating creative solutions from the Europeans.

A Deepening Relationship Across the Board

During the Cold War years, the U.S. understood Finland's precarious geopolitical position, which required a peculiar balancing act between the West and the Soviet Union. Washington, therefore, quietly supported the country's liberal-democratic path. However, since the early 1990s, this relationship has been on an upward trajectory, culminating in Finland's accession to NATO in April 2023 and a subsequent bilateral Defence Cooperation Agreement.

In recent years, the U.S. has also become an increasingly important market for Finnish businesses. In 2023, the U.S. was Finland's largest export market for the second year running, having overtaken Sweden in 2022. While the FDI balance has continued to favour the U.S. (USD 9.9 billion versus USD 4.4 billion), Finland exported considerably more goods to the U.S. than it imported (USD 8.7 billion

---

V. Sinkkonen (✉) · N. Helwig
Finnish Institute of International Affairs, Helsinki, Finland
e-mail: Ville.Sinkkonen@fiia.fi

N. Helwig
e-mail: Niklas.Helwig@fiia.fi

versus USD 2.6 billion respectively), with a roughly equal value in services (USD 1.7 billion) flowing in both directions.

Political relations between the two countries have been amicable for decades, regardless of which party has been in power either in Finland or in the U.S. Finland even managed the years of the first Trump administration relatively well. President Sauli Niinistö met Donald Trump three times—an unprecedented frequency—and the two countries deepened security cooperation across the board. After Russia's second invasion of Ukraine, the NATO membership process placed Finland unusually high on the U.S. foreign policy agenda and gathered near unanimous support in the Senate.

Political Consensus on Vital Matters

The U.S. has traditionally been viewed more favourably on the right than the left of the Finnish political spectrum. Recent upgrading of security relations, though, was met with unprecedented political unity. The Finnish Parliament voted for NATO accession on 1 March 2023, with 184 MPs in favour and only 7 against—6 of these from the Left Alliance. The Defence Cooperation Agreement cleared the floor without a vote in July 2024 and received only scattered criticism focused on sovereignty questions.

In the public debate, interest in U.S. domestic politics has been unusually high, at least since 2016. The media has sought to navigate political tremors in the U.S. by representing both liberal and conservative views. However, in a notable 2018 poll by the Finnish public broadcaster Yle, only 14% of Finns thought Trump had improved the U.S.' standing in the world, while 88% considered that he had further polarised societal debate. Criticism of the authoritarian leanings and isolationism of Trump's Republican Party and the (often unarticulated) preference for the Democrats can probably be explained by Finns' liberal views on issues such as abortion and the welfare state's role. There is also an understanding that Finland benefits from an international order based on liberal values and norms.

From Partner to Ally

On the surface, Finland's swift accession to NATO might seem like a rupture, given decades of neutrality followed by military non-alignment. The decision to seek membership was driven by a drastic shift in public opinion in favour of the alliance, which opened a policy window for political leaders. However, accession was preceded by decades of relationship-building with the U.S. and NATO, entailing defence material purchases, institutionalised cooperation and Finnish involvement in international crisis management. By the time it applied to become a NATO member, Finland was a U.S. ally in all but name.

Paradoxically, Finland has hitched its wagon to the U.S. caravan at a time when the U.S. appetite for internationalism has decreased. Washington's gaze is also gradually shifting to the Indo-Pacific and hence European allies will be asked to do more in return for U.S. engagement. Here Finland can tell a compelling story as a regional security provider with a well-equipped and large conscript force. Yet, the amount of attention Finland has received in the U.S. during its NATO accession process is hardly likely to last. Helsinki must learn how to manage its bilateral relationship and simultaneously act as a member of a 32-member alliance.

A Pragmatic Atlanticist in Europe

A deepened bilateral relationship with the U.S. has not brought discernible changes in Finland's positions within the EU. For years, Helsinki has pragmatically called for strengthening the EU's global role, particularly as a security actor, but Finland will also continue to push for increased coordination between the EU, NATO and the U.S. A long-held commitment to open markets and free trade has been espoused by the current conservative government, which translates into a critical stance on large EU-level spending increases or competition-distorting policies. While Finland has been a strong proponent of EU defence initiatives of recent years, such as Permanent Structured Cooperation (PESCO), officials have stressed that these initiatives should not undermine Finland's existing defence cooperation and industrial ties with non-EU states, such as the U.S., UK and Norway.

Although key Finnish politicians have tried to assuage fears over a transatlantic divorce, Donald Trump's second stint in the White House, as with the first, will likely be chaotic, but also marked by political appointees more willing to do the president's bidding. This means less amenable interlocutors will be available for the U.S.' European partners. Trump's transactional foreign policy approach also creates profound uncertainty over long-term U.S. commitment to European security as well as support for Ukraine and international institutions, coupled with fears regarding economic nationalism. Trump will certainly drive a hard bargain on burden sharing, suggesting it is high time for Europe to become serious about its own security, in both military and economic terms.

Recommendations

The EU should assume a more *longue durée* approach to development of the transatlantic relationship, one going beyond "Trump proofing". This would entail fostering links to new generations of leaders in Washington, D.C. and U.S. states, harnessing the contacts possessed by different EU Member States in a coordinated manner. Here the High Representative should nominate an EU special representative, whose role would be to oversee and coordinate further development of the transatlantic relationship. The EU also needs to show the U.S. that not only is greater European strategic autonomy in Washington's long-term interests, but it is also deserving of concerted American support. A regularised forum on matters of security, similar to the EU-U.S. Trade and Technology Council, would allow for frank exchanges of views and a smoother transition towards more equitable burden sharing.

Dr. Ville Sinkkonen is a Senior Research Fellow at the Finnish Institute of International Affairs, Center on U.S. Politics and Power. His research focuses on U.S. foreign policy, great-power politics, normative power and the politics of trust in international relations. His work has been published by various international outlets, including Brill, Palgrave, Routledge, the *Cambridge Review of International Affairs*, the *Journal of Transatlantic Studies*, and *European Foreign Affairs Review*.

Dr. Niklas Helwig is a Leading Researcher at the Finnish Institute of International Affairs based in Brussels. He is also an Associate Professor in International Relations at Tampere University. His research focuses on EU foreign and security policy, German foreign and security policy, as well as EU-U.S. relations. He currently co-leads an Academy of Finland-funded project on "Transforming strategic cultures in contemporary Europe" (STRAX). The Finnish Institute of International Affairs (FIIA) is a research institute whose mission is to produce high quality, topical information on international relations and the EU. It realises these aims by conducting research, organising domestic and international seminars and publishing reports on current international issues. FIIA was established by the Parliament of Finland in its centennial plenum in June 2006 and is autonomous in its research activities.

France, the U.S.' Oldest and Most Complicated Ally: A Stubborn Defender of a Truly European Industrial and Defence Policy

Marie Krpata

France, the U.S.' oldest ally, is also the EU country which most stubbornly defends genuinely European industrial and defence policies. It calls for 'strategic autonomy' in all political domains, a position increasingly difficult to hold against a hardening international climate.

Two Tightly Interknit Countries with Fundamental Political Divergences

As the first state to recognise America in the eighteenth century, France is considered to be its oldest ally. Two centuries later, the U.S.' role in France's liberation from Nazi Germany further tightened the bonds between these two countries.

However, almost immediately following the Second World War, U.S.-French priorities took divergent paths, with the Suez crisis (1956) still regarded as a major humiliation for France. In 1966, President Charles de Gaulle, who embodied a policy of autonomy, loosened France's ties with NATO by withdrawing from its integrated command. Under de Gaulle, France developed its own nuclear capacities, criticised the U.S.' presence in Vietnam, recognised China in 1964 and called for French-speaking Quebec's national independence in 1967. Almost four decades later, France opposed George W. Bush's Operation Iraqi Freedom, another important development in these two countries' bilateral relationship. The Obama years were marked by the 'Pivot to Asia' and U.S. failure to intervene in Syria. Under Trump, the U.S. grew more unpredictable and transactional. This was followed

M. Krpata (✉)
French Institute of International Relations, Paris, France
e-mail: krpata@ifri.org

by two major blows under Joe Biden: firstly, the withdrawal from Afghanistan in 2021; and secondly, the launching of AUKUS, a security partnership between Australia, the UK and the U.S.—including Australia's cancelling of a EUR 56 billion submarine deal with the French company Naval Group. However, these mishaps were compensated for by the U.S.' support to Ukraine in response to Russia's war of aggression.

In the economic sphere, Franco-American business relations are tightly interknit. Repercussions from the Russian war in Ukraine on Franco-American trade have been sensitive with France's energy imports from the U.S. having surged in 2022 as substitution for Russian energy supplies. French oil and gas imports from the U.S. though fell sharply in 2023. Transportation equipment and chemicals, mainly exported by France, are other key elements in the bilateral relationship. In 2023, the trade volume reached EUR 167 billion with a French trade surplus worth EUR 9 billion. In terms of FDIs, France is the fifth largest investor in the U.S. while the U.S. is the main investor in France. In 2022, French FDI stocks in the U.S. represented USD 360 billion, while U.S. stocks in France amounted to USD 139 billion.

Between Gratitude for American Involvement and the Aspiration for More European Autonomy

France's perception of the U.S. in the media, according to public opinion and among political parties, is ambivalent. The U.S. is often deemed to be the 'world's policeman' whose interventionism is not selfless. This criticism arose following the Second World War at a time when French and American interests in terms of global presence and influence drifted apart. While France was looking to preserve its colonial presence, the U.S. as leader of the free world took a firm stance against colonial powers. Two France-related examples stand out: Indochina and Suez.

After the Cold War, the U.S. was regarded as a 'hyperpower'. However, its hegemony was soon to be contested. Following the terrorist attacks on 11 September 2001, France's daily newspaper *Le Monde* carried the headline 'We are all Americans', but the atmosphere shifted in 2003 when U.S. President Bush decided to 'finish the business' in Iraq. Former French Foreign Minister Dominique de Villepin's speech at the UN opposing intervention still resonates today.

Under the Obama presidencies, following two George W. Bush terms, the U.S. has been trying to embrace a more multilateralist approach. In France, where Obama was highly popular, he was nicknamed 'Obama, the European'. The Obama terms were, though, overshadowed by the Arab Spring, which unfolded from 2011 onwards and where the U.S. became increasingly hesitant to become involved, as the Syrian example shows.

So far, against the current geopolitical backdrop with the war in Ukraine, though, the U.S. and NATO were regarded as reliable partners (64% of the French surveyed by the German Marshall Fund of the U.S.), with a U.S. involvement in European defence and security generally welcome according to French public opinion (62%). In contrast, most French see Russia's and China's influence in global affairs negatively (71% and 58%, respectively).

France's Call for Action Every Time the U.S. Withdraws from Global Leadership

As a permanent member in the UN Security Council and a nuclear power, France is championing international regulation and cooperation on major challenges that cannot be dealt with at state level. This is echoed by Biden's promise 'America is back' as he was elected to power, after a Trump presidency where the U.S. had withdrawn from several multilateral organisations and agreements.

Some examples of converging interests are: cooperation in the fight against terrorism in the Sahel region; cooperation on climate issues, where Biden decided to rejoin the 2015 Paris Climate Agreements echoing Macron's call to 'Make Our Planet Great Again'; food and energy security which have become subject to collateral damage from the war in Ukraine, issues tackled by France and the U.S. in fora such as the G7 and G20; as well as regulating the five U.S. tech giants Google, Amazon, Meta, Apple and Microsoft, which former French EU Commissioner Breton and U.S. President Biden both eagerly worked on.

Nuances in approaches between France and the U.S. which relate to security and defence may be spotted when it comes to the perception of NATO's role and we can recall the debate that flared in 2019 when Donald Trump called the Organisation 'obsolete' while Emmanuel Macron framed it as 'brain-dead'. Between France and the U.S. three key issues remain about NATO. Firstly, the U.S. would be much more in favour of EU enlargement to include Ukraine, whereas France would find it more comfortable that Ukraine is protected by the NATO (and thus American) umbrella. Secondly, France refuses to accept that NATO be driven into the U.S.-China rivalry. Thirdly, Macron stated that the sending of troops to Ukraine could not be excluded claiming 'strategic ambiguity', while this option was dismissed by President Biden from the outset.

France's Sovereigntist Stance Partly Directed Towards the U.S. is not Consensual in the EU

France played a major role in defining the EU's industrial strategy, which aims at boosting the EU's competitiveness in response to the challenges of offensive Chinese and American industrial policies. In its endeavours, it sometimes had to face headwinds from other European states opposing a too statist approach. Macron has also been very vocal in his criticism of the IRA, while other Member States are wary of France's proposals to retaliate.

On defence, France laments that other European states rely too much on American technology and hence pushes for a strengthening of the European Defence

Technological and Industrial Base (EDTIB). Other Member States fear that this is driven purely by self-interest.

Overall, France's capacity to influence the European debate as it has in the past years is likely to diminish against the backdrop of rising instability in domestic French politics. Following the 2024 U.S. elections, it may be worthwhile taking a glimpse into how EU-U.S. relations might develop and what that could mean for France.

After Trump's victory in the U.S. presidential elections, it is likely that the U.S. will adopt a tougher tone, increasing tariffs against European products in line with his continuing 'America first' policy. He is likely to carry on with Biden's IRA in one way or the other in so far as his goal will be to maintain the U.S.' competitive edge—the central objective within this programme—given that some Republican states are hugely benefitting from it. Furthermore, Elon Musk, who heads the electric vehicle company Tesla and is thus interested in benefitting from favourable conditions for his business, may play a role in influencing the President to maintain advantages for the green technologies sector in general. However, Trump is also likely to further the U.S. fossil fuel industry.

Under Trump, it is also likely that NATO will become more unpredictable. Trump's statement that he could encourage Russia to attack those countries which do not spend 2% of their GDP in military spending, which he called 'delinquent', has caused much concern.

Trump is likely to carry on with his unilateral and transactional approach. In such a context, EU countries will be eager to seek privileged communication channels on a bilateral level. Their leverage towards the U.S. would be incomparably weaker than that of a truly united EU.

Trump will try to put his promise to end the war in Ukraine into action and may ask Ukraine to make difficult concessions to Russia. As he may generally increase pressure on European allies to comply with Washington in terms of strategic priorities, tensions with France are to be expected on Ukraine, China and the EDTIB.

Recommendations

On Europe's defence policy, various proposals at EU level were raised recently to strengthen the EDTIB, such as the European Defence Industrial Strategy. The latter foresees that by 2030, EU countries should: buy at least 40% of their defence equipment by working together; spend at least half of their defence procurement budget on products made in Europe; and trade at least 35% of defence goods between EU countries instead of with other countries. Further convergence should also be sought.

Beyond that, the EU needs to accelerate work on new European security architecture. That set out by the Helsinki Final Act (1975) and the Charter of Paris for a New Europe (1990) was shattered by Russia's invasion of Ukraine and Europe cannot stand idly by when its security is at stake. One major concern for France is to be sidelined by Russia and the U.S. during the post-war settlement. To avoid such a scenario, the EU needs to work on a common position among its Member States.

To further European competitiveness, the EU should work towards creation of a European Capital Markets Union, a topic amply discussed by Enrico Letta in his report 'Much more than a market' (April 2024) and echoed by Mario Draghi in his report 'The future of European competitiveness' (September 2024). EUR 300 billion of European savings feed the U.S. market every year. These investments could be put to good use in the European market instead.

Marie Krpata is Research Fellow at the Study Committee on Franco-German Relations (Cerfa) at the French Institute of International Relations, Ifri, where she dedicates her research activities to the EU and the external relations of the Franco-German couple.

The French Institute of International Relations, Ifri, founded (1979) and chaired by Thierry de Montbrial, is the leading independent research and debate institution in France dedicated to the analysis of international issues and global governance. Its director is Thomas Gomart. Over the past 45 years Ifri has gained worldwide recognition among its peers.

A Tested Friendship: Ensuring the Resilience of U.S.-German Relations in a Changing World

Tobias Hofelich, Klara Stecker, and Funda Tekin

Germany's economic and security interests demand cultivating its close transatlantic ties despite the U.S. having become a volatile partner. Against the backdrop of mounting geopolitical challenges, Germany must work towards enabling the EU to take more responsibility in foreign and security policy.

Transatlantic Ties: Strong but Strained

The U.S. and Germany have a long and deeply intertwined relationship, shaped by various waves of migration from Germany to the U.S. In 2022, almost 12% of the American population was of German ancestry, which has positively affected U.S. policy towards Germany ever since the establishment of bilateral relations in 1871. The U.S. was not only hesitant to join the allied forces fighting Germany in both world wars, but was also among the first to reestablish amicable relations with Germany afterwards. Following the Second World War, the U.S. became a key player in Germany's post-war recovery with funds from the Marshall Plan and support for its integration in multilateral institutions such as NATO and the UN.

T. Hofelich (✉) · K. Stecker · F. Tekin
Institut für Europäische Politik, Berlin, Germany
e-mail: Tobias.Hofelich@iep-berlin.de

K. Stecker
e-mail: Klara.Stecker@iep-berlin.de

F. Tekin
e-mail: Funda.Tekin@iep-berlin.de

Today, the two states enjoy strong ties in various sectors. As a NATO member, Germany is a vital partner in U.S. security policy. It hosts over 50,000 U.S. soldiers at numerous military bases and wields significant influence in the EU as its most populous state and largest economy. Berlin and Washington also share strong economic bonds. In 2024, according to the U.S. Census Bureau, Germany exported goods worth USD 159.27 billion to the U.S., while importing USD 76.70 billion, resulting in a trade surplus of USD 82.57 billion. Cultural influence in both directions has a long history. Notably, during the post-war years West Germany saw an enormous influx of American music, TV shows, films as well as fashion and food.

Nevertheless, transatlantic relations have been under strain for some time, *inter alia* due to Germany's long reluctance to meet NATO's military spending target of 2% of GDP. In contrast, U.S. military interventions have been met with significant resistance and criticism in Germany. Berlin's refusal to participate in the 2003 invasion of Iraq marked a key point of tension and highlighted divergent foreign policy approaches. During the Trump administration, relations further soured as the U.S. abandoned international agreements, cast doubt on NATO and imposed tariffs on European steel and aluminium, threatening also to target the automotive sector—Germany's industrial heart. However, President Biden has since made efforts to repair relations with Berlin. His administration suspended Trump's tariffs and, in response to Russia's full-scale invasion of Ukraine, reaffirmed U.S. commitments to European security.

The war in Ukraine has caused Germany to adopt a much tougher stance on Russia, bringing its position closer to that of the U.S. Nevertheless, differences in foreign trade linger, particularly with regard to China. Although the German national security strategy generally identifies China as both a partner and a systemic rival, Berlin's approach is more pragmatic. This is primarily due to the significant economic reliance on China, which forbids taking as strong a confrontational stance as the U.S. currently does. In addition, the U.S. IRA has sparked controversial debate and calls for similar efforts to support German industries.

German Perceptions of the U.S.

Among mainstream German political parties, the U.S. is seen as a key international partner. However, the recently founded far-left party Alliance Sahra Wagenknecht (BSW) and the far-right Alternative for Germany (AfD) are more critical. Both parties denounce recent plans to station American long-range missiles in Germany. The AfD goes as far as characterising the U.S. as a *raumfremde Macht* (a foreign power) and has suggested that Russia's full-scale invasion of Ukraine is a defensive response to U.S. actions.

Although both fringe parties are becoming increasingly popular, German public opinion on the U.S. is largely positive after a noticeable slump during the Trump years. Some issues, such as the perception of U.S. interventionism, occasionally spark public debate. However, the importance of transatlantic relations as well as the American presence in Germany and Europe is not questioned *per se*. Both Americans (85%) and Germans (77%) see their countries as having very good relations; furthermore, Germans see the U.S. as their country's most important foreign policy partner.

Volatile Commitments to Security

The U.S. remains the most important financial and strategic contributor to NATO; hence Germany has built its entire security structure around American guarantees. In recent years, though, the U.S. has shifted its attention towards the Indo-Pacific. Responding to China's ever-more assertive posture against Taiwan and other regional actors and tapping into the world's most dynamic markets are priorities shared by both major parties in the U.S. and will likely remain so in the near future.

As a result, Europe is expected to take more responsibility in its neighbourhood. In the EU, this has refuelled debate about developing a joint military capacity. Germany has so far been hesitant, highlighting the importance of NATO and the transatlantic partnership. However, Russia's full-scale invasion of Ukraine prompted the German government to proclaim a *Zeitenwende*, a geopolitical turning point that was accompanied by a pledge to invest more in defence, not only to support Ukraine, but also to protect the European security order. For the first time in decades, Germany now meets NATO's spending target.

The war also marked a shift in energy policy. As Germany has strenuously been seeking to reduce and eventually end its reliance on Russian gas, the U.S. emerged as a key supplier of LNG. Extracted via fracking, this has not unexpectedly sparked controversial debates on both sides of the Atlantic. These tie in with the broader issue of climate change and shared security concerns arising from the increasing amount and severity of natural disasters.

In many security-related areas, relations between Washington and Berlin are complicated by diametrically opposed positions maintained by the Republican and Democratic Parties in the U.S. On the one side, Democratic President Biden was key in delivering and coordinating financial and military aid for Ukraine and pledged to uphold NATO's security guarantees. On the other, Republican President Donald Trump wants to limit support for Ukraine and has toyed with the idea of abandoning the defence alliance. The positions on energy and climate security are equally diverse. While the Biden administration temporarily paused new LNG export approvals early in 2024 due to climate risks, many in the Republican Party go so far as to deny climate change. Moreover, Trump has vowed to expand U.S. exports of fossil fuels and to abandon the Paris Climate Agreement a second time.

Balancing the Transatlantic Partnership and EU Strategic Autonomy

Historically, the U.S. has aimed for a united and strong Europe and supports Germany's commitment to the EU as a key factor in reaching this goal. Today, Germany's unique relationship with the U.S. influences Germany's preferences at EU level concerning economic, foreign and security policies. Regarding the last of these, Germany's reliance on U.S. security guarantees is no outlier in the EU. Despite previous hesitation, the wars in Ukraine and the Middle East, as well as the U.S.' unpredictable role, have moved Germany closer to the idea of strengthening European defence capabilities.

Likewise, Germany has warmed up to the concept of European strategic autonomy, which bridges security and economic aspects to reduce dependencies on foreign actors—including the U.S. Under the previous government, Germany was already embracing an industrial policy, which had long been considered taboo, and worked together with other EU Member States to reshore the production of key technologies and increase the EU's economic competitiveness.

Trade between the EU and U.S. is likely to remain a point of contention. Trump has promised to impose general tariffs of up to 20% on all imports and at least 60% on Chinese trade goods. The EU has shown determination to respond to U.S. trade barriers in kind, but opted for a more measured approach towards China to avoid being drawn into a major trade dispute. Protectionist policies on either side of the Atlantic are expected to harm Germany's export-oriented economy.

Against a backdrop of the U.S.' unstable international role, Germany would benefit from a stronger and more self-reliant EU in matters of security and trade. To advance the idea of strategic autonomy, the EU may need to adapt its competition policies accordingly and create a regulatory framework that facilitates more cooperation in security and defence. Moreover, the EU's role in foreign affairs should be strengthened by allowing for qualitative majority voting in CFSP.

Recommendations

With geopolitical tensions on the rise and shifts in global power relations, a U.S.-led NATO remains a crucial security actor in Europe and its neighbourhood. Germany should strengthen security relations with Washington, setting a positive example within the alliance by meeting its spending requirements and taking on more responsibility. Importantly, this does not preclude advocating for stronger security capacities at European level.

The U.S. and China are both important trading partners for the EU and Germany. Thus, Berlin and Brussels must find a way to maintain sound relations and trade links without being drawn into an escalating trade dispute between the U.S. and China. To justify a balanced approach, Europe can rely on international law and adherence to WTO rules as a key argument for relatively open trade with both the U.S. and China without being forced to choose sides. Simultaneously, Europe should strengthen other existing partnerships and explore alternative markets.

Ultimately, transatlantic relations must become more resilient to U.S. government shifts. Germany should lead efforts to strengthen cooperation between the EU and the U.S. in areas of mutual dependence such as digital technologies and the mechanical engineering sector, as well as the protection of democratic institutions and practices from foreign interference together with shared security concerns in the traditional sense. Institutions such as the Trade and Technology Council provide an example of pragmatic cooperation beyond party politics and ideology.

Dr. Tobias Hofelich is a Research Advisor at the Institut für Europäische Politik (IEP). He holds a Ph.D. in Political Science from the University of Agder and his research deals with European integration, international organisations and comparative regionalism.

Klara Stecker works as a student assistant at IEP. She holds a Bachelor's degree from Lund University and pursues a joint Master's degree at SciencesPo Paris and Freie Universität Berlin.

Prof. Dr. Funda Tekin is Director of the IEP and Honorary Professor at University of Tübingen. She earned her Ph.D. in Political Science from the University of Cologne with a research focus on differentiated integration and enlargement. Prof. Tekin is a member of the TEPSA Board.

The Institut für Europäische Politik (IEP) is a non-profit, non-partisan organisation focused on European integration. It provides an accessible, European, interdisciplinary forum and a platform for expert debates on European policy. The institute is one of Germany's leading research institutions for foreign and European issues.

From Myth to Reality: The Odyssey of U.S.-Greek Relations Finding Safe Harbour

Dimitris Tsaknis and Athina Fatsea

This chapter examines the status of U.S.-Greece relations, which have undeniably reached a generational high, a trend that is reflected in many fields of common interest and seems set to continue over the coming years.

Greece and the U.S.: Friends or Foes?

As both researchers and politicians, including U.S. Secretary of State Antony Blinken and President Joe Biden, have repeatedly stated, Greek-U.S. relations today are better than they have ever been. This is confirmed by ever-closer cooperation at all levels: military, energy, commercial, economic and cultural. However, in the past, relations between the two nations have been tested and characterised by various difficulties, although Greece's position in siding with the transatlantic alliance was never in doubt. With the Truman Doctrine in 1947, the U.S. aimed at keeping Greece anchored to the West, for fear of the country moving towards communism. However, treating Greece as a service hub for U.S. interests in the Eastern Mediterranean basin, combined with the U.S. stance on Turkey's invasion of Cyprus and its relations with the military junta, caused strong dissatisfaction according to public opinion. Over time, this led to anti-American feelings. In 1982, following these events, polls showed that an overwhelming 80.6% of Greeks had a negative view of the U.S., compared with a European average of 45.21%.

D. Tsaknis (✉)
EPLO, Athens, Greece
e-mail: dtsaknis@eplo.int

A. Fatsea
ELIAMEP, Athens, Greece

'Rising Like a Phoenix': The Rebirth of U.S.-Greece Ties

The Greek debt crisis was a catalyst for change in Greece-U.S. relations, as Barack Obama's administration supported the huge rescue programme required by the IMF for the Greek economy in 2015. It was then that almost all political parties recognised the importance and depth of bilateral relations between the two countries. Two more developments contributed to a further deepening and shifting of public opinion. Firstly, Turkish aggression towards Greece softened, following adoption of a revisionist strategy by the ruling Justice and Development Party (AKP) of Recep Tayyip Erdoğan after the failed *coup d'état* attempt in 2016. This new strategy is also largely due to the continuing expansion of military cooperation between the U.S. and Greece, as reflected in the Mutual Defence Cooperation Agreement and its two following amendments. Secondly, with the blessings of the U.S. and the EU, resolution of the long-standing sensitive name dispute with North Macedonia through the Prespa Agreement during the Tsipras administration proved in practice that all major Greek parties recognised the value of cooperation with the U.S.

Furthermore, increases in the volume of trade and investment in recent years have shown that the two allies' relationship has entered a new upward trajectory. The U.S. was among the top 10 countries investing in Greece during the period from 2013 to 2023 with the bilateral trade in goods amounting to USD 3.8 billion in 2023. The U.S. has also invested in areas such as: defence (acquisition of Neorio Syros and discussion about the Elefsina shipyards); technology (Microsoft Data Center, Pfizer, CISCO); and energy. Especially with regard to energy transition and autonomy, it seems that the U.S., NATO and Europe are relying largely on Greece, whose position can realise the pressing need to replace Russian gas with LNG from elsewhere. Increase in the capacity of the Revithoussa liquid gas terminal combined with the floating natural gas storage unit in Alexandroupoli highlights the strategic value of Greece in a vulnerable region that stretches from the unstable Eastern Mediterranean to war-torn Ukraine and the Black Sea.

The New Reality

A Pulse survey, conducted in February 2024 by Kathimerini, demonstrated the complete conversion of Greek public opinion on relations with the U.S. Based on this poll, 54% of Greeks evaluate positively the stance and role of the U.S. on issues related to Greece. The same poll shows Greeks trusting their allies at a rate of 76% in the event of a military crisis with Turkey, confirming the very strong security ties that have been built between the two nations in recent years. Finally, the poll also answers the question of Biden (Kamala Harris) or Trump, with 42% of respondents answering that they do not see any change in relations with Greece after the elections on 5 November 2024.

The result, especially in the light of Trump's victory, is certainly expected to affect Europe's transatlantic relations with the U.S. However, the impact specifically as regards Greece can be unpredictable, especially in relation to Turkey, as an American intervention cannot be taken as granted in the case of a crisis between the two countries. Trump lacks familiarity with the Cyprus issue, contrary to the outgoing President Joe Biden. However, Trump had previously excluded Turkey from the F-35 programme under the Countering America's Adversaries Through Sanctions Act legislation and furthermore imposed economic sanctions on Turkey after the imprisonment of Pastor Andrew Brunson. Moreover, Trump's Secretary of State Mike Pompeo visited Greece and sent a letter containing security guarantees for the country in 2020. Regarding the dynamic Greek diaspora, close to Donald Trump is Nicole Malliotakis, the only Republican elected official in the New York area.

The shift in Greek public opinion is also reflected in the Pew Research Centre survey, according to which 56% of Greeks have a favourable attitude towards the U.S., with 42% arguing that the U.S. contributes to world peace and stability. Furthermore, based on data from the Transatlantic Periscope (2022–2024), the trend of Greek-U.S. relations averages 8.5/10, which ranks Greece among the U.S.' closest allies in the EU. As for the Greek parties and media, as can be seen by the former's stance in the voting process of military procurement from the U.S. and of the latter in covering related events, most of the political spectrum seems more favourable to the U.S. than in the past, mainly centre-right and centre-left parties (New Democracy and PASOK-KINAL).

Indicatively, during the Greek financial crisis, the Obama administration played a crucial role in avoiding Grexit. The U.S. stance was appreciated by the then governing leftist party, Syriza, which later negotiated the Prespa Agreement with North Macedonia and agreed to expand the U.S. military presence in Greece. However, in 2022, the party's leader, Alexis Tsipras, did not support the second amendment to the Mutual Defence Cooperation Agreement. The Communist Party of Greece (KKE) and its related media increasingly fail to support American intervention; the same seems to apply for the far-right *Elliniki Lisi* (Greek Solution), which also failed to back the Mutual Defence Cooperation Agreement.

Undoubtedly, the Greek strategy has been developing consistently over recent years, emphasising the values and rules of international law. Greek foreign policy is fully aligned with U.S. interests and vision for the Eastern Mediterranean region, Europe and the world. The two countries' shared commitment to the transatlantic alliance is demonstrated by the fact that, together with Poland, they are the three NATO countries with the highest defence spending as a percentage of their GDP in 2023. In any event, Greece's defence spending is traditionally high, exceeding 3% of GDP even during the Greek economic crisis. Greece is, therefore, reintroducing itself as a reliable partner, with the ability to intervene in its wider geographical neighbourhood and with a view to resolving disputes in a peaceful manner, as required by the spirit of international law. This presupposes an emphasis on both external and internal means of balancing, with Greece having significantly strengthened its armed forces by purchasing state-of-the-art fighter aircraft, helicopters and frigates, on the basis of defence agreements signed with countries such as the U.S. and France.

Recommendations

Greece is a reliable NATO member, with the prospect of becoming a cornerstone of the common European defence and security policy. Greece's capabilities, as well as those of other Member States with remarkable performances in the field of defence, should be utilised in order to develop deterrent capabilities. This will strengthen the EU's role as a provider of security not only in its own region, but also beyond in the midst of major crises and wars, such as the conflict in Gaza and Russia's invasion of Ukraine, in Europe's 'backyard'.

The EU's purpose is not to replace NATO, as its action is complementary in nature. Thus, it is able to increase its global influence, without competing with the U.S., which has realised the futility of its role as the world's border guard. However, the time is long overdue for more steps to be taken in the area of autonomy, skills development and the European defence industry. Trump's second term as President could alienate the U.S. from Europe and may test its commitment to Europe's defence armour, as indicated by his election campaign statements. Emphasis should also be placed on new technologies and their use for deterrent purposes.

Finally, the EU should consider a proposal for the creation of a common European air defence shield to protect the continent and its population, based on the proposal submitted to the President of the European Commission Ursula von der Leyen by the Greek Prime Minister Kyriakos Mitsotakis together with his Polish counterpart Donald Tusk in May 2024. In addition, incentives should be provided for joint defence procurement to be developed cooperatively in Member States within common defence planning.

Enhancing the sense of security within the EU is of primary concern for a community defined by the 'persecuted' democracy. In a rapidly changing environment, it is necessary for the EU to adjust to developments and create mechanisms that will safeguard the security of its Member States and its neighbourhood—all these in cooperation with the U.S., as the EU currently does, as long as conditions remain favourable.

Dimitris Tsaknis is a Research Associate at EPLO. He holds a Master's Degree in International Relations from the National and Kapodistrian University of Athens. His research focuses primarily on European defence questions, terrorism and the Middle East.

EPLO is an international organisation, based in Athens, dedicated to the creation and dissemination of knowledge in the area of Public Law *lato sensu* and Governance. 17 countries have already ratified the International Treaty establishing EPLO.

Athina Fatsea is a Research Assistant and Project Manager at ELIAMEP, curating the Greek version of the Transatlantic Periscope, a project of Bertelsmann Foundation. She is also a Ph.D. candidate at the Ionian University, Greece.

ELIAMEP is an independent, non-governmental, non-profit think tank, established in Athens, in 1988. Its mission is to conduct policy-oriented research and provide authoritative information, analysis and policy recommendations, for the development of evidence-based responses to major European and foreign policy challenges.

The U.S. and the Future of Europe: Is There a Quest for Plan B in Budapest?

Ádám Kerényi

Hungary's relationship with the U.S. affects its position within the EU, as its alignment with American security policies and occasional divergence on democratic values can create friction with EU Member States that prioritise European unity and shared governance principles. Facing mounting criticism and even sanctions under the Obama administration as a result of his government's poor democratic track record, mounting corruption and friendliness towards Russia, Prime Minister Viktor Orbán had every reason to root for change in the Oval Office.

Relationship between the U.S. and Hungary

The U.S. first established diplomatic relations with Hungary in 1921 following dissolution of the Austro-Hungarian Empire after the First World War. With the later collapse of communism, Hungary then played a pivotal role in Central Europe's market economy transition during the early 1990s and dependencies have since emerged, particularly in security cooperation through NATO. Hungary became a member in 1999 and is now viewed by the U.S. as a strategic ally in Central Europe, especially with its participation in NATO missions within Afghanistan, Iraq and the Balkans.

Political relations continue to experience tensions because of differing views on major issues, such as democracy and the rule of law. Since Russia invaded Ukraine

---

Á. Kerényi (✉)
Institute of World Economics of HUN-REN CERS, Budapest, Hungary
e-mail: kerenyi.adam@krtk.hun-ren.hu; kerenyi.adam@szte.hu

University of Szeged, Szeged, Hungary

© The Author(s), under exclusive license to Springer Nature Switzerland AG 2025
M. Kaeding et al. (eds.), *The United States and the Future of Europe*,
https://doi.org/10.1007/978-3-031-83350-2_13

in 2022, Hungarian-U.S. relations have deteriorated even further, the country's close cooperation with Russia and China having already caused concern in Washington. Prime Minister Orbán has repeatedly stressed that the war would not have happened if President Donald Trump had still been in power.

Yet economic relations between the two nations have flourished, with the U.S. being not only one of Hungary's top investors, accounting for nearly USD 10 billion in FDI, but also Hungary's biggest export market outside the EU. Indeed, Hungarian-American bilateral trade set a new record in 2023 by exceeding USD 9 billion, alongside continuing U.S. investment. Moreover, the trade structure is diverse. Culturally, the U.S. exerts considerable influence on Hungarian society through media, education and business practices, while Hungarian-American communities in the U.S. foster cultural exchanges and promote Hungarian traditions abroad. Hungarian Citizens born in Hungary, who hold a Hungarian passport, may apply for admission to the U.S. using the Electronic System for Travel Authorization for the purpose of tourism or business travel to the U.S. for 90 days or less. Under the Visa Waiver Program, visa-free travel is granted, albeit since 1 August 2023, it has become more difficult for Hungarian citizens to enter the U.S. The validity of travel authorisation has been limited to one year so that thereafter Hungarian citizens must reapply for entry.

On Public Perception

In Hungary, public perception of the U.S. is mixed, influenced by political, historical and cultural factors. Major media outlets often reflect the political leanings of their ownership. Pro-government media sometimes express scepticism towards U.S. policies, particularly regarding criticism of Hungary's domestic governance, while non-government media platforms tend to adopt a more favourable tone, emphasising democratic values and international cooperation. Pro-American sentiment is often motivated by Hungary's desire for strong economic ties and security cooperation through NATO. Conversely, anti-Americanism can be driven by concerns about perceived U.S. interference in Hungarian domestic affairs, cultural dominance and geopolitical influence. A survey in March 2024 found that 51% of all respondents thought Hungary would benefit if Donald Trump won the U.S. presidential election in November. Among right-wing supporters, 78% said they would welcome a Trump victory, while only 26% of leftist respondents shared that opinion.

Security and Defence Issues

Cooperation between the U.S. and Hungary flourished throughout the 1990s on security and defence issues. In 1992, the Hungarian government authorised the use of its airspace for NATO's Airborne Warning and Control System reconnaissance aeroplanes, which proved vital in ending the Balkan crisis. The U.S.

and Hungary signed a Defence Cooperation Agreement in 2019 to help modernise military cooperation between the two countries. Relations are expected to improve following Trump's success in the U.S. elections. Prime Minister Orbán publicly expressed his support and extended congratulations following the Republican victory, highlighting the significance of the outcome for future bilateral relations.

Policy Implications for the EU

Prime Minister Orbán was the only EU head of government who embraced candidate Donald Trump in the 2016 election. Facing mounting criticism and even sanctions under the Obama administration as a result of his government's poor democratic track record, mounting corruption and friendliness towards Russia, Orbán was eager for change in the White House. The Hungarian prime minister was the only European leader to declare unequivocal support for Trump prior to the 2020 election, telling the press that his victory was a certainty. Should Trump have lost, Orbán had no plan B.

Hungary's government believed all along that the only chance to improve relations with Washington would come if Donald Trump returned to power in the 2024 presidential elections. Accordingly, it invested considerable resources in building relations with the Trump-affiliated part of the Republican Party before the elections, seeking to find common ground mainly on an ideological level. Journalists asked the prime minister why he was so openly in favour of Trump, while the EU's diplomatic approach is not to interfere in other countries' elections. Orbán responded by saying: "What I am doing is exactly the same level of interference by the Hungarian prime minister in the U.S. elections as the Democrats' government has interfered in Hungarian domestic affairs". Under a U.S. administration led by Kamala Harris, Hungary would certainly have faced more pressure to align with broader EU democratic norms and governance, with specific emphasis on human rights and rule of law issues. In contrast, a Trump victory could strengthen Hungary's nationalist stance within the EU, potentially emboldening Prime Minister Orbán's government to resist EU policies still further, which are perceived as infringing on sovereignty, given Trump's past support for similar populist leaders.

Recommendations

The EU and Hungary should deepen cooperation with the U.S. in key sectors such as technology, energy and green innovation, leveraging American investment to enhance competitiveness and sustainability across Europe while ensuring fair trade practices. Hungary should advocate for a balanced approach where NATO remains a central pillar of European security, but simultaneously push for a more autonomous EU defence policy, promoting initiatives such as the European Defence Fund to reduce over-reliance on the U.S. Both Hungary and the

EU should seek stronger U.S. cooperation on global challenges such as climate change, cybersecurity and international regulatory standards, but Hungary should also encourage the EU to assert its independent leadership in multilateral organisations such as the UN and WTO, to ensure European interests are represented even when U.S. policies diverge.

Ádám Kerényi is a Researcher at the HUN-REN Centre for Economic and Regional Studies, Institute of World Economics, and at the University of Szeged Faculty of Economics and Business Administration. The Institute of World Economics hosted the Hungarian Pre-Presidency Conference on 13–14 June 2024 in Budapest.

The Institute of World Economics of HUN-REN CERS, founded in 1973, is a leading research institute focusing on global economic trends and regional integration processes. As part of the Centre for Economic and Regional Studies (HUN-REN CERS), the institute conducts in-depth analyses on topics such as international trade, the impacts of globalisation, the economic dynamics of emerging markets and the socio-economic effects of European integration. The institute plays a key role in providing expert insights contributing to both national and international economic discourses.

Ireland: An Unusual Transatlantic Partner

Andrew Cottey

Since it gained independence in 1921, Ireland has had generally good relations with the U.S., which has been central to Ireland's Celtic Tiger economic model in recent decades, as a key source of FDI and as a major trading partner. Ireland's policy of neutrality marks it out as distinctive amongst the U.S.' European partners (mostly NATO members), but this has not disrupted the overall political and economic relationship between Ireland and the U.S.

History

Ireland has had generally positive, indeed warm, relations with the U.S. since it gained independence from the UK in 1921. The U.S. established diplomatic relations with the recently formed Irish Free State in 1924—the second state to do so after the UK in 1923. Economic relations were limited in the early decades of the relationship by Ireland's economic under-development and dependence on the UK.

Ireland's policy of neutrality was established at the beginning of the Second World War, although its origins can be traced to the longer struggle for independence from the UK. At various points during the Second World War and later the Cold War, the U.S. was critical of Irish neutrality. In practice, though, Ireland has always leaned Westwards in its neutrality, for example allowing U.S. troops (albeit not weapons) to transit through Shannon airport, in particular during the

---

A. Cottey (✉)
University College Cork, Cork, Ireland
e-mail: A.Cottey@ucc.ie

U.S. wars in Afghanistan and Iraq in the 2000s and 2010s. U.S. concerns about Irish neutrality have thus not disrupted the overall Irish-U.S. relationship.

Northern Ireland (which, of course, remained part of the UK from 1921) has been an additional factor in Irish-U.S. relations. Irish governments hoped that the U.S. might be persuaded to lean upon the UK in relation to Northern Ireland. However, the U.S. prioritised its relationship with Britain, arguing that this was an internal UK issue which could be resolved only bilaterally between Britain and Ireland. In the 1990s, under the presidency of Bill Clinton, U.S. policy shifted, with pro-active U.S. support for the Northern Ireland peace process. The U.S. was thus an important factor behind the 1998 Belfast Agreement and has continued to play a role in supporting peace in Northern Ireland—a role which is very much welcomed in the Republic of Ireland. More recently, in the context of Brexit, the U.S. also played a quiet back-seat role in trying to ensure that the UK's exit from the EU did not disrupt the Northern Ireland peace process.

A further factor in Irish-U.S. relations is 'Irish America'—U.S. residents claiming Irish ancestry, in particular arising from the large-scale emigration from Ireland to the U.S. in the nineteenth century. According to the 2021 U.S. census, 31.5 million people (9.5% of the U.S. population) identified as having Irish ancestry. This has created a particular cultural bond between the U.S. and Ireland, reinforced by many Americans visiting Ireland and by many Irish visiting the U.S., as well as continued Irish emigration to America.

Economics: The Centrality of the U.S. for Ireland

Starting in the 1960s and accelerating during the Celtic Tiger period in the 1990s and 2000s, the Irish economic model has been based on a combination of FDI and a strongly export-based economy. The U.S. plays a central role in this, both as a source of FDI and as a market for Irish exports. The U.S. is Ireland's largest single export market, accounting for 30% (EUR 63 billion) of Irish exports in 2022 (although Irish exports to the EU as a whole are somewhat larger). U.S. investment in Ireland was EUR 492 million in 2022, compared to EUR 339 million from the 26 other EU Member States. U.S. multinational pharmaceutical and technology companies have a prominent place in the Irish economy.

As a consequence, within the EU and in EU-U.S. trade and economic discussions, Ireland is a strong supporter of an open trade and investment relationship. In EU economic policy debates, Ireland generally advocates a more free-market liberal approach, as opposed to the more interventionist position of some EU Member States. U.S. protectionist and re-shoring policies since the 2010s have to date not had a significant negative impact on Ireland. Were the U.S. to move further in this direction, though, such a shift could pose serious challenges for the Irish economy.

The 2008–10 global financial crisis had a big impact on the Irish economy, triggering a major contraction. However, Ireland recovered well, as it also did from recession caused by the COVID-19 pandemic. Through all of this, trade with and investment from the U.S. have remained central to the Irish economy.

Our American Friends—with Imperial Tendencies

Irish public attitudes towards the U.S. are broadly positive, with the U.S. and Americans viewed as friends of Ireland. The U.S. economic presence in Ireland is also generally welcomed. At the same time, a substantial part of Irish opinion is critical of what can be viewed as the more imperial or militaristic elements of U.S. policies. There are no major political party differences within Ireland on relations with the U.S. although Fine Gail and Fianna Fáil (the two main centre-right/centre parties) take a more programmatic approach, whereas Sinn Féin (and other smaller left-wing parties) are more critical of aspects of U.S. foreign policy, in particular overseas military interventions.

Tension in Irish opinion was reflected in the shifting views of U.S. President Joe Biden. Biden—who proudly proclaimed his Irish heritage—was warmly welcomed to Ireland when he made an official visit to the country in April 2023. Biden's support for Israel in its war in Gaza from October 2023, though, led to a significant change in opinion in Ireland, where there was strong public and elite criticism of Israel's war and support for Palestinian independence. A March 2024 article in the New York Times declared 'Biden Loves Ireland. It Doesn't Love Him Back'.

Donald Trump's populist politics have not been generally popular in Ireland, but the first Trump presidency (2017–21) did not significantly disrupt Irish-U.S. relations. Ireland's non-membership of NATO and low threat perceptions *vis-à-vis* Russia mean that possible U.S. security disengagement from Europe does not prompt the high degree of concern seen elsewhere in Europe. Trump's victory in the November 2024 U.S. presidential election, though, may pose new challenges for Ireland, in particular if his second-term policies include the introduction of tariffs on imports from European countries. Strong Trump administration support for Israel may also be another point of difference with Ireland.

Security and Defence: Getting Away with Free-Riding?

Ireland's policy of neutrality marks it out as unusual amongst America's European partners, most of who are members of NATO—all the more so since Finland and Sweden's accession to NATO following Russia's full-scale invasion of Ukraine in 2022. As noted, although the U.S. has occasionally criticised Ireland's neutrality and Ireland is sometimes critical of U.S. policies, this has not derailed the overall bilateral relationship. Irish governments carefully calibrate criticism of or opposition to specific U.S. policies with broad support for good relations with America and a pragmatic approach to issues in which the U.S. has a particular interest.

Ireland is particularly weak militarily—with armed forces numbering less than 10,000 personnel, no combat air force and defence spending of less than 1% of GDP in the last decade or so. Consequently, the country might be viewed as especially vulnerable to criticism of free-riding on the collective defence provided by NATO (even if it is not a member of the alliance). However, in general, the U.S. has not criticised Ireland on this issue. Ireland is perhaps small enough to get away with free-riding, whereas larger European states, such as Germany, face more criticism from the U.S.

Larger European debates on security and defence may be understood on a spectrum of opinion ranging from Atlanticists supporting NATO and close cooperation with the U.S. to Europeanists advocating greater independence from the U.S. and a stronger EU defence role. By contrast, Ireland does not really fit into this spectrum, emphasising instead support for multilateral institutions and soft power. In this context, Dublin has been a cautious partner in the EU's Common Security and Defence Policy (CSDP), seeking to balance engagement in defence projects such as Permanent Strucutured Cooperation (PESCO) with Ireland's longstanding policy of neutrality. While Russia's full-scale war against Ukraine since 2022 has made Ireland more conscious of security threats and resulted in more active defence cooperation with the EU and NATO, the policy of neutrality remains domestically popular and there are no calls for NATO membership.

Recommendations

Ireland and the EU should prepare for a more protectionist U.S., seeking to develop an economic model which is less dependent on the U.S. while remaining open to trade and economic cooperation with America. Ireland needs to do more to address its security and defence weaknesses, for instance in the maritime sphere, air defence and cyber security. Other European states should seek to help Ireland with this task, which can best be done through a variety of frameworks, including the EU, Ireland's partnership with NATO and bilateral or mini-lateral arrangements with Ireland's neighbours, including in particular the UK, France and the Nordic states.

Andrew Cottey is a Professor and an EU Jean Monnet Chair in the Department of Government and Politics, University College Cork, Ireland. An expert on European security, his publications include *Security in 21st Century Europe* (Bloomsbury), *The European Neutrals and NATO: Non-aligned, Partnership, Membership?* (Palgrave Macmillan) and articles in journals such as Journal of Common Market Studies, International Affairs, the British Journal of Political Science and International Relations and European Security.

University College Cork is one of Ireland's oldest universities with a dynamic learning environment with a global outlook and makes a major contribution to Ireland's economy and cultural identity.

Italy, the EU and the U.S.: A Multifaceted Bond

Riccardo Alcaro

Italy's relationship with the U.S. is marked by strong social, economic and political ties. Over 17 million Americans are of Italian descent and hundreds of thousands of Italians work in the U.S. Bilateral trade exceeds EUR 100 billion, while political-security cooperation is robust, bolstered by Prime Minister Giorgia Meloni's support for Ukraine. Despite differing views on some issues, Italy generally supports transatlantic collaboration, which benefits its interests within the EU. Trump's return to the White House could impact Italy's policies on Ukraine, European defence and trade, with Meloni likely to adapt her approach accordingly.

The Pillars of the U.S.-Italy Partnership

The relationship between Italy and the U.S. is characterised by deep societal connections, strong economic ties and strategic alignment.

Between 17 and 26 million U.S. citizens are of Italian descent, and 360,000 Italian citizens live and work across the Atlantic (Italy is home to much fewer American citizens—about 15,000). Economic relations are thriving. Bilateral trade in goods and services, now worth over EUR 100 billion, has grown by over 60% in 10 years. In 2023, Italian exports reached a record EUR 67 billion, making the U.S. the second largest destination market for Italian goods (after Germany), while imports from the U.S. hovered around EUR 25 billion. The stock of U.S. direct investments in Italy in 2022 was stuck at a modest EUR 24 billion, but Italian investment in the U.S. was more substantial (EUR 36 billion in stock and

R. Alcaro (✉)
Istituto Affari Internazionali, Rome, Italy
e-mail: r.alcaro@iai.it

EUR 4.8 billion in flows). Political-security cooperation is similarly strong. Prime Minister Giorgia Meloni's support for Ukraine and hera decision to quit China's Belt and Road Initiative won her significant goodwill in Washington as well as with Republicans.

In short, the relationship with the U.S. remains an unshakable organising principle of Italian foreign policy, widely shared across the political spectrum. Even parties that are home to critical U.S. voices—most notably the anti-establishment Five Star Movement—did not question the bond when in power (2018–22). Notably, U.S. domestic politics reverberate in Italy much louder than they used to. Particularly, Italy's right-wing parties, the *Lega* (League) and Meloni's *Fratelli d'Italia* (Brothers of Italy), are ideologically close to the native, intolerant and protectionist form of conservatism espoused by 'Make America Great Again' Republicans.

Elite support for the transatlantic relationship is reflected in public opinion, which by January 2024 generally expressed warm feelings towards the U.S. (with a score of 70/100) and NATO (74/100). This said, Italians of any political colour tend to be lukewarm at best towards US foreign policy activism, including the policy of arming Ukraine championed by the Biden administration and followed by successive Italian governments. This in part stems from the strong pacifist tradition within Italy's civil society. However, a measure of mistrust with U.S. foreign policy—a legacy of Italy's catholic, communist and post-fascist traditions, all of which had issues with U.S. political and cultural hegemony—lingers on in public opinion, despite the generally Atlanticist orientation of mainstream media.

The U.S. Factor in Italy's Engagement with the EU

For governments in Rome, as with others in the EU, developing synergies and containing tensions between the Atlantic and European dimensions of their international action have always been a strategic imperative.

Italy generally supports U.S. foreign initiatives within the EU, in the belief that transatlantic collaboration gives European foreign policy greater impact (as was the case in the Balkans or handling of the Iranian nuclear issue during the Obama years). On issues of less geopolitical relevance, though, Italy accords preference to intra-European over transatlantic consensus. For example, Rome opposed neither the adoption of counter-tariffs on U.S. goods in response to the duties adopted by the first Trump administration, nor the EU's carbon adjustment border mechanism in spite of the Biden administration's aversion. Italy remains nonetheless reluctant to take positions that could be perceived negatively in Washington. It has consequently avoided public controversy on issues such as the extraterritoriality of U.S. sanctions or risks to European industry from the subsidies and tax breaks for green energy contained in the 2022 U.S. IRA, which have generated so much tension in the EU.

The link with Washington has rarely prevented Italy from supporting a policy of greater EU cooperation, a line followed with few exceptions even by the rhetorically more Eurosceptic parties. After all, the three most pressing issues for Italian governments—fiscal spending capacity, migration control and trade—can better, or only, be pursued through greater European collaboration. However, even here Italy tends to pursue a level of integration that is acceptable in Washington, for instance being more open to the fact that strengthening the European defence industrial base would not cut out U.S. corporations.

The Impact of the 2024 U.S. Election

U.S. Democratic administrations have not looked favourably on a divided EU, and in this sense, the relationship with Washington has also worked as a brake on the Eurosceptic excesses of some Italian political forces, including the two main parties within the current government coalition, *Fratelli d'Italia* and *Lega*. Instead, Donald Trump's victory in the November 2024 election is likely to embolden European far-right parties to promote a vision of a Christian and illiberal (and implicitly white) West of sovereign nations. The transatlantic constraint on Meloni's EU policy may well vanish and she could have domestic incentives (including pressure from the more openly Eurosceptic *Lega*) to confront Brussels. However, while Meloni's foreign policy might align with Trump's transactional approach, his likely withdrawal of support for Ukraine would force her to adjust her position within a shifting European consensus. Trump's return could also spell trouble due to his focus on military spending, where Italy's low contributions regarding the NATO-set 2% of GDP minimum (soon to be raised to 3%) might easily draw criticism. Trade could be another major issue, as Trump's penchant for tariffs would risk hitting Italy's export-dependent economy hard.

Recommendations

In the light of the (opportunities and (many) risks that have opened up with Trump's re-election, Italy must prepare to act on three priorities: Ukraine and European security, European defence and trade. In each of these areas, Rome should move within the European framework.

Italy has an interest in containing Russian imperialism and denying Russian President Vladimir Putin's intolerant, anti-liberal regime a victory. Italy should insist with the second Trump administration that Europeans be included in any negotiations between Washington and Moscow. Italy should advocate for giving Ukraine, at the very least, guarantees that the flow of Western weapons will continue even if Kyiv has to give up on NATO membership. The Italian government should back this up with a firm commitment to participate in the effort, which is of the utmost importance as Ukraine will need a stable security environment to focus on the political and economic reforms necessary for EU accession. The latter should be presented to Trump as a way to reduce—over time—the need for assisting Ukraine financially.

A leap forward in defence industrial integration is functional for the EU's ability to manage the crisis in Ukraine and sharpen its credentials as a security actor. Especially with Trump back in the White House, Italy has every interest in championing the cause of European defence integration in Washington, including opening up the participation of U.S. companies in the process.

Finally, Italy should refrain from seeking bilateral talks with the Trump administration to defend itself against tariffs and instead join other Europeans in making it clear that the EU is ready for a trade war with the U.S., so as to strengthen Brussels' negotiating position in the inevitable negotiations that would follow.

Riccardo Alcaro is Research Coordinator and Head of the Global Actors Programme at the Istituto Affari Internazionali (IAI). His main area of expertise is transatlantic relations, with a special focus on U.S. and European policies in Europe's surrounding regions. Riccardo has been a Visiting Fellow at the Brookings Institution in Washington, D.C. and a Fellow of the EU-wide programme European Foreign and Security Policy Studies (EFSPS).

The Istituto Affari Internazionali (IAI) is an independent, private, non-profit think tank that studies international issues of strategic importance such as European integration, security and defence, international economics and global governance, energy and climate, Italian foreign policy; and cooperation and conflict in the Mediterranean and Middle East, Asia, Eurasia, Africa and the Americas.

A Friend in Need Is a Friend Indeed: Latvia and the U.S

Karlis Bukovskis and Aleksandra Palkova

Latvia's trust in the U.S. as strategic partner stems from geopolitical pragmatism together with small state foreign and security policy choices. The symbolic value of Latvia's economic development and democratisation for U.S. decision-makers coincides with Latvia's search for a major country's military and political patronage to counter Russia's unsolicited advances.

Founding the Evolution

The foundations of official Latvian-U.S. bilateral relations can be traced back to the U.S. Senate's resolution of 10 December 1918 supporting the Baltic states' independence, albeit the *de jure* recognition of Latvia took place only on 28 July 1922. This was followed by accreditation of the first ambassador with missions opened in Riga and Washington. During the interwar period, bilateral relations were robust and notably characterised by NGO assistance to Latvians in their state-building process. Subsequently, in the late 1930s, the U.S. embassy, seeking to gather intelligence on the Soviet Union, arranged political and cultural exchanges with visits to Riga by the then-former U.S. President Herbert Hoover and future U.S. President John F. Kennedy.

The most important moment with lasting consequences in bilateral relations was the U.S.' refusal to accept Soviet annexation of the Baltic states as announced in

1940. This non-recognition policy allowed Latvia's diplomatic mission in Washington, D.C. to operate as a symbol of the country's continued *de jure* existence and lobby for Baltic independence. Full diplomatic relations were re-established on 5 September 1991 following the collapse of the Soviet Union. Signing of the U.S.-Baltic Charter in 1998 and Latvia's NATO accession in 2004 marked significant milestones in deepening this partnership. Politically, the U.S. helped Latvia to regain its independence, with: the withdrawal of Russian troops early in the 1990s; NATO membership; provision of security guarantees; as well as financial and humanitarian assistance since Latvia's re-establishment. Latvia has been visited by sitting U.S. Presidents Bill Clinton and George W. Bush. In addition, the country has also hosted the then-Vice President Joe Biden and various U.S. state secretaries. Hence, the U.S. has been and is still seen as Latvia's strategic partner both politically and militarily.

However, economically the position is far from desirable. Aggregated U.S. FDI in Latvia in 2024 was only just above EUR 400 million, but even that constitutes historically the highest amount in more than three decades. Over the same period, Latvia's exports to the U.S. have traditionally amounted to twice the value of imports, with a total trade turnover exceeding EUR 800 million. In broad terms, this makes the U.S. Latvia's 10th largest trade partner. Exports of timber products, radio broadcasting equipment and other IT products constitute the greatest share of exports to the U.S., while U.S. exports mainly consist of aircraft products.

Culturally, the U.S. has played an essential role in promoting democratic practices in Latvia, especially following its independence in 1991. American organisations such as the National Democratic Institute, the International Republican Institute (IRI) and many others have supported Latvian civil society in enhancing political engagement, transparency and human rights. Educational exchanges, facilitated by programmes such as Fulbright and Baltic American Freedom Foundation, have fostered connections with Latvian students and professionals. American media has also deeply influenced Latvian culture, with U.S. television, films and music shaping local entertainment and lifestyles.

Polarisation of Society

Public perception of the U.S. in Latvia has generally been positive throughout the decades, shaped by a combination of political, historical and media influences. Since the beginning of the 1990s, the political scene has been dominated by pro-Western, pro-NATO, pro-EU and pro-U.S. parties. A few pro-Russian political parties, such as Harmony, have been taking a U.S.-sceptical stance, resonating with the Kremlin's views. However, the leading group of pro-Western parties have always been in decision-making positions and consequently, Latvian-U.S. relations have maintained a strong, uninterrupted and friendly character.

Public sentiment varies in a similar fashion. While ethnic Latvians (around 65% of the population) appreciate U.S. support for democracy and security and only around 15% see the U.S. in a negative light, among ethnically non-Latvian citizens the negative attitude is almost 50%. Nevertheless, on average most Latvians see the U.S. in a positive light, as the negatives are clearly caused by the Kremlin's traditional anti-U.S. narratives. The media plays a crucial role in shaping these views, with coverage ranging from supportive portrayals of U.S. military cooperation and democratic values to critical perspectives on U.S. cultural influence and global hegemony in Kremlin-supported media outlets available in Latvia until recently. Historical factors, such as the Soviet occupation and the U.S. role in supporting Latvian independence, contribute to both pro- and anti-U.S. sentiments. Many Latvians value U.S. assistance, but there is also a wariness linked to over-reliance on any foreign power.

Security in Partnership

The U.S. role is a cornerstone of Latvia's national defence strategy, covering a broad spectrum of issues. Latvian-U.S. partnership has grown in significance, especially since 2014, and the U.S. promises to protect the Baltic states unilaterally in case of NATO's inactivity. When Russia attacked Ukraine for the first time in 2014, not unexpectedly anxiety levels among Latvian people grew enormously. Of utmost importance has been the support displayed by then-President Barack Obama not just in the form of words, but also by sending U.S. troops to the Baltic states as part of Operation Atlantic Resolve as well as negotiating the Enhanced Forward Presence multinational battlegroups for NATO's Eastern flank countries since 2016.

Operation Atlantic Resolve aims to reassure NATO allies of U.S. commitment and includes the deployment of company-level units and helicopter units to conduct joint training exercises with Latvian forces and strengthen interoperability among NATO allies. In addition to military deployments, the U.S. has increased its defence assistance to Latvia through the Baltic Security Initiative, which in 2023 allocated over EUR 200 million to projects. Money is put towards improving Latvian military capabilities, including advanced training programmes and infrastructure enhancements. The rise in cyber threats, particularly from hostile state actors, has necessitated robust defences for critical infrastructure. Hence, the U.S. Cyber Command has been actively involved in Hunt Forward operations in Latvia aimed at detecting and mitigating cybersecurity threats.

Understandably, the political climate in the U.S. influences Latvia's security dynamics. The U.S. presidential elections always create worries about potential shifts that can impact the transatlantic security landscape. While President Joe Biden has reinforced transatlantic ties and increased military support for Eastern European allies, including Latvia, the administration of President Donald Trump saw relations with NATO as more transactional, creating uncertainty among European allies about the U.S.' long-term commitment to European security. Arguably, any uncertainty of this kind impacts Latvia's security planning and strategic alignment, given its dependence on U.S. military and political support. The same logic of more certainty also remains at the core of Latvia's outlook on the results of the

2024 U.S. presidential elections. Latvia will work with election winner President Donald Trump, as dictated by its geopolitical and national interests. Continuity, predictability and reliability on both the future of NATO and support for Ukraine by the next U.S. administration are the preferred option.

Recommendations

The EU needs to accept the importance of NATO and non-EU members in traditional defence. It should build its capacities in non-NATO areas, mindful that hybrid war tactics are becoming increasingly prominent. The EU has sole responsibility for dealing with attacks outside the traditional military domain, such as weaponisation of migration, abuse of the international legal system, spreading propaganda and misinformation, character assassinations of decision-makers and so on.

On economic matters, the robust U.S.-Latvia trade relationship provides a foundation for expanded and more reliable cooperation. The EU should leverage Latvia's dynamic economic ties with the U.S. to promote investment, entrepreneurship and a level playing field for businesses on both sides of the Atlantic. Increasing mutual investments between Latvia and the U.S. is of importance as it represents another level of security.

Building a positive image of Latvia and the Baltic countries in the U.S. is essential. Not only familiarising U.S. citizens with the EU, the Baltic states and Latvia, but also building a positive image via the entertainment industry and cultural exchanges is paramount to raise awareness not just of the existence of Latvia and the Baltics, but also of the need to protect its uniqueness.

By pursuing a balanced approach of selective cooperation and principled independence, the EU and Latvia can navigate any difficulties encountered with the transatlantic relationship in a manner that advances their shared interests while preserving their ability to act autonomously when necessary.

Karlis Bukovskis is the Director of the Latvian Institute of International Affairs and an Associate Professor at Riga Stradins University. Bukovskis was a visiting Fulbright Scholar at the Johns Hopkins University SAIS in 2021 and an Associate Researcher at the European Council on Foreign Relations from 2017 to 2021. He also produces and co-hosts a programme on Latvian Radio 1 in which he analyses the political economy of various countries.

Aleksandra Palkova is Head of the EU Research Programme at the Latvian Institute of International Affairs. She is a Guest Lecturer at Riga Stradins University, specialising in EU affairs and security. Since 2021, she has been an Associate Researcher at the European Council on Foreign Relations. From 2023 until 2024, she has served as a NATO Parliamentary Assembly Researcher on the Political Committee. From 2022, she is PhD Student at Riga Stradins University.

Lithuania's Transatlantic Dilemma: How to Maintain U.S. Interest in Baltic Security?

Ramūnas Vilpišauskas

Since the early 1990s, Lithuania has regarded the U.S. and NATO membership as vital for its security. It has been a strong supporter of transatlanticism within the EU, although the presidency of Donald Trump in 2016–2020 led to a reassessment of the country's cautious stance towards security and defence cooperation within the EU. Domestic politics in the U.S. and the presence of threats from authoritarian Russia are likely to continue pushing Lithuania's political elites to search for ways of maintaining American interest in Baltic security, while at the same time stepping up military cooperation with European NATO partners such as Germany, Poland and the UK.

Freedom Aspirations Complicated by Geopolitics

The U.S.-Lithuanian official relationship dates back to the interwar period in the 1920s and 1930s. The U.S. was among the first countries to recognise the independent state of Lithuania on 28 July 1922, albeit that was some years after the official declaration of independence by Lithuania on 16 February 1918. Broader geopolitical changes in the region, which followed the First World War and the Bolshevik revolution in Russia, were behind the initially cautious approach of the U.S. towards recognising independent Baltic states.

Following the Second World War, America's policy of non-recognition of the Baltic states' occupation by the Soviet Union provided an important anchor for the Lithuanian population that one day the country's sovereignty and freedom

---

R. Vilpišauskas (✉)
Institute of International Relations and Political Science, Vilnius University, Vilnius, Lithuania
e-mail: ramunas.vilpisauskas@tspmi.vu.lt

© The Author(s), under exclusive license to Springer Nature Switzerland AG 2025
M. Kaeding et al. (eds.), *The United States and the Future of Europe*,
https://doi.org/10.1007/978-3-031-83350-2_17

would be restored. For many households, it was a daily ritual of trying to listen to the Voice of America radio news broadcasted from Washington, D.C. in Lithuanian, despite Soviet jamming of the radio waves. During that period, Lithuanian diplomatic representation continued in the U.S.

In the second half of the 1980s, in Lithuania and other Baltic states popular movements for restoring statehood gathered pace. In Lithuania, many were hoping for political support from the U.S. after the country's parliament declared the re-establishment of independence on 11 March 1990. However, although U.S. administrations have been continually supporting the freedom aspirations of the Baltic nations, the changes in Lithuania were just one small piece of a much bigger geopolitical puzzle which included shifts taking place as the Cold War ended such as the reunification of Germany, the Soviet Army's withdrawal from Central and Eastern European countries followed later by enlargement of the EU and NATO.

It was only after the failed *coup d'état* in Moscow in August 1991 that most Western countries recognised Lithuania's independence. The U.S. established diplomatic relations with the government of Lithuania in September 1991 and at the end of that year Lithuania started enjoying the most-favoured treatment in relations with the U.S. The agreement on bilateral trade and intellectual property protection followed in 1994 and a bilateral investment treaty in 1997. In 1998, the U.S. signed a charter of partnership with all three Baltic countries, establishing working groups on regional security, defence and economic issues.

Economically, the U.S. has been less important for Lithuania as a trade partner compared to neighbouring EU Member States. According to the Ministry of Foreign Affairs, in 2022 the U.S. was the seventh most important export market for Lithuania and the fourth most important source of imports, including fossil fuels (LNG). In terms of FDIs, the U.S. was the 12th largest investor in Lithuania, but it was the top destination for investments from Lithuania. The U.S. was seventh regarding the number of tourists who visited Lithuania in 2022. There is also a Lithuanian migrant diaspora in the U.S., which, according to the population census of 2022, exceeds 620,000 people and has been characterised by the Lithuanian government as forming a key pillar of pursuing priorities of the bilateral relationship. Lithuanian migrants in the U.S. played an important role in advocating for Lithuania's interests in the U.S., some of them returned to Lithuania after 1990 to participate in its politics or as investors.

Instinctive Transatlanticists

The Lithuanian public generally can be characterised as transatlanticist and supportive of a partnership with the U.S. as well as the country's membership in NATO. This can be seen from various surveys, which have been undertaken on the subject. For example, the Eurobarometer surveys conducted at the time of U.S.-EU negotiations on the TTIP in 2014 and 2015 showed that Lithuania (and Malta) had 79% of respondents indicating their approval of TTIP—the highest share among all EU Member States—with only 7% indicating their disapproval. According to the NATO survey of November–December 2023, 91% of Lithuanian respondents indicated that they consider the transatlantic bond important in dealing with security challenges (second highest share among all NATO members).

This strong popular support for transatlantic relations has also been reflected in a robust agreement of parliamentary parties about the importance of the U.S. presence in the region for Lithuania's security and policies pursued by successive governments. Accession to NATO along the accession to the EU has been the key priority of Lithuania's foreign policy since the early 1990s. After it was achieved in 2004, the agreement on foreign policy priorities for 2004–2008 adopted by the country's political parties declared further strengthening of Lithuania and the EU's transatlantic relations and developing cooperation with North America, in particular, the U.S., as its first goal, with the provisions on the importance of supporting EU integration coming afterwards. It also stressed that NATO was considered the most important collective security organisation for Lithuania.

Most recently, in May 2024, the Lithuanian government adopted strategic guidelines on Lithuania's relations with the U.S. It stated that the strategic partnership with the U.S. is based on common fundamental values and remains key for Lithuania's security and welfare. It pledged to do everything it takes to ensure U.S. attention and presence in Lithuania and its region in these times of geopolitical shifts, at the same time acknowledging that a U.S. pivot to Asia is likely to continue and that due to political polarisation within America, its policies and decision-making processes are becoming increasingly unpredictable.

It's Security, Stupid

Thus, in Lithuania relations with the U.S. are seen mostly through the prism of security, especially after Russia's attacks on neighbouring Georgia and Ukraine. The perceived need to convince the U.S. to support Lithuania's NATO accession and later to increase its military presence in the region affected other policies ranging from investment promotion to alignment of the country's positions with the U.S. in various matters of international affairs. Some policies proved controversial and were politicised domestically. For example, sale of the oil refinery 'Mažeikių nafta' to the U.S. company Williams, initially seen by supporters as an additional incentive for the U.S. to support Lithuania's NATO aspirations, eventually led to the resignation of Prime Minister Rolandas Paksas in 1999, arguing that it was a costly deal for Lithuania. Another controversy was related to the presence of the secret CIA prison in Lithuania in 2005–2006, where the U.S. allegedly kept suspected terrorists.

Lithuania has been among those Central and Eastern European countries which expressed their support for U.S. intervention in Iraq, following the terrorist attacks of 11 September 2001 against the U.S. It was also active in contributing special forces for the NATO operations in Afghanistan, which was provided as evidence of the country's contribution to the alliance's collective security at a time when Lithuania's defence expenditure was well below 2% of the country's GDP. However, after Russia's war against Ukraine in 2014, Lithuania's successive governments started increasing defence expenditure, expected to reach around 2.7% of GDP in 2024. There are suggestions that this expenditure should continue increasing to match the same proportion of GDP as America's share of military spending (3%) or even reach 5–6% of GDP.

Lithuania has also been receptive to shifts in U.S. foreign policy, in particular re-aligning its policy towards China. It was among the first in the EU to introduce restrictions on the use of certain technologies and investments from China around 2018–2019. The decision which attracted particular international media attention (and domestic criticism from opposition parties, which is unusual concerning foreign policy issues) was the decision of the centre-right coalition government in 2021 to allow the opening of a Taiwanese representative office in Lithuania. Many observers saw this as an effort of the country's government to signal to the U.S. that it is keen to develop relations with democracies in the Indo-Pacific region, even in the face of diplomatic and economic sanctions imposed by China.

Similar aspirations to cooperate with the U.S. in strengthening relations with the Indo-Pacific region to counter authoritarian China are expressed in the recently adopted strategic guidelines. They outline further directions of strengthening bilateral cooperation with the U.S. as well as working together with other Baltic states, the Nordic-Baltic 8, the Bucharest 9 countries and through the EU to maintain U.S. interest in the region. In addition, Lithuania's efforts in coordinating EU-wide sanctions concerning violators of international norms—Belarus, Russia, Iran—including via the G7 format, could also be seen as another forum for trying to align its policy with the U.S.

Hedging and Diversifying

For a decade after joining the EU, Lithuania advocated transatlanticism in trade, investment and security policies. It was cautious towards proposals regarding a stronger EU in terms of security and defence, seeing this as a potential weakening of America's role in European security. However, the election of Trump in 2016 and his transactional approach towards allies resulted in a twofold change in Lithuania's policy. While it continued signalling to the U.S. about its policy alignment, it doubled down on increasing defence expenditure and investing in areas such as cyber security. At the same time, it became more supportive of cooperation with EU countries in security and defence matters. A stronger EU role in this field, especially more defence spending by European NATO members, started to be seen as an argument to convince the U.S. that European countries were shouldering their fair share of the collective burden, and it serves U.S. interests to remain part of the alliance. This view is likely to be strengthened even more after the election of Donald Trump in 2024.

The decision from NATO's Warsaw summit in 2016 to establish enhanced forward presence in Lithuania from 2017 led by Germany further strengthened security and defence cooperation with Germany and other European NATO members. This trend was further reinforced by the agreement of Germany and Lithuania, in response to Russia's full-scale war against Ukraine in 2022, to work towards establishment of a German brigade in Lithuania by 2027. At the same time, Lithuania continued its active efforts to maintain and increase the U.S. military presence in the country, with its rotating military forces stationed since 2019 (from 2022 increased to the size of a battalion), by announcing a series of purchases of different types of weapons produced in the U.S. The military presence of both the U.S. and Germany is seen as mutually reinforcing and necessary for credible deterrence of any potential aggressor.

Lithuania should seek to maintain a good working relationship with administrations of either U.S. political parties. Although the Trump administration is remembered for its transactional and occasionally unpredictable decision-making, it was under this administration that the U.S. increased its military presence in the region. At the same time, while the Biden administration was appreciated for its strong initial leadership in supporting Ukraine, there was a growing disappointment with its too incremental and conditional provision of military assistance and reluctance to accelerate the country's NATO accession.

Recommendations

For decades, Lithuania has viewed the U.S. as the most important security actor in the region, a perception only strengthened since Russia's full-scale invasion of Ukraine in 2022. Hence, EU institutions need to understand the concerns of Lithuania and other Eastern flank NATO members in not only further developing coordinated security and military policies, but also trying to prepare for any future U.S. foreign policy changes following Trump's election in 2024.

The EU has been relatively active and united in its response to Russia's violations of fundamental international norms, although from Lithuania's point of view, more and faster decisions could have been taken concerning sanctioning the aggressor and assisting Ukraine. As the new European Commission starts its work, it is important to focus on overcoming fragmentation around producing weapons and dual-use goods inside the EU single market and more coordination of their procurements (without discriminating purchases from the U.S.). The choice of Lithuania's former Prime Minister Andrius Kubilius as a defence commissioner provides an opportunity to contribute to improved coordination of military equipment standards and procurement efforts among European NATO members.

The main dilemma for Lithuania will be how to find the right balance between bilateral efforts to signal to the U.S. that it remains a reliable partner, contributing its fair share to collective defence while being attentive to U.S. global concerns, and coordinated efforts within the EU to strengthen collective efforts to invest in European security and defence. Unfortunately, domestic politics in Germany and France with the rise of parties hostile to the U.S., the EU and international cooperation more generally might become a major new obstacle for those efforts.

Ramūnas Vilpišauskas is a Professor at the Institute of International Relations and Political Science (IIRPS) of Vilnius University. In Autumn 2024, he was a Konrad Adenauer Visiting Scholar at Carleton University (Ottawa) teaching a course on transatlantic relations. In 2020–2023, he was a Jean Monnet Chair Professor at Vilnius University. From 2009 to 2019, he was Director of the IIRPS. In 2004–2009, he worked as Chief Economic Policy Advisor to the President of Lithuania, Valdas Adamkus. The Institute of International Relations and Political Science of Vilnius University is one of the most prominent social sciences institutions in Eastern Europe and the Baltic region. IIRPS is also a member of TEPSA.

Malta and the United States: A Common Interest in Mediterranean Security

Mark Harwood

A relationship between the world's only remaining superpower and one of Europe's smallest countries would seem unlikely, but Malta-U.S. relations stretch back over two hundred years to a time when Malta was governed by the Knights of Malta (the Knights Hospitaller). In 1783, Benjamin Franklin requested that American ships be granted access to Maltese ports, with the first U.S. Consul to the Knights of Malta being appointed in 1796. By 1800, Malta had come under British control and bilateral relations with the U.S. ended. However, increased American interest in European security during the Second World War saw a growing appreciation of Malta's strategic importance in the Mediterranean and it was in Malta that George H. W. Bush and Mikhail Gorbachev declared the end of the Cold War in 1989. However, Malta's strategic position at the centre of the Mediterranean, its neutrality and view of NATO as a means of facilitating EU membership (rather than as an opportunity for collective defence) have meant that the U.S. represents a different type of partner for Malta compared with many countries' views of the U.S. from continental Europe.

Bilateral Relations as Opposed to Collective Defence

Following Malta's independence, diplomatic relations with the U.S. were established in 1964. The ruling Christian Democrats had already signed a defence agreement with the UK in that same year and the U.S. government made clear that it was not in favour of Malta joining NATO as long as its military pact with

M. Harwood (✉)
Institute for European Studies, University of Malta, Msida, Malta
e-mail: mark.harwood@um.edu.mt

the UK protected the country from becoming part of the Soviet sphere of influence. This position was short-sighted, as NATO's Mediterranean Headquarters was shut down in 1971 when the Socialists took government. As is typical in Malta's two-party, highly polarised politics, the pro-West policy of the Christian Democrats was quickly reversed by a Socialist government, which favoured non-alignment and swung heavily towards cooperation with Libya. Following the eventual closure of British military bases in 1979, Malta declared itself neutral in 1980, with this being incorporated into its constitution by 1987 with specific reference to the position that its ports could not be used by either superpower.

While prickly at times, Malta-U.S. relations have endured, based on bilateral trade and a common understanding of the importance of Mediterranean security. Regarding trade, in 2020 the U.S. supplied 2.2% of Malta's total imports while buying 3.7% of Malta's total exports, making the U.S. Malta's eighth most important export market, but a far less significant import partner. In terms of exports, these are dominated by medicines, electronic integrated circuits, semiconductors and aircraft parts, while imports focus on fuel and gas, aircraft engines and navigation instruments. Various U.S. companies operate in Malta, including major hotel chains, light manufacturing, commercial banknote printing facilities and pharmaceutical companies, with the Americans estimating that one in thirty jobs in Malta is linked to their businesses. To facilitate economic relations, a double taxation agreement was signed in 2008.

Beyond economic relations, bilateral cooperation is grounded in a common perception of the need for regional security. As stated by the U.S. government, 'the Mediterranean has long been a global crossroads, Malta's strategic position underlines its role as one of our key international partners in finding solutions to issues of global transnational importance'. To this end, there is a U.S.-Malta partnership on the Central Mediterranean Security Initiative and Malta hosts the co-sponsored International Institute for Justice and the Rule of Law. Much of America's financial and technical support has focused on the Maltese Customs Department, to strengthen export control, border security and non-proliferation of weapons of mass destruction (as Malta became an important transport hub in the Mediterranean in the 1990s). There is also support for the armed forces, focusing on cooperation to uphold safety of life at sea, maritime security and freedom of navigation in the Mediterranean.

In this way, Malta and the U.S. enjoy an enduring bilateral relationship, united by economic interests as well as a common concern with the security of the central Mediterranean and its importance for neighbouring regions. That said, areas of discord do persist. These include: American concerns over Malta's financial regulations; the high number of Russians granted Maltese citizenship through the 'golden passport' scheme; as well as continuing differences in foreign affairs, with Malta retaining extensive links with various factions in Libya. However, the overall relationship is cooperative and this is echoed by public perception of the U.S. which remains consistently positive though support can fluctuate, as occurred during the Trump administration. While data is sparse, 68% of Maltese expressed a negative opinion of Trump when he was elected in 2016, compared to 72% with a positive opinion of Biden in 2020. In 2020, Malta's Prime Minister described the Biden-Harris victory as 'inspiring'.

NATO as a Dimension in Malta's EU Membership

Most EU countries view relations with the U.S. through an economic and security lens, with NATO featuring as an important component in the latter, as an opportunity for collective defence. For Malta, its neutrality has limited its participation with defence organisations, and hence, NATO has been seen mainly as a means of facilitating Malta's EU membership; Malta joined NATO's Partnership for Peace in 1995, so as to address EU concerns that Malta's neutrality made its EU application problematic (in terms of foreign and security cooperation). Once elected in 1996, the Socialists withdrew Malta from Partnership for Peace, but the country re-joined in 2008, as a means of facilitating its participation in the EU's External Relations' Council, where NATO-related documents are circulated, but unaffiliated Member States are precluded from accessing.

In 2024, Malta signed the latest framework with NATO, the Individually Tailored Partnership Programme, representing an enhanced level of cooperation, including human security, countering hybrid threats and cyber defence. As stated by NATO itself, Malta is believed to offer much to NATO in terms of its special expertise in international maritime law, diplomatic studies, search and rescue as well as Arabic culture and language training. These areas reinforce the long history of bilateral cooperation between Malta and the U.S. where the focus avoids areas of military cooperation. The wider discussion of European security cooperation, collective defence and the role of NATO in European defence do not feature prominently in Maltese politics. Ultimately, Malta cooperates with the U.S. to strengthen regional security, participates in NATO as a means to lubricate its membership of the Union's CSDP and sees little urgency to change the *status quo*.

Recommendations

In viewing the future of bilateral relations, it is clear that the emphasis will remain squarely geared towards mutual cooperation. That said, Malta should support a global rebalancing that gives greater prominence to the EU, as with reform of the UN Security Council and the promotion of other international fora such as the Organisation for Security and Co-Operation in Europe. On a regional level, the Socialists once advocated for Malta as a 'Switzerland in the Mediterranean'. Maybe the time has come for a different model, possibly a 'Geneva in the Mediterranean', for Malta to invest in being a host for regional bodies, supported by the EU, operating as a real bridge in the Mediterranean, further strengthening Malta's strategic importance for both the EU and the U.S. Finally, while far from popular with the Maltese people, Trump winning the 2024 presidential election is unlikely to destabilise bilateral relations which have always been technical, low-key and underscored by mutual interests. Neither Trump's lack of enthusiasm for NATO nor his foreign policy goals in the Mediterranean region will raise eyebrows in Malta with the result that, as in the past, bilateral relations will continue with 'business as usual'.

Mark Harwood is a Professor of European comparative politics at the University of Malta within the Institute for European Studies. Having previously worked for the European Commission as well as the Maltese Government, his area of research is the impact of EU membership on Malta.

The Institute for European Studies was founded in 1991 as a teaching and research institute within the University of Malta. Offering a full range of degree programmes up to Ph.D. level, the Institute has over 1000 alumni. The Institute is also a member of TEPSA.

Dutch-U.S. Relations: Navigating Atlanticism under Pressure

Giselle Bosse, Lion Lehmbecker, and Lia Spornraft

The Netherlands has a long-standing pro-Atlanticist orientation, which in the post-Cold War era has gradually evolved within a dual-track foreign policy strategy, through which the Netherlands maintains close transatlantic relations while at the same time placing a strong focus on European cooperation. However, over the past decade, this dual-track strategy has increasingly come under pressure: from within the EU as Member States increasingly strive for more autonomy from the U.S.; and more recently also domestically, where the new right-wing government led by Prime Minister Dick Schoof has announced cuts in spending on diplomatic relations. Furthermore, there are struggles to maintain foreign policy coherence as the leader of the far-right Freedom Party (*Partij voor de Vrijheid*—PVV), Geert Wilders, looks to pursue his own foreign policy objectives.

The Dutch Dual Strategy of Atlantic and European Cooperation

The Netherlands has a long-standing tradition of Anglo-American orientation, dating back to the very foundation of the U.S. Dutch solidarity with the U.S. which was further reinforced in more recent history, often appearing closer to the U.S. than to its European neighbours. This sentiment was particularly evident during the Cold War, during which the Netherlands maintained a stance that supported Atlantic unity. In the post-Cold War era, the Netherlands gradually reoriented its focus towards fellow European countries while retaining close transatlantic relations, thus developing a dual-track foreign policy strategy of Atlantic and European cooperation.

These historical connections persist to this day. Economically, the U.S. is the largest foreign direct investor in the Netherlands, with investment totalling USD 885 billion in 2021, while the Netherlands ranks as the seventh-largest investor in the U.S. Dutch companies in the U.S. are responsible for creating over 600,000 direct jobs. Additionally, with a bilateral trade surplus of USD 18.2 billion in 2021, the U.S. holds its second-largest trade surplus with the Netherlands.

The Dutch dual strategy of commitment to both European and transatlantic relations continues to influence the political landscape. Nevertheless, earlier Atlanticism has gradually evolved into a more pragmatic approach, both economically and militarily, in response to changing societal values and political developments in both countries. Over the past decade, The Hague has also become more European, which is visible in its active participation in PESCO, in the European Defence Fund and in the European Intervention Initiative, for example.

This shift is also evident in the evolution of Dutch trade policies. Under Prime Minister Rutte, the traditionally liberal Netherlands has begun to adopt a French-inspired stance on strategic autonomy in trade. This change is further illustrated by the rise of political parties that oppose a free trade agreement with Mercosur, advocating instead for the protection of Dutch farmers.

Atlanticist Consensus No More? The Positions of Dutch Political Parties and Public Opinion

In 2024, some of these trends are reflected in the positions of major Dutch political parties, which range from traditional pro-Atlanticist views to pro-European stances more critical of the U.S. The centre-right People's Party for Freedom and Democracy (*Volkspartij voor Vrijheid en Democratie*—VVD) and New Social Contract (*Nieuw Sociaal Contract*—NSC) unequivocally affirm the transatlantic relationship's value, strongly linking it with NATO and security prerogatives.

In contrast, other parties predominantly focus their policy orientation on the EU, for instance by advocating for a more assertive EU role within NATO. The Green Left (*GroenLinks*—GL) and Labour Party (*Partij van de Arbeid*—PvdA) still raise concerns about the damage inflicted on NATO by the U.S. under President Trump, while the social liberal and progressive political party Democrats 66 (D66) cautions against uncritical alignment with the U.S. The latter parties' current stances thus represent a visible departure from the traditional Dutch Atlanticism. The position of Geert Wilders' far-right populist PVV remains ambiguous on foreign policy issues more generally. Wilders as leader of the PVV has previously expressed support for Russia's war against Ukraine, yet the new government coalition, of which the PVV is part, commits firmly to NATO and military support for Ukraine.

The Dutch population's view of the U.S. was severely impacted by Trump's presidency. However, it recovered speedily after Biden was elected president. In 2016, with Obama still president, 65% of the Dutch viewed the U.S. positively. In 2017, after Trump was elected, this number plummeted to 37% and reached a new low during Trump's last year in office with just 30% of Dutch people thinking favourably about the U.S. With the beginning of Biden's term, the numbers recovered quickly. In 2021, the number of Dutch people with a positive opinion about the U.S. jumped to 57%. By 2022, nearly 90% of the Dutch population looked upon the U.S. as a reliable partner for their country. Generally, conservative-leaning respondents tended to have a more favourable view compared with those leaning to the political left. Nevertheless, domestic political tensions in the U.S. are clearly recognised, with over 90% of Dutch citizens perceiving the partisan divides in U.S. society as strong or very strong.

Dutch-U.S. Security Relations and the U.S. Elections

The U.S. and NATO serve as principal security providers for the Netherlands. This is clearly visible in the Dutch approach to security. At the same time, the EU has become an important secondary framework for Dutch security, which moved successive governments led by former Prime Minister Mark Rutte to pursue a dual strategy on Atlantic and European cooperation. The Netherlands advocates for a stronger transatlantic security relationship through EU defence initiatives. By participating in EU defence discussions, the Netherlands can influence U.S. policies while at the same time also reinforcing NATO commitments.

The election of Donald Trump to the White House is expected to significantly alter the U.S. approach to NATO and its commitment to the European theatre. While the specifics of his presidency remain uncertain, it is likely that a Trump administration will reduce U.S. military involvement in Europe, potentially redeploying most U.S. ground troops stationed there. This reduction could be accompanied by pressure on European states to increase their military spending, linking the use of Article 5 to bring about a minimum defence expenditure equivalent to 2% of GDP. Such measures would probably undermine the credibility of NATO and Article 5, leading to a more transactional nature of NATO with European states, including the Netherlands, facing increased pressure to compensate for this shortfall.

These developments pose a significant challenge to the Dutch reliance on NATO and the U.S. for security, as the Trump administration may not wish to sustain this relationship. At the same time, many of these challenges are not new and were already present during Trump's previous term from 2017 to 2021. Throughout that period, the Netherlands remained committed to a close relationship with the U.S., though there is a debate among analysts about the extent to which this relationship was damaged during the Trump years.

Were the U.S.-Dutch security relationship to deteriorate as a result of a Trump presidency, then there would be significant pressure on the Netherlands to shift a greater focus on further European security cooperation and integration.

Dutch-U.S. Security Relations and the New Dutch Government

With the exit of the pro-Atlanticist UK from the EU and developments in a wider geopolitical context, the EU has already embarked on achieving greater EU autonomy in security and defence. However, this did not come at the cost of intergovernmental cooperation in security between the EU and UK, which has seen an uptick since Russia's invasion of Ukraine. As a result, the Netherlands has found it increasingly challenging to maintain its traditional pro-Atlanticist position within the EU. With Trump as president, the trend towards EU security and defence integration will not only continue but also accelerate. Calls for greater strategic autonomy and European military independence are likely to become more pronounced.

While the increasing pressures of Europeanisation would make it harder for the Dutch government to maintain its dual strategy on transatlantic relations, Dutch foreign policy towards the U.S. will also be contingent upon developments in Dutch domestic politics. In its government programme published on 13 September 2024, the new right-wing Dutch government of PVV, VVD, NSC and the Farmer-Citizen Movement (BBB) reaffirms its commitment to NATO and the EU, including the dual strategy, confirming that it wants Europe to cherish and strengthen the transatlantic bond, while at the same time taking more responsibility for its own security.

Yet, the government has also announced cuts in spending on Dutch diplomatic representation abroad, thereby placing greater emphasis on Dutch interests in the context of its relations with the EU. Moreover, governing parties' adherence to the government programme remains uncertain.

The PVV, in particular, has traditionally opposed further European integration in the defence sector and has even called for reversal, casting doubt on its commitment to European integration. Furthermore, the decision by Geert Wilders to meet Ukrainian President Zelenskyy in early September 2024, which took place without the approval or knowledge of the Dutch government, suggests that the government programme could be bypassed again in the future, with potentially detrimental effects on the credibility and reliability of Dutch foreign policy.

Trump's election is likely to influence the PVV's rationale, particularly given its long-standing ties with Trump's campaign team and alignment on issue such as migration. It is conceivable that Wilders may view the Trump presidency as an opportunity to hinder European security and defence integration by focusing on bilateral relations with a 'sympathetic' U.S. president.

Recommendations

In the short and medium terms, the Dutch government should maintain its dual strategy of transatlantic and European cooperation, to signal continuity to partners on both sides of the Atlantic. The Netherlands' approach to the first Trump presidency has shown that cooperation can continue even at a time when Euro-Atlantic relations have come under significant strain. In the longer term, though, the Netherlands must prepare for a dual strategy that is tilted more strongly towards strengthening European security and defence cooperation as part of NATO, as it is likely that the U.S.' commitment to Europe will continue to diminish. The Netherlands continues to be ideally placed as a mediator between the EU and the U.S., as well as between pro-Atlanticist EU Member States and those favouring greater EU strategic autonomy.

At the same time, the Dutch government must strive to play a central role in European defence cooperation formats, to avoid being sidelined in major European defence initiatives and projects. While the new Dutch government has pledged to increase defence spending, words also have to be turned into deeds at European level. Decreasing spending on diplomatic relations and development aid, as well as internal contestation over foreign policy leadership, is likely to reduce the credibility of the Netherlands as a reliable and consistent foreign policy actor, not only within Europe, but also in transatlantic relations and the wider world.

Giselle Bosse is a Full Professor and holds a personal chair in EU External Democracy Support, as well as the Jean Monnet Chair in EU Foreign Policy and International Relations at the Faculty of Arts and Social Sciences, Maastricht University. She is also, a Fellow at the European Democracy Hub in Brussels and Visiting Professor at the College of Europe in Bruges, and (co-)leads work packages on EU democracy support in the EU Horizon projects InvigoratEU and EMBRACE. Bosse is an expert in EU and Dutch foreign policy, EU relations with Eastern Europe and EU enlargement.

Lion Moritz Lehmbecker is B.A. European Studies Honours student at Maastricht University. He is specialising in European foreign policy and international relations with a focus on EU foreign policy decision-making and EU-Ukraine relations. He is a research assistant in Maastricht University's team participating in EU Horizon Project InvigoratEU.

Lia Spornraft is studying B.Sc. Global Studies at the Faculty of Arts and Social Sciences, Maastricht University. She is a research assistant in Maastricht University's team participating in the EU Horizon Project InvigoratEU. Additionally, she is a student assistant for the Centre for European Research in Maastricht (CERiM).

Devoted Atlanticists in Warsaw, Irrespective of Circumstances?

Magdalena Góra

The U.S. occupies a special place in Polish strategic culture. Polish security is built on the premise of an American presence in Europe. Poles are strong Atlanticists, claiming common historical and value-based foundations for U.S. cooperation and promotion in Europe. The special status that Poles want to see in this relationship is anchored as much in historical experiences as in contemporary, vibrant economic and security cooperation. Poles see themselves as U.S. protegees as well as reliable allies within NATO and bilateral cooperation. That also often impacts cooperation with European partners, particularly in terms of security. The new dynamic in U.S. domestic politics and negative trends in international relations as the country pivots more towards the Pacific demand some adjustments in Poland's approach to transatlantic relations.

Distant Friends

The U.S. is one of very few 'distant friends' that Poland counted on in dealing with its difficult geopolitically sandwiched position between German and Russian imperialism. The strong pro-American disposition of Poles and the Polish state originated during the American Revolution, when many Poles participated in the revolutionary efforts drawn by their own experience of partitions and imperialism. Most notably, Tadeusz Kościuszko—leader of the failed Polish uprising against partitions of Poland in 1794—joined the American Revolution and befriended

M. Góra (✉)
Institute of European Studies, Jagiellonian University, Kraków, Poland
e-mail: mm.gora@uj.edu.pl

Thomas Jefferson. Kościuszko and Kazimierz Pułaski—another Polish and American hero fighting in the American independence war—became a reminder of commonalities in how freedom and independence were perceived and prioritised by Poles and Americans. During the period of Poland's partition at the end of the eighteenth century, the U.S. became a destination for emigration (including for Polish Jews). It is estimated, albeit unconfirmed, that up to the First World War around 2.2 million people had left Polish territories and emigrated to the U.S. Ultimately, the Americans also played an important role in how Poland regained its independence in 1918. Among 14 points raised in the U.S. Congress by Woodrow Wilson in January 1918, one demanded that Poles should be granted an independent state, a goal which was achieved in November of that year.

The U.S. officially recognised Poland and initiated diplomatic relations in 1918. Despite much less attention during the interwar period, the Polish diaspora in the U.S. was a significant actor in developing closer ties between the two countries. The importance of the U.S. in Polish foreign policy increased during the Second World War, particularly as a target of a political campaign by the London-based Polish government in exile. Despite support for the government of national unity that was supposed to govern Poland following the war, American diplomacy could do little to save the country from Soviet occupation and ultimately its position behind the Iron Curtain. However, Poles can certainly remember American efforts to provide independent news through the famous Radio Free Europe and even Soviet propaganda could not really overcome the Polish pro-American attitudes.

The U.S. government became especially active in the late period of Soviet dominance in Poland, particularly during the Polish Crisis when General Wojciech Jaruzelski imposed martial law against the Solidarity movement led by Lech Wałęsa. Not only were Americans in covert operations supporting Solidarity before the violent suppression of the free trade unions by the Polish communist government, but Ronald Reagan's administration imposed severe sanctions against Poland as well as against the Soviet Union. Even if these led to a deepening economic crisis in Poland, Poles supported it. It also actually contributed to the ultimate weakening of the Soviet Union. The U.S. became an indispensable supporter during the Round Table negotiations and in the early days after the democratic government of Tadeusz Mazowiecki was formed following the first (semi)free elections in post-war Poland in June 1989. All Polish governments since have put relations with the U.S. high on their lists of priorities, thereby confirming the country's deeply rooted Atlanticist position.

Strong Value-Based Atlanticism

Poles continue to believe that they have a special relationship with the U.S., which is reflected in how they perceive the U.S. and Americans. Over the past 30 years, most Poles have consistently displayed a positive view of the U.S. and Americans. In 2023, the Pew Research Centre indicated that 93% of Poles had positive attitudes towards the U.S.—the highest in the world. While this support dropped by 7% in 2024, Poles remain global leaders in positive assessments of the U.S. Moreover, Poles confirm (particularly older generations) that there is a 'special relationship' between the two countries. There is little criticism of American foreign policy, with respondents usually positively assessing American leaders. Most Poles also perceive the state of Polish-American relations in positive terms. Interestingly, Poles were among the few Europeans who also positively assessed the presidency of Donald Trump during his first term in office, with the highest level of trust towards this American leader in the entire EU, according to Pew Research Center (2019).

American Protégée and Reliable Ally

The U.S. was the most responsive of the Western allies to Polish security needs immediately following the fall of Communism in 1989. In key security issues, such as the status of the Polish western border during the 2 + 4 negotiations on the unification of Germany, Americans were sensitive towards Polish fears. Ultimately, U.S. political actors developed the idea of NATO enlargement, providing Poland (and other countries in the region) with what they desperately wanted—security guarantees. In response, over time, Poles developed one of the most stable aspects of Polish strategic culture—strong Atlanticism prioritising the U.S. role as a security provider in Europe.

In addition, following the principle that 'a friend in need is a friend indeed', Poles were building a portfolio of reliable and trustworthy ally supporting Americans even in such controversial endeavours as the 2003 war in Iraq, despite opposition from (some) European partners. Over the years, despite varying ideological profiles, Polish governments have shared these elements of Polish foreign policy. The key instrument of Polish-American security relations has been NATO, but bilateral relations have also been developed with significant American military equipment contracts for the Polish army. Since 2022, Poland is one of the countries spending the most on modernising its army, reaching much above the 2% of GDP target set by NATO (4.2% in 2024 and planned 4.7% in 2025). One of the most significant developments in Polish-U.S. military cooperation was to send of American troops to Poland as part of NATO allied deployment securing the Eastern flank. Despite the differences in how Polish governments were seeing the key components of country's security and its key allies—there was very little criticism about Polish-American relations. The key lines of the debate were how to structure relations with European defence arrangements so as not to jeopardise America's dominant position. The new Donald Trump's administration in White House brought significant shifts in American approach to security in Europe, especially reversing its support for Ukraine in its fight against Russian aggression. It already causes a concern in Poland and in Europe.

The U.S. was not just the main security partner of Poland after 1989. Economic relations between both countries were also crucial for Poland in rebuilding its economic standing, with the first trade treaty already being signed in 1990. The

Polish economy not only thrived through utilisation of American and Western investments as well as development aid, but also implemented a more neoliberal orientation in the economy than mirrored many Western-oriented models.

While Polish-U.S. trade relations have been and remain asymmetrical, despite new themes of energy and environmental investments, Poland remains a key U.S. partner in Europe. The U.S. is the eighth highest export destination in Polish trade (all other countries are in the EU) and fourth in terms of imports to Poland. In 2023, Poland's exports were valued at USD 11.8 billion and imports at USD 16.2 billion. Poland is also attracting significant American capital investment. American companies are the biggest investors among non-EU countries in Poland and the second globally after Germany. Among the most visible is Discovery—an owner of the leading TV news station in the country, TVN. However, since Poland is a member of the EU, most of the trade relations are governed by the bloc's collective decisions.

The most debated recent investment concerns the American contribution to the building of Poland's first nuclear power plants. As reiterated by leaders of both countries in 2024, cooperation in developing Poland's nuclear energy is a strategic matter for both sides. Polish-U.S. economic relations are vibrant and dynamic, yet growing tensions between the U.S. and the EU and the transactionalist approach of new Trump administration will put a pressure on Poland. In addition the perspective of tensions in American relations with China are also creating possible difficulties for Poland. The Minister of Foreign Affairs Radosław Sikorski clearly stated in 2024 that Poland hopes to play a role in mitigating Sino-American tensions, but if Poland is forced to choose, it will always be on the side of the U.S.

Poland puts relations with the U.S. on top of its foreign policy priorities. Frequently, this has resulted in conflicts with EU partners, which was most notably visible during the Iraq war in 2003. More recently, the Polish position of locating NATO and the U.S. above the EU defence cooperation formats has often been criticised. However, Poland is not the only country within the EU that aspires to the special status of key U.S. ally in the bloc.

Recommendations

Firstly, Poland invests a lot in its relations with the U.S., anchoring these in historical affinities, emotional links and good cooperation in strategic sectors of security and trade. However, with a more polarised political scene in the U.S., it has become more difficult for Polish politicians to navigate relations with the Republicans, particularly Donald Trump. This is primarily because Poles strongly support American aid for Ukraine in fighting Russian aggression. On that front, Trump's stance of being critical of Ukraine and favourable towards Putin is received with reserve (if not with shock) in Warsaw. Polish authorities will need to find a formula to combine its strong Atlanticism in the era of crumbling bipartisan consensus in the

U.S. concerning transatlantic relations and under Donald Trump's second term as U.S. president.

Secondly, in more uncertain international relations, Poland must prepare for Europe, where the U.S. security umbrella is diminishing. The answer in Warsaw today is to invest in a strong and modern army. This is seen as an argument that will be heard in the U.S. under the second Trump administration and will keep assuring Poland's 'special' status among other European allies. Another strategy that will be communicated in Washington is that Poland's central position within the EU is good for American interests in Europe. The question of navigating the changing dynamics of alliances in Europe and a balancing point between Atlanticism and Europeanism is still to be resolved.

Thirdly, in the world of growing Sino-American enmity, choices are not only to be made in terms of security. In Poland and Europe, there is also the question of building a real strategic industrial autonomy that requires bold (and expensive) choices.

Magdalena Góra is Associate Professor of Political Science and European Studies at the Institute of European Studies of the Jagiellonian University. Her research deals with legitimacy and contestation in EU external relations, EU actorness in international relations, especially in the EU's close neighbourhood, and democracy challenges in the EU. She has published numerous journal articles, book chapters and co-edited volumes. She has been involved in many EU-funded research projects dealing with democracy and European integration.

The Institute of European Studies is part of the Faculty of International and Political Studies at Jagiellonian University—the oldest and leading university in Poland. IES is known for its interdisciplinary approach, combining anthropology, economy, cultural studies, political science and international relations, history, law and sociology on Europe. IES participates in research networks and international consortia, notably within the European Horizon Europe programme. Educationally, IES hosts BA and MA programmes in European Studies in Polish and a variety of BA, study abroad and international MA in English.

Portugal and Transatlantic Relations: A Bridge between the U.S. and Europe

José Gomes André and Alice Cunha

Although distant from each other geographically, with distinct features as individual countries, both Portugal and the U.S. nevertheless share common values. These are rooted in historical ties, a bilateral partnership and a certain mutual vision for addressing global challenges. However, Portugal does have mixed relations with the U.S., which can be summed up as: economically good, politically loose and defence dependent.

Distant Friends with Common Interests

Portugal was the third European country to recognise U.S. independence by the government of Queen D. Maria I, on 15 February 1783. Thereafter, the two countries have maintained a long history of diplomatic relations since 1791. These include expanded areas of cooperation with the conclusion of certain bilateral agreements, namely on social security, taxes, as well as maritime search and rescue. However, this bilateral relationship has as its cornerstone the 1995 Agreement on Cooperation and Defence that established the U.S.-Portugal Standing Bilateral Commission, which meets at a technical level and deals with subjects such as Atlantic cooperation, space, energy security and the environment.

J. G. André
Practical Philosophy Research Group, Lisbon, Portugal
e-mail: josegomesandre@edu.ulisboa.pt

A. Cunha (✉)
Portuguese Institute of International Relations, Lisbon, Portugal
e-mail: alice.cunha@fcsh.unl.pt

According to official data, the U.S. was the fourth largest customer of Portuguese exports in 2023, with a share of 6.8%, and ninth largest in terms of imports, at 2.1%. The trade balance of goods is favourable to Portugal, with a surplus of EUR 2.983 million in 2023. U.S. Foreign Direct Investment (FDI) in Portugal amounted to EUR 10.412,23 million in the second quarter of 2024, being in the top 10 countries that invest in Portugal, especially in real estate, whereas Portugal's FDI in the U.S. amounted to USD 1.2 billion in 2023, promoted by the Amigo Act (2022).

After the 1980s, Portuguese foreign policy became increasingly focused on its European Union (EU) membership and its Atlantic axis became more centred on security via NATO. However, at the same time, with the end of the Cold War the U.S. also lost some interest in the military base of Lajes, on the island of Terceira in the Azores. Both facts lead to their political relations being increasingly stretched. For example, the last Portuguese prime minister to undertake a working visit to the U.S. was José Durão Barroso in June 2003, whereas the last U.S. president on a state visit to Portugal was Ronald Reagan in May 1985.

Despite these somewhat detached political relations, there is a large Portuguese community in the U.S. (over 200,000, plus more than 1.4 million Portuguese descendants), engaged in economics and even politics. Furthermore, the U.S. soft power and cultural influence are well perceived in Portugal, mainly through the consumption of American technological products, watching Hollywood films and even Halloween is becoming increasingly popular. Moreover, after Madonna lived in the country for some time, it became a popular destination for American tourists and digital nomads.

Pro-American Views... with some Caveats

There are varying perceptions of the U.S. among Portuguese political parties, shaped by their ideological positions. Centre-right parties such as the Social Democratic Party (PSD) generally view the U.S. positively, emphasising strong transatlantic relations as well as valuing free trade and economic liberalism. The centre-left Socialist Party (PS) also supports a strong relationship with the U.S., particularly in security and trade, but advocates for multilateralism and balanced EU integration, aligning more closely with U.S. Democratic policies on climate change, social justice and human rights. Left-leaning parties, such as the Portuguese Communist Party (PCP) and Left Bloc (BE), are often critical of U.S. foreign policy, especially in relation to military interventions and capitalism, criticising the U.S. as a dominant global power.

Portuguese media present a generally well-balanced tone towards the U.S., with a prevailing pro-American sentiment. This positive view is driven by historical alliances through NATO, economic ties, cultural influence (mainly films, music and technology) and shared democratic values. Anti-Americanism is rare, though critical perspectives do arise from time to time when U.S. foreign policy disregards multilateralism, or when American leaders push strict immigration policies or neglect environmental issues, both sensitive topics in Portugal. These criticisms are mainly directed at the Republican Party, while the media often praises the Democratic Party, especially on foreign policy, health, education and social rights, which align more with Portuguese values and practices.

Security and Its Costs

When the U.S. first became a superpower, Portugal's geopolitical positioning was at the core of its interest. Following the Second World War, Portugal was invited to become a NATO member and was the only non-democratic country to join in 1949. However, the authoritarian regime that then governed the country distrusted the U.S. and had difficulty in acknowledging the emergence of a new Atlantic maritime power and accepting Marshall Plan aid. Ultimately, though, Portugal ended up not only being a recipient but also becoming a founding member of the Organisation for European Economic Co-operation. That started the trend of being close to the U.S. should there be common interests.

As political preferences and security needs do not always match, Portugal signed the Lajes Agreement with the U.S., a bilateral military cooperation agreement, in February 1948. This agreement is still in force, albeit subject to periodic revision. Both the Lajes Agreement and NATO membership implied the consolidation of new alliances, either bilaterally with the U.S. or multilaterally via NATO. These remain today's key defence alliances for Portugal.

The EU is leading the clean energy transition and the regulation of digital and artificial intelligence, strategies with which Portugal is certainly aligned. Moreover, in terms of defence, a future U.S. president committed to NATO is good news for both Portugal and the EU, until such time as the EU is properly equipped to secure its own defence. In 2023, Portugal invested only 0.8% of its GDP on defence and has not budgeted to reach 2% investment (aligned with NATO criteria) until 2029.

Influence on EU Policies and a Crystal Ball after 2024

Portugal's relationship with the U.S. positively affects its position within the EU by enhancing its role as a bridge between the U.S. and Europe. Strong ties with the U.S. bolster Portugal's influence in transatlantic security through NATO, support its economic interests via trade and align on key issues such as democracy and climate change. Additionally, Portugal's robust connections with Latin America and Africa—regions where it has historical and cultural ties—offer valuable opportunities for political, social and economic cooperation with both the U.S. and the EU.

Portugal can effectively influence EU policy by leveraging its unique strengths and diplomatic positioning within the Union, particularly through its influence in the aforementioned regions, as well as its strategic role in promoting transatlantic relations and cooperation. Praised values in Portugal's foreign policy, such as social cohesion, multilateralism and cultural diplomacy, can also contribute to the development of a more consistent and globally engaged EU. As a leader in renewable energy, particularly in wind and solar power, Portugal should further influence EU energy policy by advocating for increased investment in renewable energy sources and energy efficiency.

With Donald Trump's victory in the 2024 presidential election, Portugal-U.S. relations could face challenges in areas such as trade, climate policy and multilateral cooperation. Portugal would need to balance its commitment to the EU with the necessity of maintaining a constructive bilateral relationship with the U.S., navigating the complexities of a potentially more unilateral American foreign policy.

Recommendations

The obvious recommendation is for the EU finally to choose which direction to take regarding defence: either build up a proper defence policy, with an appropriate budget and necessary instruments or simply assume that its defence requirements are satisfied by NATO and hence provide it with the proper budget, burden-sharing and distribution of duties from its side. This way, NATO will not be hostage to U.S. elections and presidents' preferences.

The EU should advocate for multilateral solutions in international diplomacy, trade and climate policy. This approach aligns with both Portugal's and the broader EU's commitment to a rules-based global order, ensuring that Europe remains a key player on the global stage.

The EU should build on Portugal's leadership in renewable energy by increasing investment in green technologies across Europe. This would not only help meet climate goals but also reduce dependence on external energy sources, thereby enhancing energy security.

Finally, the EU should also be proactive in preparing for potential geopolitical shifts post-2025, including changes in U.S. foreign policy. This means being adaptable in its strategies, namely if facing a more unilateral U.S. approach.

José Gomes André, Ph.D., is Assistant Professor at the Faculty of Letters of the University of Lisbon, where he teaches courses in Political Philosophy and American Studies. A Researcher at the Praxis-CFUL, he is the author of several papers and books on American federalism, and the political and electoral system of the U.S. He is a political analyst at RTP (a public service broadcasting organisation), for matters related to American politics.

The Practical Philosophy Research Group (Praxis) is part of the Centre of Philosophy (CFUL), a research unit of the Faculty of Letters of the University of Lisbon, founded in 1989. The Praxis group promotes scientific high-quality philosophical research focusing on the broad range of subjects and fields traditionally acknowledged to the domain of practical philosophy, namely political theory.

Alice Cunha, Ph.D., is Assistant Professor with Habilitation in International Relations at the NOVA University of Lisbon and Researcher at the Portuguese Institute of International Relations (IPRI-NOVA), where she works on European Integration, an area in which she has published extensively. Her main research interests are related to EU studies, enlargement studies, Europeanisation, European funds and Portuguese foreign policy.

The Portuguese Institute of International Relations is a research institute founded in 2003 and dedicated to advanced studies in Political Science and International Relations. IPRI-NOVA promotes scientific research, specialised training at doctoral and post-doctoral levels, knowledge transfer and social value creation. It has been recognised as a Public Utility Institution for services rendered to the community. IPRI-NOVA is a member of TEPSA.

The U.S.-Romania Relationship is Set to Stand the Test of Time in a Volatile Global Context

Mihai Sebe and Eliza Vaș

The U.S. has been a key strategic partner for Romania during difficult times. Over the years, countless efforts have been devoted to consolidating this partnership in all areas of society. EU accession added new dimensions to this complex relationship as Romania pursued consolidation of the transatlantic partnership in parallel with the deepening of EU integration.

A Match Made in... Geopolitics

The U.S. and Romania share more than a century-old relationship, which goes back to 1880, when the two countries first established diplomatic relations. During the communist regime, Romania was granted Most Favoured Nation treatment and it enjoyed the benefits of this status from 1975 to 1988, when the human rights situation worsened. In 1992, following the transition to democracy, which started after the 1989 Revolution, Romania and the U.S. signed a bilateral agreement focused on intellectual property, tourism and access to information related to foreign trade. In 1993, the Most Favoured Nation treatment was reinstated.

From that moment, Romania has proved to be firmly committed to Euro-Atlantic values and has developed its relations with the U.S., while setting a roadmap for joining the EU and becoming a NATO member. In the last three decades, cooperation between Romania and the U.S. has been focused mainly on

M. Sebe (✉) · E. Vaș
European Institute of Romania, Bucharest, Romania
e-mail: mihai.sebe@ier.gov.ro

E. Vaș
e-mail: eliza.vas@ier.gov.ro

economic affairs and foreign investments, democratic values, defence and security matters, as well as education (for instance, Fulbright exchanges). In the early 1990s, the U.S. played a significant role in fostering the development of civil society organisations and in transferring administrative know-how to the newly built democratic institutions in Romania, a twofold support that was later consolidated with the EU's assistance.

The year 1997 marked the launch of official talks for a strategic partnership between Romania and the U.S. These talks eventually concluded with the Joint Declaration on Strategic Partnership for the 21st Century between the U.S. and Romania adopted in 2011. At the turn of the century, Romania was an active player in the fight against terrorism, with its troops participating in Iraq and Afghanistan operations and even supporting NATO before becoming a member in 2004.

Subsequently, the relationship evolved organically, and in 2014, the U.S. Navy established a new military base at Deveselu (in southern Romania)—the U.S. Aegis Ashore Missile Defence System, capable of detecting, tracking, engaging and destroying ballistic missiles flying outside the atmosphere. By facilitating the access of American capabilities on its national soil (such as the Mihail Kogălniceanu airbase near Constanța that serves as a multi-modal transportation hub for U.S. forces), Romania established itself as a reliable ally for the U.S. In return, the U.S. has always endorsed Romania's Euro-Atlantic integration and has shown a vested interest in the security developments associated with the Black Sea region, most recently translated into the Black Sea Security Act that further calls for a Black Sea security and development strategy.

In June 2024, Romania and the U.S. held the ninth Strategic Dialogue in Washington, D.C. The main points on the agenda were energy cooperation, strategies for bolstering the Republic of Moldova's resilience and the war in Ukraine. On this occasion, a Memorandum of Understanding on countering foreign state information manipulation was signed. The Memorandum of Understanding serves as a basis for consolidating cooperation between the U.S. and Romania (other European countries have also signed similar Memoranda of Understanding) in five key action areas: national strategies and policies; governance structures and institutions; human and technical capacity; civil society; independent media and academia; and multilateral engagement.

The Economic Relations Gained Momentum

Romania's strategic geopolitical position is highly relevant to the security and global economic interests of the U.S. Its determination to align with EU and NATO priorities and standards has led to a dynamic investment climate that has attracted an important number of U.S. investors. According to the National Bank of Romania, the U.S. ranked fourth with a total of EUR 8.232 million (31 December 2023). American investments are oriented towards the following sectors: automotive industry, machine industry, machines and equipment, agriculture and food industry, IT, electronics, chemical and pharmaceutical industry, communications, tourism, energy and services.

As for the trade in goods and services, in 2023 Romania's imports from the U.S. amounted to USD 2.3 billion (up 5.4% from 2022), while its exports to the U.S. reached USD 4.9 billion (up 8.4% from 2022). The main American exports consisted of navigation equipment, explosive ammunition and broadcasting equipment. By contrast, top Romanian exports to the U.S. include machinery, vehicle parts, steel and metallic items as well as fertilisers. In the field of energy security, recent developments include Romania's intention to import from the U.S. and deploy small modular reactor technology, the first of its kind in Europe. The two countries are also developing their cooperation in the production of offshore natural gas and wind energy.

The U.S.: Romania's Favourite Ally?

Overall, representatives of the political spectrum generally agree that the transfer of institutional mechanisms, technologies and values from the U.S. has been beneficial to Romania. However, one of the risks identified in the 2024 U.S. Integrated Country Strategy for Romania is that 'Romanian voices challenging the U.S. model and American values are gaining ground domestically'. Consequently, the U.S. 'risks... losing or weakening its position as domestic/regional moral voice and aspirational model'.

While there were some forms of discontent over this strategic partnership (especially regarding the Visa Waiver Programme for which a positive outcome is, nevertheless, expected in 2025), the attitude of mainstream media towards the U.S. remains positive.

As for public perception, with the outbreak of war in Ukraine, Romanians started to value even more the role and importance of security, affirming (53%) in 2024 that the U.S. was the most important strategic partner for Romania.

Maintaining Transatlantic Unity

Romania has tried to increase its profile within the EU, while contributing to the advancement of the European project, perceived as a guarantee for prosperity, resilience and democratic security. At the same time, the country worked on strengthening its Strategic Partnership with the U.S., seen as a symbol of security and democracy as well as economic and social progress. These are viewed as complementary because a strong EU-U.S. relationship is crucial for global stability.

Romania will continue to support the consolidation of the transatlantic relationship at EU level (in line with the guidelines for the 2024–2029 European Commission). In this regard, the EU should focus on the transatlantic relationship's fundamentals by enhancing its dialogue with the U.S. presidential administration.

For many European states, an active U.S. presence in NATO is perceived as essential for their security. At the same time, the EU should invest more in its own security and industrial capacity in order to become a European Defence Union.

Given the long-standing U.S.-Romania strategic partnership and American interests in the region, a change in the U.S. presidential administration is expected to have a low impact on U.S. policy towards Romania. From a historical perspective, the strategic partnership between the U.S. and Romania was launched during the Democratic presidency of Bill Clinton, and Romania's NATO accession took place during the Republican presidency of George W. Bush.

However, as the U.S. presidential administration is switching gears, with the second term won by Donald J. Trump, one could say that 'everything must change for everything to remain the same'. This is especially true in the area of security and defence, where Romania has a strong dependence on its strategic partner—the U.S. An increase in military spending for the upcoming period is expected to meet demands inside NATO. However, decades of close strategic partnership and the first mandate of President Trump have shown that this is a manageable situation given Romania's solid record of a pro-American stance.

Furthermore, a more transactional approach in bilateral relations can be expected, where the focus would be on economic growth. Any uncertainty derived from this change might appear in a potential tariffs dispute between the U.S. and the EU, a case Romania will have to balance carefully. An increased accent on regional cooperation (like the Three Seas Initiative) can also be expected, given its U.S. support. Romania is at its best when there is an *Entente Cordiale* between Washington and Brussels and less at ease when it has to dodge potential crossfire between the two.

At this moment, any effects are difficult to estimate with any certainty, as there is no definitive crystal-clear approach, but rather a grey area where economic and military opportunities may rise.

Recommendations

Romania's relationship with the U.S. should be based on mechanisms which are meant to eliminate the arbitrariness of national politics. It should also be grounded in respect for their common values.

Firstly, the EU could build its strategic resilience, while maintaining and consolidating the transatlantic relationship. Accordingly, Romania could be an active player in this equation given its close cooperation with American energy companies and talks of further development in its stance as a regional energy hub.

Secondly, when discussing the EU-U.S. relationship, European institutions should also take into consideration the Member States' specificities and security concerns. For instance, in Romania's case, bilateral relations with the U.S. are centred around the strategic partnership, which predates both Romania's NATO accession and EU membership.

Thirdly, for many EU Member States from Central and Eastern Europe, enhancing the EU's cohesion and deepening the relations with the U.S. are concurrent objectives. In particular, regional cooperation formats, such as the Three Seas Initiative, which brings together 13 EU Member States from Central and Eastern Europe, can simultaneously promote EU cohesion and reinforcement of the transatlantic bond.

Finally, one approach that could be slightly different in the next few years concerns the relationship with China. For instance, Romania has maintained its position on the 'one China' principle without having a strategic partnership with China, all in the context of our EU and NATO membership and support for multilateralism and rules-based international order. The U.S.-China competition could generate different reactions in the European capitals.

To sum up, the transatlantic partnership is essential to global stability and it should be reinforced to cope with old and new challenges (*inter alia*, fragmentation of the rules-based world order and climate change). The recommendation is to focus on aspects related to technology cooperation, security and defence, economic cooperation, multilateralism, cultural exchanges and energy security.

Mihai Sebe is Head of the European Affairs Department, European Institute of Romania, and Lecturer at the University of Bucharest. He holds PhD in Political Sciences. His current research interests include European affairs, the impact of new technologies and regional cooperation formats.

Eliza Vaş is coordinator of the Studies Unit at the European Institute of Romania and Editor-in-Chief of the *Romanian Journal of European Affairs*. Additionally, she holds the position of Vice President of the Young Initiative Association and is actively engaged in the European non-profit sector.

The European Institute of Romania (EIR) is a public institution, coordinated by the Romanian Ministry of Foreign Affairs, whose mission is to provide expertise in the field of European Affairs to the public administration, the business community, the social partners and the civil society. Studies, training, translations and communication are EIR's key areas of activity.

Slovak-U.S. Relations: Balancing Strategic Partnership

Kateryna Kasatkina and Lucia Mokrá

Slovakia and the U.S. share a historically significant relationship characterised by profound political and economic connections. The U.S. has been instrumental in Slovakia's transition from communism and its subsequent integration into Western institutions, though nationalist-populist rhetoric within Slovakia has at times intensified anti-American sentiments. Nonetheless, the current bilateral partnership remains strong, particularly in defence cooperation and security.

Historical, Political and Economic Relations

Diplomatic relations between Slovakia and the U.S. were established in 1993, immediately following Slovakia's independence declaration, although the ties between these nations have much deeper historical roots. Slovak immigrants significantly shaped America's cultural character in the late nineteenth and early twentieth centuries. After the First World War, the U.S. championed the principle of self-determination and hence supported the formation of Czechoslovakia in 1918, which contributed to a positive perception of Americans. In the second half of the twentieth century, relations with Washington were significantly influenced by the broader geopolitical confrontation between the U.S. and the Soviet Union during the Cold War and existed only formally, largely exercised on the level of international organisations.

K. Kasatkina · L. Mokrá (✉)
Comenius University in Bratislava, Bratislava, Slovakia
e-mail: lucia.mokra@fses.uniba.sk

K. Kasatkina
e-mail: kateryna.kasatkina@fses.uniba.sk

Following the collapse of the bipolar world order, the U.S. was instrumental in facilitating Slovakia's transition from communism to democracy and a market economy. This support was manifested through financial assistance, technical expertise and strong political backing for Slovakia's aspirations to integrate with Western institutions, including the UN, NATO and the EU.

The economic relationship between the two countries is marked by substantial trade and investment flows. The U.S. is the leading non-European investor in Slovakia, with FDI primarily concentrated in key sectors such as manufacturing, the automotive industry and technology. Conversely, Slovakia imports a diverse array of products from the U.S., including energy equipment, medical equipment and supplies, electrical and electronic machinery, components, chemical products and plastics. In 2023, Slovak exports to the U.S. were valued at approximately USD 5.24 billion, while imports from the U.S. amounted to around USD 426.82 million, reflecting a robust and mutually beneficial economic relationship.

The Polarisation of Attitudes Towards the U.S.

Public perception of the U.S. in Slovakia today is significantly influenced by the domestic political climate, characterised by political parties' polarisation through contrasting approaches to governance and international relations. Accordingly, two primary political groups can be identified, each exhibiting distinct attitudes towards the U.S., albeit at present forming the governing coalition in Slovakia.

The first group comprises programmatic parties that uphold liberal-democratic values. These parties still perceive the U.S. as a key strategic ally, especially in terms of security, economic cooperation and shared democratic values. Their stance is largely influenced by Slovakia's integration into NATO and the EU, organisations where U.S. leadership and partnership are seen as essential for maintaining regional stability and fostering economic growth.

The second group includes political parties that favour an authoritarian style of governance, leveraging populism and nationalism to mobilise voters. They display a more critical stance towards the U.S., prioritising stronger ties with Russia based on a 'common history'. Strong ties to Russia remain substantial especially in the government's rhetoric, although public opinion after Russia's war against Ukraine has shifted towards strong support for Ukraine and the EU's efforts in that regard. This stance is driven by concerns that U.S. foreign policy is in conflict with Slovakia's national interests, particularly concerning such issues as military presence and economic relationships. Notably, these parties exhibit a political style similar to that of the U.S. Republican Party, which was reflected in their support for Donald Trump and their overall positive view of his presidency.

The current broader geopolitical context also shapes pro- and anti-American sentiments in Slovak society. Russia's invasion of Ukraine in 2022 increased positive views of the U.S. as a leading NATO force and defender of territorial integrity. However, by 2023 anti-American sentiment had increased again due to economic challenges from the war, populist rhetoric from political parties and extensive pro-Russian propaganda. According to a Globesec poll, this has resulted in 50% of Slovaks currently perceiving the U.S. as a security threat, an 11% increase from 2022, contrary to the Slovak strong integration in NATO and EU. The increase in anti-American sentiment within Slovakia can potentially affect the formulation and prioritisation of strategic partnership areas between the two nations significantly.

Navigating Security and Defence

As a NATO member, Slovakia benefits from the alliance's security guarantees, integrally linked to U.S. strategic security initiatives in Europe. The Defence Cooperation Agreement, signed in January 2022, is designed to deepen and broaden defence cooperation between the two nations. This agreement allows the U.S. military to use two Slovak Air Force bases for 10 years, while Bratislava receives USD 100 million to modernise its military forces and infrastructure. Additionally, in 2023 the U.S. pledged USD 3.6 million to enhance the security of Slovakia's eastern border. This funding is directed at strengthening collective security by safeguarding Slovakia's border against the illicit movement of weapons, drugs, contraband and people, given the regional threats.

Concerns between the two countries also extend to broader issues such as energy security, digital security and countering disinformation, the third of which was present not only in the last U.S. election, but also as a strong tool in previous Slovak elections to the Parliament and president's office. Slovakia's reliance on energy imports, particularly from Russia, has made it vulnerable to external pressures. Washington has been actively supporting Bratislava in diversifying its energy sources by promoting initiatives focused on developing nuclear energy and the supply of LNG. These efforts are designed to enhance Slovakia's energy independence and resilience, reducing its reliance on external energy imports. Digital security has become an increasingly pressing issue due to the rising frequency and sophistication of cyberattacks. By collaborating with the U.S. on 5G security and signing a Joint Declaration in 2020, Slovakia is strengthening its national security and contributing to a broader NATO and EU effort to secure information and communication technologies. In response to the threats posed by hybrid warfare, both Washington and Bratislava have intensified their efforts to address pro-Kremlin disinformation campaigns, which undermine U.S. credibility among its regional partners.

Interestingly, though, the Slovak government does not criticise the U.S. for its support and supply of arms to Ukraine through the Ukraine Security Assistance Initiative to help the country protect itself from Russian aggression, but directs its criticism exclusively towards the EU. This confirms the caution in relation to the key position of the U.S. in Slovakia's foreign policy.

Recommendations

Given the strategic importance of U.S. support in strengthening NATO and enhancing Europe's defence capabilities, it is absolutely essential today and in Slovakia's best interests that security cooperation between the EU and the U.S. is expanded. Joint efforts in digital security and counter-disinformation should also be intensified to safeguard democratic processes from the multifaceted challenges of hybrid warfare. Continued collaboration on energy diversification, including nuclear energy and LNG, is crucial for enhancing Slovakia's energy security and resilience. Considering the polarised perceptions of the U.S. among Slovaks, it is important to promote initiatives for developing a more balanced EU foreign policy, with engaged Member States. This will enable the Union to address regional specifics and effectively safeguard its interests while maintaining strong transatlantic relationships.

To maintain stable and strong ties with the U.S., the Slovak government may need to emphasise a more transactional approach, focusing on economic and defence cooperation—areas likely to be prioritised under Donald Trump's administration, but also not to forget on liberal-democratic values. Slovakia should also remain cautious to U.S. perspectives on the war in Ukraine and relations with Russia, potentially assuming a more active role in regional security to signal its commitment to shared responsibilities in compliance with the EU views.

Kateryna Kasatkina is a Researcher at the Institute of European Studies and International Relations, Faculty of Social and Economic Sciences, Comenius University in Bratislava. She studied History and International Relations at Kuban State University and holds a PhD in World History from Borys Grinchenko Kyiv University. Her research interests include U.S. foreign policy, American history and international relations during the Cold War and the post-bipolar era.

Lucia Mokrá is Professor of International and European Law at Comenius University in Bratislava, Faculty of Social and Economic Sciences. She is also a Visiting Professor at other universities in Europe and Chairperson of the TEPSA Board. Her research interests include human rights, external relations, institutional settings and enforcement in international and European law.

The Faculty of Social and Economic Sciences is an integral part of Comenius University in Bratislava. Academics and researchers provide expertise in different fields of social science for national decision-makers, running research and popularisation projects in Slovakia and abroad. The faculty's foreign professors, students from abroad and European research projects give it a truly international feel. In the last decade, it has earned a reputation as one of the best social science faculties in Slovakia. The Institute is also a member of TEPSA.

Slovenes Like the U.S., but not its Politics

Boštjan Udovič and Maja Bučar

Slovenians are historically linked to the U.S. The first Slovenian migrations to the U.S. date back to the nineteenth century, accelerating at the dawn of the twentieth century and after the Second World War. Before the war, the main reasons for migrations to the U.S. were economic, but they subsequently fragmented, with political motivation becoming more relevant. Given the position and particularities of Yugoslavia in the world system after 1945, and thus Slovenia, we can say that the country developed a specific dualism towards the U.S.: a positive attitude towards the country, the culture and the people, but a negative attitude towards American politics.

A Historical Outline of the Relations between Slovenes and Americans

The first contact between Slovenia and the U.S. can be traced back to the nineteenth century when the Slovenian Friderik Irenaeus Baraga went to the U.S. and started missionary work with German immigrants and later with natives. In 1853, he became the Bishop of Michigan. Another historically important Slovene was Anton Čižman, who worked first at the American embassy in Vienna, then went to the U.S. in 1849 and eventually took up a job as a university professor.

B. Udovič (✉) · M. Bučar
University of Ljubljana, Ljubljana, Slovenia
e-mail: bostjan.udovic@fdv.uni-lj.si

M. Bučar
e-mail: maja.bucar@fdv.uni-lj.si

© The Author(s), under exclusive license to Springer Nature Switzerland AG 2025
M. Kaeding et al. (eds.), *The United States and the Future of Europe*,
https://doi.org/10.1007/978-3-031-83350-2_24

The second period of contact between the U.S. and Slovenia occurred at the turn of the twentieth century. At that time, migration from the Slovenian ethnic territory was largely economic. As the number of Slovenes in the U.S. increased, they began to settle in the neighbourhoods of certain cities, or in cities that were becoming more and more 'Slovene' (Cleveland being the most prominent among them). Self-organisation followed.

Following the Second World War, emigrations from Yugoslavia/Slovenia to the U.S. became more motivated by politics than economics. According to the 1990 U.S. census, 124,437 people declared themselves of Slovene ancestry, with 738 holding doctoral degrees. Among them are politicians, such as Minnesota Senator Amy Klobuchar, Iowa Senator Tom Harkin, Republican leader George Voinovich, as well as the Mayor of Cleveland and Ohio Governor Frank Lausche. Away from politics, other prominent people include, *inter alia*, Frank Yankovic, the American king of Polka, France Rode, who was part of the team that made the first calculator, Joe Sutter, father of the Boeing 747, and the astronaut Sunita Williams. In recent times, we can mention Stanford professor Jure Leskovec, Berkley professor Uroš Seljak, basketball players Goran Dragić and Luka Dončić, as well as First Lady Melania Trump (*née* Knavs).

Slovenia and the U.S.

From the mid-1970s, Slovenia as a part of Yugoslavia had some contacts with the U.S. when the U.S. Information Agency opened a library in Ljubljana that served as a platform for enhancing knowledge about the U.S. in this part of the Communist Bloc. In the 1960s and 1970s, certain Slovenians were already studying in the U.S., including some Slovenian critical intellectuals who were later among important figures within the Slovenian independence movement (1991). One such personality was Dimitrij Rupel, who held the post of foreign minister on a number of occasions and was also ambassador to Washington, D.C. (1997–2000).

From today's perspective, a breaking point with American politics that still resounds was the U.S. reluctance to support Slovenian independence, which was voiced by Secretary of State James Baker's '*Njet*' during his visit to Belgrade, a few days before its promulgation.

Slovenia declared independence in 1991. The states belonging to the European Communities confirmed recognition on 15 January 1992, the Russian Federation in February 1992, while the U.S. did so 'only' in April 1992. In the same year, diplomatic relations were established, and the U.S. opened its embassy in Ljubljana.

A second breaking point with American politics, as perceived in Ljubljana, was the failure to gain NATO acceptance in 1997, when Hungary, the Czech Republic and Poland all became members. Slovenia became a member of NATO only in 2004.

Regarding American official visits, Bill Clinton visited Ljubljana in 1999 and was accepted with gratitude as well as extensive applause in Ljubljana's main square. In 2001, George W. Bush and Vladimir Putin met in Brdo (close to the Slovenian capital). Bush returned to Slovenia during its first presidency of the Council of the EU in 2008. In the following years, Slovenian prime ministers and other ministers met with American leaders in the U.S. on a number of occasions. For instance, Prime Minister Pahor visited Washington, D.C., in 2011 and had talks with Barack Obama. However, no official state-to-state visit has occurred since 2008.

In 2017, when Donald Trump became the U.S. president he was expected to visit Slovenia, given his wife's Slovenian origin. However, despite some high-political lobbying, this did not happen. After the 2020 U.S. elections, government leader Janez Janša congratulated Trump for his victory, which proved to be somewhat premature. In October 2024, Prime Minister Robert Golob visited Joe Biden. This was the first official visit of a Slovenian high-ranking politician to the White House in 18 years. After Donald Trump was elected, the Slovenian authorities congratulated him. What was a little bit surprising from the Slovenian perspective was the speech of Donald Trump after he was elected in which he expressed his gratitude to his (Slovenian) wife Melania, his father-in-law Viktor and late mother-in-law Amalija Knavs. Slovenian newspapers also published a notice that Trump's son Barron speaks Slovenian fluently.

With regard to relations with the U.S. after Donald Trump's election as president, there are fewer expectations than were there during his first election. Still, it seems that Slovenian politicians (this time more tacitly) will try to establish (informal) ties with the new president.

Slovenian Perception of the U.S.

Usually, when debating Slovenia's attitude towards the U.S., one must bear in mind that the discussion is about American politics and not the country (its people, culture, nature and so on). Here, some division lines are pertinent.

More than 70% of Slovenians strongly support the EU and consequently see the U.S. as a rival, hence their reluctance towards its politics. The prevailing belief in the country is that the U.S. disregards the EU's position and it is expected that with Trump's return this will become even stronger. Many Slovenians are particularly vocal regarding issues such as Palestine, where the U.S. takes a different stance. Hence, this situation is more likely to create potential divergences, rather than similarities.

There is a majority perception in Slovenia that the U.S. sees itself as a single world leader. Due to some domestic issues and the past (socialist) legacy, Slovenians are reluctant (or even opposed) towards U.S. world leadership. These (as well as some historical experiences) lead to maintaining a negative image of U.S. politics in Slovenia. Thus, it is not surprising that, according to the Eurobarometer Spring Report of 2024, just 28% of Slovenians have a positive image of the U.S. (38% of China, 18% of the Russian Federation and 41% of Turkey). The Gallup investigation portrays a similar situation. Whereas in 2009 58% of Slovenians were in favour of U.S. world leadership, a year later this share had decreased to 34%, a decade later to 19% and then stopped in 2023 at the level of 25%. However, from 2010 more than 60% of Slovenians disapproved of such an American position. By contrast, especially among current opposition parties, along with members and followers of the Slovenian Democratic Party (SDS), U.S. politics is regarded more positively, including the support which Washington is providing to Israel. Any support provided to Ukraine is from a Slovenian perspective less problematic since on this issue it seems that the EU and the U.S. are in accord.

Recommendations

There are three recommendations that should be followed to improve the image of American politics in Slovenia.

The first is to invest more (from the American side) in its public diplomacy. Little has been done in this field over recent years and hence this potentially offers some manoeuvring space to obtain better results.

The second recommendation would be to use Slovenian media to de-link politics from a more positive experience borne out of the common history and heritage of both nations. What seems to be missing among the population is the knowledge about the past (good) relationship as well as awareness of numerous contacts in other, non-political areas such as science, culture and sports.

With regard to U.S.-EU relations, the third recommendation would concern improving communication to the public in the numerous fields of positive cooperation between the two superpowers, where the EU is treated by the U.S. as an equal partner. Cooperation in the field of scientific research would be one such example.

Boštjan Udovič is Professor in Diplomacy at the Faculty of Social Sciences at the University of Ljubljana. He is an expert in diplomatic studies and negotiations and worked extensively also on key topics regarding the EU enlargement to ex-Yugoslavia countries. He has been member of different national and international research projects and has published more than 80 peer-reviewed articles in journals, as well as a few books and book chapters.

Maja Bučar is Professor Emeritus in International Relations at the Faculty of Social Sciences at University of Ljubljana. She has worked extensively in the field of development economics as well as research and innovation policies of the EU and Member States. She participated in a number of EU and national research projects, as a reviewer and editor as well as the author/co-author of several books, articles and research papers.

Spain and the U.S.: Friends, Partners and Allies

Carlota García Encina

Spain and the U.S. have experienced a changing, close and asymmetric relationship that cannot be taken for granted. At a time of change on both sides, strengthening its bilateral relationship with the U.S. is key for Spain and not incompatible with other transatlantic and multilateral channels.

"Friends, Partners and Allies"

"We are friends, partners and allies", is the recurring phrase of U.S. and Spanish authorities when asked about the bilateral relationship. Although there is a structural asymmetry between the two powers, Spain undoubtedly features on the American list of allies. It has been so for decades, with a more or less fluid and intense relationship depending on the vagaries of history. Spain is certainly a U.S. partner, but is it the same as many other countries?

Spanish-U.S. relations began in 1778, when Spain offered military and financial assistance to the emerging nation during its war of independence. However, the current relationship stems from when the Pact of Madrid was signed in 1953 during Franco's dictatorship, which established the military bases. This agreement was controversial, especially for liberals in the U.S., democrats in Spain and Spaniards in exile. In 1988, as a member of NATO and the European Economic Community, democratic Spain signed a new Defence Agreement. It was the culmination of a prolonged effort to correct the imbalances that had existed since the 1950s. Thereafter, changes not only in the respective domestic political situations but

C. G. Encina (✉)
Elcano Royal Institute, Madrid, Spain
e-mail: cencina@rielcano.org

also in the international climate—following the Cold War and the 11 September 2001 attacks—have required constant adaptation of the bilateral relationship. Perhaps the most outstanding feature is Spain's EU membership. This necessitated an adjustment of relationships, as Madrid ceded control of its trade and monetary policy to the EU, while maintaining a sharing of military matters with NATO. As a result, issues that arose in Spanish-U.S. relations became increasingly multilateral in nature, as did their solutions.

Spain's growing pro-European leaning led it to view the U.S. through an almost exclusively European prism and to align its bilateral relationship, as far as possible, with that developed in Brussels. Despite this, for years the U.S. remained committed to strengthening the bilateral relationship by demanding from Madrid a leadership role in Europe. From the U.S. point of view this was seen as beneficial, in that Spain stood out from other European countries by being Atlanticist, Mediterranean, European, a firm NATO ally and committed to transnational challenges.

However, Spain neither wanted or knew how to accept that role and accordingly preferred to continue conducting its relationship with the U.S. increasingly through Brussels, thereby reducing their bilateral potential. It believed this to be neither a priority nor a problem for the U.S. and hence deliberately undertook not to make its interests more visible in Washington and not to develop a more strategic view of the bilateral link.

Defence and an Economy on the Rise

Defence will continue to be the main pillar of continuity in the bilateral relationship, given the strategic value of the Rota naval and air base, which harbours five AEGIS destroyers with one more on the way. The war in Ukraine and growing instability in the Middle East merely confirm its importance. This privileged area of the relationship is already adapting to growing technological changes, essential for maintaining interoperability, expanding into cyberspace, artificial intelligence, outer space and initiatives with private companies. Nor should the convergence of threats and challenges to security and defence be ignored, such as the fight against terrorism and concerns about instability in the Sahel. However, Spain's defence spending, though increasing over the past 10 years, is still around 1.2% of GDP, below the 2% guideline set within the Defence Investment Pledge of 2014. This provokes the U.S. administration's widespread and repeated criticism, despite Spanish presence in almost all NATO military initiatives and its exceeding NATO's 20% military equipment target within overall defence spending. However, this does not generally jeopardise the bilateral relationship, or the defence relationship in particular, as Spain remains strategically important for the U.S. in defence matters.

Conversely, being close to the U.S. is clearly strategic for Spain in economic terms. Indeed, excellent long-standing bilateral economic relations between the two countries, are particularly so at present. Political harmony in recent years has helped strengthen trade and investment flows that had been growing strongly for over a decade, making Spain the 11th-largest investor in the U.S. for 2022, albeit there has been a slight decline of late. Energy, finance, metallurgy, manufacturing, construction, transport and infrastructure have all featured. In an increasingly dynamic market, with huge amounts of public money, Spain's growth in investment stock is expected to continue because friction generated mainly by the U.S. IRA affects Spain much less than other European countries.

Meanwhile, the U.S. is Spain's main foreign investor, with a significant industrial presence across the automotive, aeronautics and energy sectors. In terms of trade in goods, the U.S. was Spain's seventh-largest customer (5% of total exports) in 2022 and its fourth-largest trade supplier (7% of exports).

Defence and economics highlight the increasing importance of digital issues in the relationship, reflecting broader global trends. Spain has actively engaged with U.S. companies and investors to boost its own digital economy. This includes partnerships in sectors such as telecommunications, information technology and digital services. In addition, both nations are engaged in joint research and development efforts.

It should also be noted that within improved economic relations, the energy relationship has grown considerably, both in trade and investment. The U.S. was not only Spain's main supplier of natural gas in 2022 (28.8% of the total, all LNG), but also its second-largest supplier of oil. Spain has also become a major investor in the U.S. energy sector. However, the vector with the greatest potential in this area of the relationship is renewable energies.

Latin America should also be considered. In general, Madrid has been careful not to take a position on U.S. initiatives there. It was thought that Spain could not depend on Washington when it came to deploying its presence in Latin America, although it had to take into account U.S. interests. Until very recently there were no real areas of coordination in relation to the continent, but following the signing of the Spain-U.S. Joint Declaration in 2022, the first in over 20 years, Spain committed to participating in the U.S. programme to provide legal migration channels for those attempting to move away from Central and South America. This was a milestone in the bilateral relationship, with great prospects for the future.

The Spanish response in support of Ukraine also impacted the Spain-U.S. Joint Declaration. Madrid's political response was immediate, with military, economic and humanitarian assistance being appreciated by Washington from the outset. Spain has proved to be a supportive and responsible ally, albeit prior to the conflict the bilateral relationship with Ukraine was not significant. Indeed, Spain's geographical distance from Ukraine could have implied a lower perception of Russian threat, but in reality this has not been the case.

The good progress of this exclusively bilateral relationship, with common interests in the field of defence with regard to economic, energy and digital development as well as the importance of the Rota military base is being broadly maintained. However, political harmony between the left-wing coalition governing Spain and a Trump administration would be hard sought. Moreover, it could affect specific areas such as cooperation on migration issues, or the commitment to multilateralism and the fight against climate change, key elements of the current Spanish government.

Public Opinion

To establish the elements that have shaped the vision and sentiment of Spaniards towards the U.S., we must go back to 1898, when Spain lost Cuba, Puerto Rico and the Philippines. Also to be considered is the support Washington offered Franco and the 1953 accords. Subsequently, Spain's image of the U.S. was shaped by controversial events such as the Vietnam and Cuba conflicts, the civil rights struggle and the Chilean *coup d'état*. It was a rather sour and polemic vision, which at the same time was intermingled with a great curiosity and even admiration for the American way of life. For some, the U.S. presented a vision of progress and prosperity, while for others it brought thoughts of imperialism and multinational corporations.

During the Spanish transition from dictatorship to democracy following the death of Franco in 1975, Spaniards did not clearly perceive the U.S. as an enthusiastic supporter of the democratisation process. Moreover, during the Cold War, many feared that, far from providing security, the presence of American troops made them vulnerable to possible attack from the Soviet Union. In sharp contrast, Europe became an attractive symbol of democracy, modernity and progress.

At the beginning of this century, the Iraq war led to a further deterioration of the U.S. image in Spain, which some blamed on an alleged latent anti-Americanism. However, what it really reflected was specifically profound rejection of the Bush administration's foreign policy and not the U.S. as a whole. Indeed, Spanish public opinion had for some time been distinguishing between U.S. rulers and its population. Moreover, it certainly continues to do so. It is worth noting, in this regard, that the U.S. image has never aroused such extreme evaluations as those obtained by its presidents. Thus, Bush was assigned a very low evaluation in Spain, while the country's image was always somewhat better. Conversely, when opinion of Obama reached its highest levels, the country's image was at a lower level than that of its presidents. Most Spaniards gave Donald Trump such low evaluation that it even translated into a decrease in the value of the U.S. as a country, albeit not markedly. However, it should be noted that Spanish confidence in Trump's handling of international affairs went from 7% in 2018 to 21% in 2019.

A second Trump administration will not achieve the approval levels of Joe Biden among Spaniards, considering that in 2024 69% considered that Biden would be a better president than Trump. However, if Trump can refrain from starting any new wars or inflaming those that already exist, surely Spaniards will have a better perception of him. If he really manages to end the war in Ukraine, regardless of how, Spanish public opinion will be on his side. However, if instability in the Middle East increases or the situation in Gaza deteriorates, it will be against him, taking into account that Spaniards have historically supported the Palestinians.

Recommendations: And Now, What?

For the U.S., Spain has for many years been more of an ally than was apparent, but less than it should have been. Politicisation of Spain's relationship with the U.S., as during the war in Iraq, has at times meant a step backwards in how the country is considered as an ally, while Spain's absence from the U.S. political agenda has had more to do with U.S. presidential priorities than any bilateral disagreement. Although Spain's EU and NATO memberships strengthen it as a U.S. ally, its absence from other institutions, such as the G7 or the G20 (although it is currently a permanent guest), places it on a lower scale than other allies that do form part.

Nevertheless, any uncertainty about the U.S. and its future should not prevent Spain from continuing to seek better channels to make the exclusively bilateral part of the relationship more intense. Renewable energies, cooperation in Latin America and the Sahel as well as the digital economy should lead efforts in the bilateral agenda. Spain's goal should be to fulfil all the potential it has and not settle for being just another partner on the list of U.S. allies, despite the relationship's structural asymmetry. Indeed, the future of this exclusively bilateral relationship should be viewed by and large with increasing optimism. The main fear is that the bilateral relationship with the U.S. will become politicised as a result of controversies linked to the new Trump administration. In addition, the agri-food industry and other sectors are already fearing the impact of the tariffs that Trump has promised to impose. And on the defence front, there are fears of close calls from Washington for being at the bottom of the defence effort. Much will depend on how the government in Madrid manages and communicates with the new administration, something it is going to have to do, despite the lack of political affinity between the two governments.

Carlota García Encina is Senior Fellow for the U.S. and Transatlantic Relations at the Elcano Royal Institute and a Lecturer in International Relations. Her recent research topics include U.S. foreign and defence policy, the U.S.-Spanish relationship and U.S. domestic issues. She has also promoted the Spain-Israel Strategic Dialogue, coordinating it since 2018.

The Elcano Royal Institute is Spain's main think tank for international and strategic affairs and one of the leading institutions of this type in Europe and the world. Its mission is to contribute to innovative, robust, inclusive and informed responses to global challenges and governance and to analyse Spain's role in the world, with a particular emphasis on its position in Europe.

Sweden–U.S. Security Cooperation in a Changing World Order

August Danielson and Ulla Reinfeldt

The U.S. has long been one of Sweden's most significant partners and allies. Until recently, Sweden had effectively relied on U.S. support for its national defence instead of seeking NATO membership, a strategy exemplified by the 'Hultqvist Doctrine'. However, in light of global shifts such as the first Trump presidency and Russia's invasion of Ukraine, Sweden reevaluated its defence strategy, ultimately joining the alliance in March 2024. A second Trump term will have significant effects on Swedish and European security, as it risks weakening NATO and straining EU-U.S. relations. In response, policy recommendations include increasing the EU's military and financial support to Ukraine, strengthening the EU's China strategy and involving the U.S. in European defence initiatives.

An Ally and a Necessary Partner

The relationship between Sweden and the U.S. is long-standing, dating back to the American Revolutionary War. Sweden was the first state not engaged in the conflict to recognise U.S. sovereignty, following which the two countries established diplomatic relations in 1783. Mass emigration from Sweden to the U.S. during the 1800s—up to a quarter of the Swedish population—as well as strengthening economic ties through trade in iron, steel and wood led to a strong and amicable

---

A. Danielson (✉)
Swedish Institute of International Affairs, Stockholm, Sweden
e-mail: august.danielson@liu.se

U. Reinfeldt
Sweden's Youth Atlantic Treaty Association, Stockholm, Sweden
e-mail: ulla.lovcalic@hotmail.se

© The Author(s), under exclusive license to Springer Nature Switzerland AG 2025
M. Kaeding et al. (eds.), *The United States and the Future of Europe*,
https://doi.org/10.1007/978-3-031-83350-2_26

relationship between the two countries. These ties have continued to strengthen over time. Today, Sweden is a country that relies heavily on U.S. exports. The U.S. is one of Sweden's largest trading partners and Swedish companies have a strong presence in the American market, not least in machinery and chemical products. In 2022, bilateral trade in goods and services exceeded USD 25 billion. The U.S. was Sweden's largest non-European export market, accounting for around 7% of Swedish exports. Many American media and technology companies operate in Sweden and have a substantial influence as their products are widely adopted across the country.

Likely due to the strong economic and cultural ties between the countries, the Swedish public perception of the U.S. is, as of 2024, overall very positive. For instance, in a 2023 poll conducted by the ECFR, 82% of respondents from Sweden held that the U.S. should be regarded either as an ally or a necessary partner—the third highest score among the eleven EU Member States included in the poll. The Swedish public perception of the U.S. temporarily decreased during the first Trump administration. According to a 2020 report by the Pew Research Centre, 81% of Swedes had 'no confidence' in Trump doing the right thing in world affairs. However, this negative perception was largely associated with Trump's personal policies and administration, rather than a permanent shift in Sweden's overall stance towards the U.S.

From the 'Hultqvist Doctrine' to Sweden's Pivot Towards NATO

The strong relationship between the two countries is also clearly reflected in Sweden's national security doctrine. During the Cold War, the country adopted a strategy of publicly upholding its strict policy of neutrality, while unofficially maintaining close relations with the U.S. Despite later abandoning its political neutrality and instead adopting a strategy of military non-alignment, the doctrine that underpins Swedish territorial defence has since the Cold War departed from the assumption that it would receive external support—primarily from the U.S.—in the event that it would be attacked by another state—most likely the Soviet Union/Russia. This assumption has not only had a tremendous impact on Sweden's strategic military posture, but also affected its political relations. For instance, although Sweden has had a history of a relatively strong independent defence industry, it has also chosen to procure military equipment from the U.S., such as the Patriot missile defence system, despite cheaper, European options being available. The strategy of strengthening Sweden's bilateral relationships, most notably with the U.S., as a means of enhancing its national defence instead of applying for NATO membership, later became known as the 'Hultqvist Doctrine', named after the Social Democratic defence minister Peter Hultqvist.

During Trump's first presidency, this strategy faced criticism in Sweden due to his transactional approach to bilateral relationships in general and his negative perception of Sweden specifically. For instance, in February 2017 Trump made a provocative statement about 'what happened last night in Sweden', falsely suggesting a terror incident had occurred. The Trump presidency highlighted the inherent fragility of a security strategy dependent on the strength of a single bilateral relationship, which was only further emphasised following Russia's invasion of Ukraine and the West's unwillingness to provide direct military assistance to the country. In addition to the necessity of following in the footsteps of Finland, Sweden's choice to apply for NATO membership in 2022 was thus largely based on the notion that a military doctrine based on non-alignment and a strong bilateral relationship to the U.S. would be insufficient to deter Russia.

Recommendations

The U.S. remains an extremely important partner for Swedish security, not least due to Sweden joining the NATO alliance. Hence, the outcome of the U.S. presidential election was highly significant for Sweden. Trump's repeated questioning of the U.S. commitment to Article 5 has already undermined NATO allies' confidence that the U.S. would support them in the event of an attack. Consequently, a second Trump presidency poses a significant risk of further weakening NATO, thereby jeopardising European—and Swedish—security. In light of this, three policy recommendations for policy-makers in Europe and Sweden are proposed.

Firstly, Europe should proceed from the assumption that the Trump administration will reduce or even completely strip its military and financial support to Ukraine. The EU, UK and other partners outside Europe that are invested in Ukraine's survival, such as Canada, South Korea and Japan, should therefore aim to compensate fully for a hypothetical U.S. decision to withdraw aid to Ukraine. Additionally, concrete steps should be taken to ensure Ukraine's future membership in both the EU and NATO. Anything less could embolden Russia's aggression and undermine the territorial sovereignty of other European states.

Secondly, Europe should assume that the second Trump presidency will be even more transactional than the first. Trump may seek to promote bilateral relationships with states that act in line with the U.S.' foreign policy interests, such as a hardened approach to China (not least in its trade relations). Such tactics would risk further fragmenting the EU's common foreign policy. One way to guard against this would be to forge and establish a new EU strategy on its relations with China. While the EU's current China policy is focused on its bilateral relations with the country, a renewed policy document should clarify the EU's stance and actions in the context of increasing competition between the U.S. and China.

Thirdly, while the EU is ramping up its security and defence initiatives, it should actively try to involve the U.S. in this process. This would enhance transatlantic cooperation and make the Euro-Atlantic area safer. For instance, the EU should enable full third-party involvement in the European Defence Fund to partners beyond the European Economic Area (EEA). By allowing funding through this scheme the EU could find better synergies in the Euro-Atlantic defence industrial base and thus fend off accusations of European protectionism.

August Danielson is an associate research fellow at the Europe Programme, Swedish Institute of International Affairs (UI) and a postdoctoral researcher in Political Science at Linköping University.

Ulla Reinfeldt is the chair of Sweden's Youth Atlantic Treaty Association (YATA Sweden) and works at the Swedish Ministry of Defence. Previously, she worked as an analyst at the Swedish Institute of International Affairs (UI).

EU Neighbours

From Staunch Enemy to Strategic Partner: Albanian-American Relations in Transition

Albert Rakipi

In 1919, Vatra, a pan-Albanian association functioning as something of a shadow Albanian government in the U.S., made an unprecedented request to Secretary of State Robert Lansing: Albania should become an American protectorate. Just three months later, at the Paris Peace Conference, President Woodrow Wilson rejected the Secret Treaty of London, which would have effectively erased Albania from the map as an independent state. Thereafter, in the autumn of 1946, Albania issued an ultimatum to the U.S. to withdraw its diplomatic mission, forcing its members to flee under the protection of American warships. For the next 50 years, the U.S. was branded Albania's greatest and most dangerous enemy by the communist regime. Yet, through it all, two generations of Albanians held onto the hope that one day 'the Americans would come to liberate the country from communism'. In 1991, Albania and the U.S. re-established diplomatic ties and today Albania is perhaps the most pro-American country in the world, as well as being the only aspiring EU member with near-unanimous support for membership.

Throughout modern Albanian history, relations with the U.S. have either been exclusive and privileged or non-existent. To understand and explain contemporary Albanian-American relations, it is essential to deconstruct myths and explain paradoxes as a necessity for encouraging democratisation of the asymmetric relations between a great power and a small state so as to protect and develop these relations in the years ahead.

A. Rakipi (✉)
Albanian Institute for International Studies, Tirana, Albania
e-mail: arakipi@aiis-albania.org

"Myths are Lies that Tell the Truth"

On 5 June 2007, President George W. Bush was greeted in Prague by 2000 protesters opposing U.S. plans to install a missile defence system in Europe. Five days later, tens of thousands gathered to welcome him in Tirana's main square, decorated for a grand celebration with portraits, Albanian and American flags and slogans for the occasion. For the older generation, this might have evoked memories of similar receptions during communist times when Soviet leader Nikita Khrushchev or Chinese Premier Zhou Enlai visited Albania in 1959 and 1965, respectively. This resemblance, along with Albania's history of asymmetric relationships with great powers, leads some scholars to categorise Albania-U.S. relations as 'client-patron'. As with many small states, over the past 100 years Albania has sought various alliances, first with the Soviet Union, then China and finally the U.S.

However, careful observation of Albania's foreign relations does not necessarily support this pattern, with Albanians' love for the U.S. at first glance seeming irrational. Looking back over a century of relations, this love has certainly been grounded in rationality—even as it was becoming a myth. As the ancient thinker Aphthonius noted, "Myths are lies that tell the truth". However, where does the rationality lie in Albanians' love for America and what are some of the truths behind the myth? Regardless of their asymmetry, Albania's ties with the U.S. have always revolved around crucial issues vital to the Albanian state and nation. For instance, in 1919 President Wilson became a national hero for Albanians when he intervened to save the country from partition. Relations with the U.S., in Albania's case, have defined its relations with the West. After the Second World War, Albania's society was split: pro-Western Albanians, which were in the majority, looked to the U.S. for economic and cultural guidance, while pro-Eastern factions turned to the Soviet Union. It is important to note that at this time, when the country had less than one million inhabitants, more than a quarter of a million Albanians had either emigrated to the U.S. or had family there.

As mentioned earlier, in modern Albanian history, relations with the U.S. have been either exclusive and privileged or non-existent. When they have existed, they have been deeply rooted in principles of freedom and democracy. Hence, in 1945 the U.S. refused to recognise rigged elections and the communist regime of Enver Hoxha, with the result that less than a year later Albania's new communist government forced the U.S. to withdraw its diplomatic mission. In 1991, restoration of relations hinged on America's demand for the existence of a democratic opposition in Albania. Hence, from 1992 Albania embraced democratic reforms and strengthened ties with the West. In 2008, Washington championed Albania's NATO membership, the greatest achievement of modern Albania since the fall of communism, thereby firmly linking Albania's present and future with the West and as such becoming the U.S.' most reliable Balkan ally.

As a sign of its gratitude, all Albania's governments over the past 30 years have supported U.S. foreign policy and moreover have become actively involved, for example in Afghanistan and by joining the U.S.-led coalition against ISIS. During the 1999 Kosovo crisis, America spearheaded NATO's intervention and supported Kosovo's subsequent independence in 2008. Albania's strategic partnership with the U.S. was formalised in 2013, when Tirana and Washington signed a strategic partnership agreement. In popular sentiment, the U.S. is perceived by Albanians as their country's most important strategic ally, a relationship more valued than that with the European powers, including the EU, with which Tirana claims strategic relations.

According to annual surveys conducted by the Albanian Institute of International Studies, both the U.S. and the EU enjoy strong public support in Albania, with approval ratings of 90% and 91%, respectively. They are regarded as the most important strategic partners in Albania's international relations.

"It's (not) the Economy, Stupid!"

For decades, Albanians believed that the U.S. would one day liberate them from communism. This hope endured for 50 years, until it finally happened in 1991, when Secretary of State James Baker was welcomed in Tirana with much popular fanfare. Since then, Albania has established solid links with the U.S., a relationship which is contributing to Albania's democratic transformation. Yet, one key area remains underdeveloped, namely the economy.

Despite various economic agreements, trade between the two countries remains minimal and U.S. investments in Albania continue to be small. The reasons can be attributed to Albania's unattractive investment environment, weak rule of law and high corruption levels. Moreover, Albania's small market size makes it of peripheral interest for American companies and other FDI. However, Western countries dominate in foreign investments. Moreover, other Balkan states have much stronger economic ties to the U.S. than Albania. Over the past 20 years, U.S. investments in Albania amounted to USD 232 million, while U.S. investments in Serbia were USD 4 billion for the same period.

Back to the Future

More than 30 years after re-establishing ties, Albania-U.S. relations are in transition. What does the future hold at a time when foreign policy is becoming increasingly transactional, raising concerns that a strategic partnership can become a 'client-patron' relationship? A century ago, Albanian leaders lobbied in Washington for the establishment of Albania as an independent sovereign state. In April 1939, just 48 h before fascist Italy invaded Albania, King Zog tearfully summoned the U.S. ambassador for an urgent and special audience, asking for help, saying that "only the U.S. can save Albania and its independence". Against this historical legacy and in sharp contrast to how foreign democratic powers such as Germany or Norway gain influence in Washington, contemporary Albanian leaders, caught in an extreme zero-sum game for power, try to buy support in Washington to gain advantages over their political opponents at home.

How will this strategic partnership develop? Will Albania continue to say 'yes' to every U.S. request, as it did when it sheltered the People's Mojahedin Organisation of Iran, a former terrorist group and Afghan refugees fleeing the Taliban regime? Will Albania continue to favour the U.S. over Western Europe, as it did in 2003 when it chose an alliance with 'New Europe' against 'Old Europe'? Moreover, how will this affect Albania's EU ambitions, when the U.S. itself supports Albania's future in the EU? This readiness to agree to every request risks transformation into a client-patron relationship, thereby making it harder to maintain a strategic partnership.

Besides being the 'guardian angel' of Albania's independence and statehood, the U.S. has known since the rigged 1945 elections that only a democratic Albania can be a partner to the U.S. and the West. Moreover, only a democratic Albania can join the EU. Sliding into autocracy and failing to build a democratic and functional state undermines the strategic partnership. Albania's economic relations with the U.S. shone brightly 75 years ago, but today must be regarded as poor. The reasons can be found in Albania's market economy not functioning properly as the rule of law is not being strictly enforced.

Finally, with a culture of total dependency, Albania behaves as if it were a protectorate or as if it has just emerged from a colonial regime. Every group or individual with a grievance—students, unions, prisoners, LGBTQIA + groups, minorities, journalists, women's organisations, veterans, political parties and their leaders, the mayor, the chief justice, the opposition leader—even the head of Parliament and the president—pen letters of complaint or clarification to the international community. This starts with the U.S. ambassador, who is at the centre of media attention as if they were the country's viceroy.

A potential turning point in U.S.-Albanian relations might emerge with the new U.S. administration. It is difficult to believe that President Trump would give significant attention to the Western Balkans, given the more pressing preoccupation with Russian aggression against Ukraine and a worsening crisis in the Middle East. However, geopolitically, the Balkans are significant in light of Russia's proxy policies in its confrontation with the U.S. and the West. As such, it is not impossible for the Trump administration to mediate a resolution to the frozen conflict between Serbia and Kosovo, thereby neutralising the main source of tensions in the region and Russia's proxy policies. In 2020, Trump personally engaged in an agreement between Serbia and Kosovo, while over the past four years Washington and the EU have encouraged dialogue between Belgrade and Pristina on vehicle licence plates and other peripheral issues, hoping that a bottom-up approach would end their dispute. It is not impossible that, with a top-down approach typical of Trump's style, the two states could move toward mutual recognition as two independent states during his second term.

Changes are also expected in terms of intrastate relations. In recent years, we have seen a growing trend toward a more transactional approach in U.S. foreign policy. Washington and the West, in general, have turned a blind eye to increasingly autocratic regimes in the Western Balkans, including Albania. Although such a trend may strengthen, moving forward, a reflection and a more neutral role for Washington in Albania's internal politics is needed.

After the Cold War, Albania managed to establish a privileged and exclusive relationship with the U.S., mainly due to its unparalleled influence and role it played in an unstable Balkan region. Unfortunately, over the last 10 years, this role has gradually diminished. The future of relations with the U.S. will depend on Albania's ability to regain the key role it once held in the Balkans, at a time when Serbia has almost restored its relations with the U.S. and the West.

Recommendations

Albania is crucial for Western Balkan stability, impacting European security directly. U.S. intervention helped end conflicts here after the Cold War, but lasting peace now depends on U.S. and EU efforts to resolve the Kosovo-Serbia dispute.

Albania's leaders risk authoritarianism, which could strain U.S. relations. Given Albania's close ties with the U.S. and EU, both can help prevent a shift to one-party rule. Short-term strategies may only entrench authoritarianism, rather than fostering democracy and responsible governance.

A new generation of Albanian leaders must move beyond dependence on international influence. They should focus on sustainable ideas to keep U.S. and EU support, avoiding influence-buying. U.S. and EU envoys can support democracy without being perceived as being external rulers of the country.

Albert Rakipi is the chairman of the Albanian Institute for International Studies. He holds a PhD in international relations from Bilkent University. Before assuming this position, he had previously served as Albania's Deputy Minister of Foreign Affairs. He is the founder and Editor of the *Albanian Journal of International Relations*' 'Tirana Observatory'. His latest books include *The Perils of Change, Albania's Foreign Policy in transition*.

The Albanian Institute for International Studies is a one of the oldest and most prestigious think tanks in Albania and is internationally recognised among the best in Eastern and Southern Europe for its expertise in EU integration, foreign policy, security studies and democratisation. AIIS has been decisive in bringing about the Tirana campus of the College of Europe through a special inception proposal and dedicated advocacy by its senior management figures. Since 2023, AIIS is an associated member of the European Security and Defence College.

The U.S. and Bosnia and Herzegovina—Ties that Do (not) Break?

Vedran Džihić

The U.S. played a crucial role in stopping bloodshed and war in 1995. However, the subsequent U.S.-designed Dayton Constitution failed to reunite the country. The different constitutive people in Bosnia and Herzegovina—Bosniaks, Serbs and Croats—even today engage in deep political infights. They also disagree on how they view the U.S.'s engagement in the country. While the U.S. keeps criticising secessionist forces in the country, both the U.S. and the EU remain somewhat reactive when it comes to major trends in Bosnia. In order to contribute to a more democratic, secure and European Bosnia, the U.S. and EU must engage closely in coordinating their policies and start implementing a more robust, proactive and future-oriented plan for the country.

Up for a Bumpy Start—Ending the War and Starting a New

Imagine a country that has fought a lengthy bloody war with thousands of victims and severe destruction, while the world's most powerful nation continues to watch these horrible events unfold for years. After starting a major diplomatic and military initiative to stop the war and forge a peaceful new state, this country received a new constitution not only from outside its borders, but also in a foreign language. Subsequently, it then started its new existence as a protectorate of the international community with a major power in command. This country is Bosnia and Herzegovina and the powerful nation is of course the U.S.

V. Džihić (✉)
Austrian Institute for International Affairs, Vienna, Austria
e-mail: vedran.dzihic@univie.ac.at

The U.S. and NATO allies played a crucial role in stopping the bloodshed after more than three years of war in 1995 by deploying force against the military of Bosnian Serbs. The constitution was decided upon towards the end of 1995 outside the country in Dayton, Ohio, which became the birthplace of Bosnia and Herzegovina as we know it today. The U.S., together with major Western allies and NATO resources—60,000 NATO troops were deployed to the country—managed to stop the killing and guarantee security in the country. Yet the country was left divided with three constitutive people—Bosniaks, Croats and Serbs—as major political subjects in the country. Many claim that the war's results were merely codified in Dayton and the constitution, which divided the country into two entities and provided for a highly complex political system, with ethnic quotas in all parts of the Bosnian state and institutions. The U.S. believed that military support for a secure environment, massive financial investments and repeated elections would deliver results and be able to reverse the ethnic cleansing. Yet even the father of the Dayton agreement, the American diplomat Richard Holbrooke, admitted one major mistake a few years after the war: by granting the smaller entity of the country, Republika Srpska, far-reaching competencies including the term 'republic' in its name, the seeds of later problems and political conflicts were planted without any power from outside to exercise control over the situation.

It was during the war and its immediate aftermath when Bosnia and the U.S. started their close, intensive and protracted partnership which has continued with various twists and turns right from 1995 until today. Bosnia's sovereignty depends on guarantees from the U.S. in any event, but even more so today in times of geopolitical turbulence. Following the cessation of hostilities in 1995, with the EU having provided EUR 3.7 billion in direct assistance, the U.S. has delivered USD 2 billion of financial support since 1995 and helped rebuild the war-torn country, developing the economy and institutions, as well as protecting the communities and human rights of all people in Bosnia. Ever since the end of the war, the U.S. has been and still is Bosnia's most powerful partner, albeit also the most disputed and controversial.

The U.S.—Divergent Perceptions Reflect Deep Cleavages in the Country

A quick look at the figures about public perceptions of the U.S. in Bosnia reveals major contradictions behind the U.S. engagement. Just as the country itself is deeply divided in political terms, so it is for the citizens of Bosnia and Herzegovina who very much disagree on major political issues as well as the government's partners and allies, including the U.S.

On the one hand, Bosnian Serbs bear a strong anti-American sentiment. This dates back both to the U.S. air campaign against the Serbian military as the war was ending in the 1990s and the NATO air campaign against Serbia in 1999 to stop the war in Kosovo. In 2022, 53.2% of Bosnian Serbs would place the U.S. as the biggest malign threat to Serbs. In a poll from May 2024, conducted by the IRI, the figures are similar: for 50% of Bosnian Serbs, the U.S. represents the biggest threat, while 88% of Bosnian Serbs have a very negative opinion about the U.S. There is an additional, new surge of anti-Americanism among Serbs in Bosnia and Serbia against the background of Russian aggression against Ukraine. Many Serbs believe that Russia is the victim of an aggressive posture by the U.S. and NATO, going along with the dominant political public discourse about Russians in general and Vladimir Putin in particular being the closest friends and allies of Serbs.

On the other hand, a fundamentally opposite perception of the U.S. can be found within the biggest constitutive people of Bosnia and Herzegovina, the Bosniaks. Here we see largely favourable perceptions of the U.S. with 75% of Bosniaks holding a positive opinion. At the same time, the U.S. is seen as an ally by only 21% of Bosniaks, following Turkey with 42%. Despite the still predominant positive perceptions of the U.S., there is a tendency among parts of the Bosniak population to see the U.S. more and more critically. Some Bosniaks criticise the U.S. for not doing more to protect the country's sovereignty, which for years has been under constant attack by the President of Republika Srpska Milorad Dodik. An additional negative impact on perceptions of the U.S. among Bosniaks stems from the U.S.'s strong support for Israel in events following the attack of Hamas on Israel on 7 October 2023. Given that the vast majority of Bosniaks sympathise with the situation of Palestinians in Gaza, the U.S. support for Israel drives increasing anti-U.S. sentiments. For instance, according to the IRI poll from 2024, 24% of Bosniaks stated that their view of the U.S. is rather negative.

When it comes to Bosnian Croats, criticism of the U.S. is also increasing. 20% of Croats see the U.S. as the biggest threat to Croatian interests in Bosnia, which places the U.S. in second place behind Serbia. Yet, overall sentiment regarding the U.S. is positive among 68% of the population, while 25% see the U.S. negatively. The main reason for growing criticism of the U.S. among Croats can be found in the country's rather critical stance towards the major party of Bosnian Croats in Bosnia, the Croatian Democratic Union of Bosnia and Herzegovina (HDZ BiH), run by Dragan Čović. Early in 2024, U.S. Secretary of State, Antony Blinken, directly attacked Čović for putting an important natural gas pipeline with Croatia at risk.

The U.S. *'Ultima Ratio'* in Case of a New Conflict?

From a security point of view, almost 30 years after the end of the war, the U.S. and NATO allies remain the major guarantors of security and stability in the country. Even though the military mission in Bosnia, until 2004 run by NATO but taken over by the EU (Operation Althea, formally the EU Force Bosnia and Herzegovina), most people—primarily Bosniaks, and to some extent Croats—see the U.S. and NATO as the only force that could prevent Bosnia from slipping back into conflict in the case of escalation. This is mostly true when it comes to the inherent threats of secession by Republika Srpska and Milorad Dodik, as well as periodic displays of force by the special police troops of Republika Srpska.

When Milorad Dodik organised a parade in Banja Luka to celebrate the unconstitutional 'National Day of Republika Srpska' on 9 January 2024, the U.S. sent a strong message one day before the celebration by letting two F16 fighter jets perform exercises over the sky of Bosnia. The following statement by the U.S. Air Force Lieutenant General Steven L. Basham, deputy commander of the U.S. European Command, was meant to communicate to political leaders of Bosnia and Herzegovina, and Milorad Dodik specifically, that the U.S. stands firmly behind the sovereignty and territorial integrity of the country: 'Joint military events like this are a demonstration of the U.S.' enduring partnership with the Armed Forces of Bosnia and Herzegovina'. The U.S. national guard of Maryland and the Bosnian army have recently intensified their cooperation, which once again contributes to strengthening U.S. ties with Bosnia and Herzegovina. The U.S. keeps repeating that Washington 'will act' if any faction tries to secede from Bosnia in violation of the state constitution and the 1995 Dayton peace agreement. Yet is there a common transatlantic strategy behind this *ultima ratio* threat for the case of secession?

The Pandora's Box of Ethnic Partition and the U.S.' Role

In general, from the U.S. perspective different sentiments and political positions of the three constitutive peoples in the country keep producing internal friction. This is intensified by the U.S. having placed economic and financial sanctions on Milorad Dodik, members of his family and parts of the Republika Srpska's government. Financial sanctions are also in place against some Croat and Bosniak individuals, yet the Biden administration's pressure has been greatest against Milorad Dodik and his party's government in the state's smaller entity. The U.S. embassy keeps publicly criticising Dodik for his rhetoric and political obstruction, which merely results in partly harsh attacks on U.S. embassy and officials by Dodik. The political infighting between Republika Srpska and Dodik on the one hand and mostly Bosniaks together with pro-Bosnian political parties in Sarajevo on the other hand keeps the country dysfunctional and in a state of political blockade and crisis. Hence, the U.S. policy of criticising Dodik feeds into divisions within the country, contributing to a vicious political circle.

The whole paradox of Bosnia and Herzegovina and its political landscape is very much visible when it comes to attitudes towards results from the U.S. elections—while Milorad Dodik kept his fingers crossed for Donald Trump, the Bosniaks hoped for Kamala Harris and an even stronger stance towards all secessionist forces in the country. Dodik, who before the elections even said that he prayed for Trump's win, was more than happy and celebrated what he hoped to be the return of pragmatic transactionalism in the Balkans. He believes that Trump's administration will open the window for lifting the sanctions against him and his inner circle and create the opportunity for a 're-integration' of Republika Srpska into Serbia. The last time Trump was in office, the U.S. was seeking to redraw borders in the Balkans by supporting the idea of exchanging territories between Kosovo and Serbia and opening up a question of a possible pragmatic partition of

Bosnia. This would have meant opening the Pandora's box of new ethnic conflicts in the Balkans. Today, with Trump back in office, there are no signs that the Western Balkans will be high on the agenda of his new administration. However, the danger of partition in the country keeps looming and the Pandora's box of unresolved issues has certainly not been closed indefinitely. Another possible effect of the new Trump term might be a strengthening autocrats global alliance, with Hungary—an important regional player in the Balkans—exercising a decisive role, which could also have a negative impact on the fate of democracy in the region.

As Bosnia and Herzegovina keeps struggling internally and remains far behind in the process of EU integration, one particular still unanswered question remains high on the agenda. Do the U.S., beyond its security-oriented posture, and the EU, beyond the rhetorical commitment to the EU integration of the country, really have a common transatlantic strategy and vision for the future of the country? In political terms, limits to the EU enlargement promise on internal reforms in Bosnia are obvious. For example, in 2024 it was only the Bosnian government which did not manage to agree on the reform agenda needed for the financial support through the EU's Growth Plan for the Western Balkans. This was due to obstructions by Republika Srpska and four of the ten cantons within Bosnia and Herzegovina.

In essence, both the U.S. and the EU remain clearly reactive when it comes to policies towards Bosnia, failing to orchestrate and implement a common and forward-looking approach for the country. This opens up some space for other 'third actors' such as Russia and Republika Srpska to step up their destructive game as spoilers of liberal democracy and the rule of law.

Recommendations

The U.S. and EU should strongly reconsider their current reactive approach to Bosnia and start engaging proactively and more decisively against those political players who are endangering the country's future. This might sound illusionary given Donald Trump's re-election, but it is the best way forward for the West to keep the country stable. Given the region's volatility, a stepping-up of EU Force Bosnia and Herzegovina and NATO operational plans for a possible deterioration of the situation should be considered as one part of a new proactive strategy across the region generally and in Bosnia and Herzegovina specifically.

The U.S. and the EU should make a stronger and more pronounced commitment to pro-democratic and civic voices in Bosnia, seeking to create alliances and working with political forces that aim at democratic and European reforms in the country. Further development of the Dayton framework or evolution of the constitution towards a more functional nation-state might be one of the options to unblock this situation. Whether this might be possible during the new Trump administration remains questionable.

Even under the most difficult global circumstances, Bosnia needs a positive vision for its future supported by the U.S. and the EU. This is why both should work more closely on their policies and approaches to Bosnia. If, under the new

Trump administration the U.S. retreats from stronger engagement in Europe, the EU must be ready to develop its capacities to step in and do its utmost to bring the country closer to democracy, honouring the rule of law and finally to EU membership.

Dr. Vedran Džihić is currently a senior researcher at oiip—Austrian Institute for International Affairs. He teaches political science, international relations and human rights at the University of Vienna as well as the University of Applied Arts, Vienna. Džihić is a co-director of the Centre for Advanced Studies, South East Europe and a co-founder of the IDESE—Institute for Democratic Engagement Southeast Europe, Belgrade.

The oiip—Austrian Institute for International Affairs is an independent research institute founded in 1979 and committed to fundamental research in the field of international politics. The oiip is Austria's leading institute on international politics at the juncture of academic and policy-oriented research. Aside from international academic publishing, the institute's researchers are also engaged in teaching, policy consultancy and raising public awareness on a variety of important issues.

Changing Times, Changing Priorities: Will the U.S.-Georgian Partnership Weather the Storm?

Irakli Sirbiladze and Giorgi Khishtovani

For some decades now, the U.S.-Georgian partnership has been deepening across many domains, even if Georgia would have welcomed stronger security, economic and people-to-people ties. The war in Ukraine and Georgia's undemocratic actions at home—including the failure to hold free and fair elections—have tested the partnership's strength. The storm is likely to be weathered if Georgia chooses democracy over autocracy and re-commits to its close ties with the U.S. and the EU.

Strong Record of Partnership now on Hold

Since regaining its independence in 1991, Georgia has built strong political, security, economic and people-to-people ties with the U.S. Yet, Georgia expected and sought more tangible results in each domain. Amid the war in Ukraine and Georgia's democratic backsliding, though, the partnership has come under significant strain.

U.S.-Georgia political relations have been underpinned by a shared commitment to democracy. The U.S. has supported Georgia's democratic development throughout, particularly during the country's pivotal moments of democratisation in 2003 and 2012. Following Russia's aggression against Georgia in 2008, Georgia and the U.S. signed the Charter on Strategic Partnership in 2009, envisaging

I. Sirbiladze (✉) · G. Khishtovani
PMC Research Centre, Tbilisi, Georgia
e-mail: isirbiladze.ydc@gmail.com

G. Khishtovani
e-mail: g.khishtovani@pmcginternational.com

cooperation across domains such as security, economy, democracy and people-to-people ties. Georgia aspired to EU and NATO membership, which the U.S. consistently endorsed. In 2023, 79% and 67% of Georgians supported EU and NATO membership, respectively.

However, Georgia sought even more tangible political-security support from the U.S. to contain Russia. In 2024, Georgia's democratic backsliding tested the partnership's strength, leading the U.S. to impose travel restrictions on the ruling elites and suspend financial assistance to the government. Amid the war in Ukraine, Georgia's ruling party prioritised multi-alignment in foreign policy over Georgia's default pro-Western orientation, making Tbilisi a less reliable partner for Washington. Disputed parliamentary elections further strained the relationship between the two countries. Calming the storm in this partnership now depends on Georgia's developmental choices: democratisation or autocratisation.

U.S.-Georgia economic and political relations evolved alongside each other. The two countries signed various trade and investment agreements and put relevant institutional arrangements in place, leading to substantial investments in infrastructure, regional development and enterprise growth. The U.S.-Georgia Charter on Strategic Partnership further strengthened the economic ties, launching in 2012 a High-Level Dialogue on Trade and Investment aimed at identifying ways to boost trade and investment between the two countries. The U.S. Agency for International Development has operated in Georgia since 1992, contributing a total of USD 1.9 billion in funding over the years *inter alia* to: support economic reforms; promote private sector investment; help diversify energy sources to improve security and sustainability; and enhance education and skill development. Signing the free trade agreement, establishing direct flights and introducing a visa-free regime remain important building blocks for further strengthening of economic cooperation.

The people-to-people relations between the U.S. and Georgia have also been strengthening. The various educational and professional exchange programmes increasingly facilitate ties between Georgians and Americans, yet geography as well as the absence of direct flights take its toll on the partnership's depth.

Perceptions of the U.S.: Still Georgia's Main Friend

The major political parties in Georgia have cultivated close relations with the U.S. and see it as key supporter of the country's sovereignty and territorial integrity. The ruling Georgian Dream party similarly cherished the partnership with the U.S., but that changed amid the war in Ukraine and growing anti-democratic developments at home. Georgia's ruling party refrained from strong alignment with the West regarding the war in Ukraine. Its adoption of the 'foreign agent' and anti-LGBTQIA + propaganda laws targeted pro-democracy voices and undermined the rule of law. The ruling party in Georgia has made the U.S. an external scapegoat to mobilise the electorate and maintain its hold on power. However, the major opposition parties continue to see the U.S. as Georgia's top strategic partner.

The U.S. has also enjoyed a positive perception among the Georgian public and in the media. Public opinion polls consistently show that Georgians see the U.S. as the main friend of the country while Russia is seen as the main enemy. As Georgia's media landscape mirrors the political picture, the pro-government media has recently grown critical of the U.S., while independent and pro-opposition media display a more U.S.-friendly tone in their reporting.

Security Cooperation Now Threatened

Georgian-U.S. security cooperation has been deepening over the decades, yet the Georgian ruling party's turn away from democracy is threatening its continuation. Georgian military forces contributed significantly to the U.S.-led international security missions in Iraq and Afghanistan and held annual joint military exercises with U.S. and other NATO members. Over the years, the U.S. provided funding, training and military equipment necessary to bolster Georgia's defence capabilities, yet Georgia still lacks credible security guarantees either from NATO or the U.S. The security cooperation weakened as Georgia's ruling party turned increasingly undemocratic, deploying anti-U.S. and anti-Western propaganda together with conspiracy theories as part of its electoral strategy. In July 2024, the U.S. announced that it would 'indefinitely postpone' military exercises with Georgia, demonstrating unprecedented difficulties in the partnership.

The weakened U.S. commitment to European security—widely expected as Trump won the U.S. presidential elections—threatens Georgia's long-term security goals and will have democracy and security related implications for the country. Under Trump, transactional approaches rather than democracy concerns are likely to guide the relations, further emboldening Georgia's autocratising government. However, Georgia's close ties with China and Iran could create tensions with the Republican administration. Trump's potentially accommodating policies with the Kremlin are likely to affect Georgia's long-term security interest in seeing a weakened Russia.

Economic Relations Trail Behind

Trade, money transfers and FDI dominate U.S.-Georgian economic relations. However, these relations can be boosted only if political differences are resolved.

Between 2015 and 2023, there was an overall increase not only in Georgia's trade turnover with the U.S., but also in the inflows of remittances and FDI, although the COVID-19 pandemic disturbed the latter. Trade grew sixfold in this period, achieving a compound annual growth rate of 22% largely due to imports of automobiles especially in 2023. The U.S. share of Georgia's trade turnover in 2023 amounted to 9.9%—the highest percentage in the last decade. Remittance inflows from the U.S. to Georgia have also consistently increased during the same period. In 2023, these inflows surged by 40.8% year-on-year, totalling USD 460 million and representing 11.1% of all remittances to Georgia. These impressive growth rates reflect an increase in the number of Georgians emigrating to the U.S. Furthermore, the FDI flows from the U.S. to Georgia have consistently grown, with the exception of 2020 and 2021, when investment levels were affected by the COVID-19 pandemic. During this period, the 53% U.S. FDI in Georgia was directed toward the information and communication technology sector. Significant investments were also made in real estate, professional, scientific and technical activities, as well as education sectors. The U.S. share in Georgia's 2023 FDI amounted to 10%.

The main economic indicators above suggest that economic relations between Georgia and the U.S. remain relatively modest. Trade is increasing, but remains highly dependent on a single product, namely automobiles. Although FDI is also on the rise, it is still at a relatively low level. The main factor strengthening economic relations is primarily related to migration flows between the two countries. Due to the increased level of emigration from Georgia to the U.S., money transfers have reached new highs and also boosted trade relations.

Georgian-U.S. Relations: Implications for the EU

Georgia's democratic backsliding has brought about a deterioration in its relations both with the U.S. and the EU. Historically—and particularly amid Georgia's attainment of the EU membership perspective—the U.S. expressed strong support for Georgia's EU accession. In general, the U.S. sees Georgia's progress on the EU path as indicative of its democracy consolidation and as the basis for taking U.S.-Georgian relations forward.

As Trump approaches the presidency, the transatlantic relations are likely to deteriorate with the U.S. becoming more hostile and unilateral in its engagement with the EU. If Georgia's ruling party—whose legitimacy following the disputed parliamentary elections has not been recognised by the opposition parties while the Western countries take a wait-and-see approach—continues to govern, Georgia's relations with the U.S. might be guided more by transactional calculations than democracy concerns, leaving Georgia more attuned with the U.S. and further detached from the EU and its accession process. With Biden/Harris gone and Trump/Vance incoming, the EU may lose the key partner that is proactively interested in seeing Georgia's democracy consolidated and its ties with the EU expanded. As the U.S. is increasingly walking back from its global commitments, the EU must now learn to act alone in ensuring its security and defending its model of governance.

Recommendations

Given the weakening U.S. role in world affairs, the EU should strengthen its geopolitical role to improve its security and that of its candidate countries. Deepening defence integration within the Union while also stepping up security support to accession countries would be a good first step.

The future Georgian government should genuinely commit to democracy consolidation and seek to improve political, security and economic ties with the U.S. This will at the same time help strengthen EU-Georgia relations.

The new U.S. administration should further support Georgia's security, its economy and democracy. This includes leveraging the country's adherence to basic tenets of democracy such as holding free and fair elections; providing tangible security guarantees to the country; launching intensive talks on free trade agreement and strengthening economic assistance; introducing visa-free regime and establishing direct flights; as well as widening the scope of cultural and educational activities.

Irakli Sirbiladze is Affiliated Researcher at the PMC Research Centre and holds an MA degree in International Relations from Queen Mary University of London. His research interests include Georgia's foreign policy, the EU and Eurasia.

Giorgi Khishtovani is Research Director at the PMC Research Centre, an Associate Professor at Ilia State University, and holds a PhD in Economics from the University of Bremen. His research interests include Georgia's economic policy, political economy, international trade, the EU and Eurasia.

Founded in 2010, the PMC Research Centre undertakes studies in the fields of economics, politics, energy, good governance and social security. By combining global and local expertise, the Centre elaborates research-based policy options focused on economic development and accountable and transparent democratic governance. Through international cooperation, research and advocacy activities, PMC brings together representatives of academia, civil society, government and industry. The Centre is also a member of TEPSA.

The Icelandic-U.S. Relations: Back on Track

Baldur Thorhallsson

Icelandic-U.S. relations are being strengthened after a serious setback in 2006 with closure of the U.S. military base in Keflavík. The governing elite in Iceland is delighted that its security relations with Washington are back on track (in the light of enhanced security risk in the North Atlantic) and has, therefore, abandoned all moves towards China. However, the country is again considering joining the European Union.

The American Period

The period from 1941 to 2006 has been referred to as 'the American period' in the history of Iceland's external relations, with substantial political, economic and societal shelter being provided by Washington, including military and diplomatic support during the Cold Wars. In 1941, Iceland signed a sweeping arrangement regarding defence, trade and economic assistance with the U.S. and a bilateral defence agreement 10 years later. Iceland's governing parties prioritised relations with Washington rather than working across multilateral organisations, such as NATO. The country has always had substantially more trade with Europe than the U.S. However, significant American economic aid (until the late 1960s) and activities in Iceland, including earnings from the military base and running of the only international airport in Iceland until 2006, contributed to Iceland's small economy.

B. Thorhallsson (✉)
Institute of International Affairs, University of Iceland, Reykjavík, Iceland
e-mail: baldurt@hi.is

However, in 2006 the U.S. did close its military base in Keflavík, there being no immediate security threat to Iceland. This move was regarded by the political elite as an act of betrayal, as Iceland was left as the only NATO member state without an army on its soil. Thankfully, from 2016 Washington showed greater interest in the North Atlantic, with the result that Iceland's defence has been strengthened with a considerable military build-up in the Keflavik Security Zone, due to increased Russian activities and a potential future threat from China.

In 2023, Iceland's exports to the U.S. amounted to USD 674.1 million and its imports from the U.S. amounted to USD 328.4 million. The previous year, there was a trade surplus of USD 121 million. In 2023, U.S. direct investment in Iceland (on a historical-cost basis) amounted to only USD 1.186 million, down from USD 54 million in 2022. Iceland's investment in the U.S. amounted to only USD 5 million in 2023. Hence, Europe continues to be Iceland's most important trading partner.

Icelanders Overwhelmingly Backed Harris

Since the turn of the century, Icelanders have overwhelmingly supported Democratic presidential candidates in the U.S. presidential elections. For instance, an opinion poll indicated that 9 out of 10 Icelanders preferred Harris to Trump in the 2024 U.S. presidential elections. Nevertheless, the only daily newspaper in the country—*Morgunblaðið*, edited by hardline conservatives—loudly supports Trump, with its editorials repeating some of his false and misleading claims. Other news outlets also cover Trump's policies and rallies quite extensively, but they are critical of him and his conspiracy theories. The Icelandic government will try to continue its relations with Washington under President Trump—mindful of the fact that the U.S. again started its military build-up in Keflavík under his leadership.

U.S. policy towards the Israel-Palestinian war is extensively followed in the news and regularly criticised by commentators and activists. It is the main motive for anti-Americanism in the country. However, most Icelanders did support the Biden administration's stand on Ukraine, as indicated by opinion polls. Finally, there is only limited discussion in the media about enhanced defence and security cooperation between Iceland and the U.S., although some news outlets occasionally publish detailed reports. That said, the main motives of pro-Americanism in Iceland continue to be the U.S. defence commitment, which most Icelanders support, and 'the American dream' which many in the newly rich Icelandic society aspire to.

U.S. Relations Hinder Further European Engagement

Historically, until the late 1960s direct economic assistance from the U.S. to Iceland resulted in limited motives to liberalise trade and take part in European integration. In 2009, Iceland applied for membership of the European Union in wake of its economic crash. After a swift recovery, Iceland put the accession negotiations on hold in 2013—after the closure of 11 out of 23 chapters. A new government that consists of the Social Democratic Alliance (SDA), the pro-EU liberal Reform Party and the populist People's Party has announced that a referendum on the continuation of Iceland's European Union accession talks will be held no later than 2027.

U.S.-Iceland security and defence relations have hindered Iceland's engagement in the European project. Iceland has not taken up EU offers to participate in some aspects of its security and defence policy—offers which Norway, another non-member, always opts for with open arms. The current government will most likely alter this policy and seek security and defence guarantees from the EU. However, renewed interests from Washington in the North Atlantic and its current military build-up in the Keflavík security zone have further reinstated the Icelandic elite's commitment to the U.S., believing that the EU cannot supplement the U.S.-Icelandic security and defence relations.

Closer Security and Defence Ties

There is a broad consensus about Iceland's Atlanticism across the political spectrum in Reykjavík and the Icelandic government continues to advocate for closer U.S. security involvement in Europe. Iceland, without an army and a non-member of the EU, has more to lose than any other NATO member if the U.S. decides to scale down its activity in Europe, particularly in the North Atlantic. Hence, Iceland is taking a more active part in the Alliance decision-making and works closely with the other Nordic states to strengthen their security and defence cooperation. However, Iceland continues to free-ride when it comes to paying for its own defence, spending only about 0.1% of its GDP.

At present, only a relatively new liberal party—the Reform party—advocates rapid transformation of Iceland's European policy and closer engagement with the EU's foreign and security policies. Nevertheless, the Reform party is in line with most other political parties on building closer security and defence ties with the U.S. The SDP is in favour of joining the European Union but, at present, does not prioritise its European policy. The SDP and the established centre-right Independence Party and the agrarian centre Progressive Party are united in their pro-American stance. Furthermore, the newly established populists parties, the Centre Party and the People's Party are in line with them, putting aside their populist outbursts. The Left Green Movement (LGM), which lost all its seats in the Althingi (the national parliament) in November 2024, formally still opposes the bilateral defence treaty with the U.S. and membership of NATO, but has not made any demands to alter these arrangements within the three government coalitions which they have been party to over the last fifteen years. Two governments under their leadership, in the period from 2017 to 2024, were in fact responsible for the military build-up in Keflavík. The Pirate Party, which also lost all its seats in the

Althingi, formally opposes military build-up in the North Atlantic and the Arctic, with some of its parliamentarians tending to be critical of the U.S.

Recommendations

Firstly, Iceland and the main EU institutions need to strengthen their relations with Trump's wing of the Republican party. They must keep them as close as other policymakers in Washington. Otherwise, policymaking in D.C. may cause Europe and the U.S. to drift further apart.

Secondly, Iceland and the EU should revisit the close cultural and educational ties that existed between Western Europe and the U.S. during the Cold War. Educational and cultural programmes between the bodies should be strengthened to bring the societies closer together, given that they have been drifting apart for some time. Enhanced social communication and better understanding of each other's societies is the way forward to closer international collaboration. The European Commission is in an ideal position to take the lead in these fields.

Thirdly, the EU-U.S. trade ties must be strengthened and EU institutions, particularly the European Commission, need to steer clear of disputes with the U.S. Closer economic and trade ties between the powers is of fundamental importance in their increased number of quarrels with other world actors. EU institutions also need to make sure that Iceland is firmly embedded in the internal market and has a greater say on EEA rules to enhance EU/EEA solidarity (also see the final recommendation). This might make Icelandic policy makers stop fantasising and contentiously exploring the possibility of a free trade agreement with the U.S.

Finally, European states and EU institutions must show a united front towards policymakers in Washington. Iceland needs to be kept in line and the EU must grant Iceland greater access to policymaking within the EEA Agreement and Schengen. This is nowhere near as important as it is in the field of EU/EEA foreign policy. The EU should set up proper channels of political dialogue on foreign policy within the EEA (as determined under the EEA Agreement) to strengthen European solidarity. Giving Iceland, Norway and Liechtenstein a voice with opportunities to shape EU/EEA foreign policy statements would reinforce the EU's diplomatic arsenal.

Baldur Thorhallsson, Ph.D., is Professor of Political Science at the Faculty of Political Science, as well as Programme and Research Director at the Centre for Small State Studies at the Institute of Institute of International Affairs, University of Iceland. His research focuses primarily on small state studies, European integration and Iceland's foreign policy. He has published extensively in international journals and written and edited several books on small states.

The Institute of International Affairs (IIA) is a research, teaching and service institute in the field of international relations, European integration and small states at the University of Iceland. IIA is a member of TEPSA.

The U.S. Impact on the Future of Europe: Views from Kosovo, the Newest State in Europe

Labinot Greiçevci

This chapter examines Kosovo's relationship with the U.S. and its implications for EU policy. In doing so, the following matters are considered: firstly, the U.S.' role in the birth of Kosovo's statehood; secondly, public perception of the U.S. in Kosovo as well as its involvement in the country's security and defence sector; and thirdly, the implications of these relations for EU policy. Hence, light is shed on the U.S.' impact on the future of Europe based on existing experience and U.S. policy actions in Kosovo, as well as their implications for EU institutions.

Background: The American 'Midwife' of the Newest State in Europe

To elaborate on the relationship between Kosovo and the U.S., one needs to return to the time of Yugoslavia's violent breakup. Back then, as claimed famously by Luxembourg Foreign Minister Jacques Poes in 1991, it was thought that the crisis in Yugoslavia was 'the hour of Europe, not the hour of the U.S.'. Unfortunately, the EU failed to manifest its ability during the Yugoslav crisis, which was ultimately considered more like the hour for the U.S. than the EU. This was particularly evident with NATO's interventions in Bosnia and Herzegovina in 1995, followed by Kosovo in 1999, both under U.S. leadership. In Kosovo's context, three milestones can be mentioned in its relations with the U.S. during the 1990s: the U.S. delegation's visit to Kosovo in August 1990 chaired by U.S. Senator Bob Dole—which

---

L. Greiçevci (✉)
Research Institute of Development and European Affairs, Pristina, Kosovo
e-mail: labinot.greicevci@ridea-ks.org

was seen as the first step in internationalising the Kosovo issue; a letter to Slobodan Milošević in 1992 from the former President George H. W. Bush in which he warned the Serbian government that if it planned to start a conflict in Kosovo, Serbia would be facing U.S. military force; and under the leadership of President Bill Clinton in 1999, NATO bombings against Serbia which culminated with the Serbian government's capitulation on 3 June 1999, when Milošević accepted peace accord terms.

Following the withdrawal of military and paramilitary Serbian forces from Kosovo in June 1999, an international administration (i.e., the UN Mission in Kosovo) in Kosovo was installed jointly with a NATO-led force dubbed Kosovo Force (KFOR). The U.S. continued to contribute to this process by establishing not only one of the largest European military bases in Kosovo, which was named Bondsteel Camp, but also through its contribution to the international administration until Kosovo declared its independence in 2008, albeit even here American footprints are in evidence. It was President George W. Bush who, during his visit to Tirana in August 2007, stated that negotiations for Kosovo's status should be brought to an end and he famously stated, 'sooner rather than later, you've got to say enough is enough, Kosovo is independent'. A few months later, in February 2008, Kosovo's Assembly declared independence, following which the U.S. was one of the first countries in the world to announce its recognition. The U.S. has also supported international recognition of Kosovo and its accession to various international organisations ever since. In September 2020, under President Trump's leadership in Washington, an agreement on economic normalisation was reached between Kosovo and Serbia. In the economic aspect, through the U.S. Agency for International Development, the U.S. government since 1999 has provided over USD 1 billion to consolidate the democratic system and economic development of Kosovo.

Public Perception of the U.S. in Kosovo

According to a poll published by the IRI in May 2024, 97% of respondents in Kosovo consider the U.S. to be the country's most important political partner. Similar numbers can also be found in various polls conducted by credible institutions and organisations over recent years. These highlight citizens' support for the U.S. Likewise, no significant contradictions existed between government policies in Kosovo and the U.S. from 2008 to 2019. However, since 2020, with elevation of the left-leaning *Vetevendosje* (LVV) party into government, there have been divergences and differences between Kosovo and the U.S. as well as other Western allies (key EU Member States) regarding the dialogue process between Kosovo and Serbia. This was also followed by antagonistic rhetoric from certain activists within *Vetevendosje* towards various U.S. officials and envoys involved in the dialogue between Kosovo and Serbia.

The U.S. Input on Kosovo's Security and Defence Sectors

The U.S., in conjunction with the EU and other international actors, has consistently supported the establishment and development of Kosovo's police force since the war, to the extent that it is today considered one of the most professional institutions in the Western Balkans region. Similarly, the U.S. has not only supported establishment of the Kosovo Intelligence Agency in the aftermath of Kosovo's independence, but also contributed to the training and development of the Kosovo Security Force, or in other words the country's army. Moreover, the U.S. input on Kosovo's security and defence sector is also linked with the presence of its soldiers in the Kosovo Force and its military camp (Bondsteel) in Kosovo since 1999.

The EU, U.S. and Kosovo

Donald Trump's return to the White House could engender new unilateral initiatives, as with the Washington Agreement in September 2020. Until now, the EU was not such a productive facilitator in this process, given that since 2011, whilst around 40 agreements between Kosovo and Serbia have been reached, only a few have been fully implemented. As it stands, the full normalisation of relations and mutual recognition between Kosovo and Serbia are still far away. Hence, in considering the present situation, EU policy should include a strict timeline and concrete process that will lead toward these goals. Constructive ambiguity and some specific agreements on 'technical issues' do not help in this respect, as evidenced over the last 13 years. A unified EU policy, coordinated with the U.S., as well as a concrete and tangible 'carrot' (namely, a European integration process for both parties) can facilitate and speed up this process.

Recommendations

The EU needs to learn lessons from past failures in the Western Balkans region during the 1990s by making the European perspective clear and tangible for all six Western Balkans countries. There is more space for coordination and clarity within the EU to clarify its policy goals towards the Western Balkans in the next 5–10 years. The empty rhetoric of the 'European perspective' since the 2003 Thessaloniki Summit needs to be transformed into a concrete action plan achievable within the next decade for all six Western Balkan countries as a group, similarly to the accessions in 2004. Moreover, the EU should seek support from the U.S. in modernising and transforming leadership of the Western Balkans region.

In particular, regarding Kosovo, the EU should seek to harmonise its policies with the five 'non-recognisers' (Spain, Slovakia, Cyprus, Romania and Greece), and there is no doubt that the U.S. can play a role in this respect. The EU should also collaborate with the U.S. to promote Euro-Atlantic integration of the entire region, particularly Kosovo's integration into NATO, together with Bosnia and

Serbia's integration if they prefer to join NATO. Such an approach would radically transform the security architecture in the Western Balkans region. This would require decisive and bold decisions on the EU side. Failure to do so and utilise the U.S. presence to reach these political objectives in the region, would leave the current *status quo,* whereby populist politicians continue to dominate the political scene, which could easily destabilise further into a violent conflict. This would also further open the door for other international actors' malign influence. The 'hour' of Europe in the region is now—tomorrow could be too late for the European future of the Western Balkans.

Dr. Labinot Greiçevci is Executive Director at the Research Institute of Development and European Affairs (RIDEA) and Senior Research Fellow at CIFE—Centre international de formation européenne. Labinot has more than 12 years of teaching experience at different higher education institutions in Kosovo, the Western Balkans and Europe. He has also held research posts as an Honorary Research Fellow at Manchester University, Visiting Researcher at Oxford University, together with other academic positions.

The Research Institute of Development and European Affairs (RIDEA) is an independent think tank devoted to promoting and improving the quality of debate and analysis on development and European affairs in Kosovo and the broader region. In doing so, alongside its research, RIDEA organises debates, seminars, workshops, conferences, training and other related projects to engage scholars, researchers, as well as policy-makers in its work.

The U.S. and Liechtenstein: Intensifying Relations Between Unequal Partners

Sieglinde Gstöhl

Liechtenstein's relations with the U.S. developed late, but have intensified recently, with the focus on trade and investment expanding to more strategic aspects. The two unequal partners are cooperating both bilaterally and in global multilateral fora.

Diplomatic and Economic Relations

Direct bilateral diplomatic interactions between the U.S. and Liechtenstein were rare in the past because the small country had for much of the twentieth century delegated various aspects of its foreign affairs to neighbouring Switzerland. The U.S. accredited its first ambassador to Liechtenstein (who is also the ambassador to Switzerland) only in 1997 and subsequently Liechtenstein opened its first embassy in Washington, D.C. during 2002.

With a territory of 160 km^2 and a population of around 40,000 people, Liechtenstein is the fourth smallest state in Europe. In the nineteenth and early twentieth century, when Liechtenstein was still a poor country, many inhabitants (around 15% of the then population) emigrated to North America. Yet today, its gross national income per capita is higher than that of the superpower U.S. Despite an important financial services sector, the legal foundations of which were established in the 1920s, Liechtenstein's manufacturing sector accounts for around 40% of its gross national product, which is among the highest worldwide.

S. Gstöhl (✉)
College of Europe, Bruges, Belgium
e-mail: sieglinde.gstoehl@coleurope.eu

© The Author(s), under exclusive license to Springer Nature Switzerland AG 2025
M. Kaeding et al. (eds.), *The United States and the Future of Europe*,
https://doi.org/10.1007/978-3-031-83350-2_32

Liechtenstein's economy is highly export dependent. In 1995 it joined the European Economic Area (EEA) and Europe is its biggest export market. With over 10% of trade in goods during 2023, the U.S. is the most important destination overseas, although Liechtenstein's trade with China has lately grown considerably. For the members of the Liechtenstein Chamber of Commerce and Industry, which include the major industrial companies and banks, the U.S. constitutes the second most important export market after Germany and before Switzerland, with these companies providing several thousand jobs in the U.S. Data on Liechtenstein's trade in services is currently not available due to the lack of an own balance of payments, given that it shares a customs and currency area with Switzerland. The U.S. is also an important destination for direct investments and about three times higher than U.S. investments in Liechtenstein. As a member of the European Free Trade Association (EFTA), Liechtenstein participates in the EFTA-U.S. Trade Policy Dialogue.

Political and Security Relations

The Principality of Liechtenstein is a constitutional, hereditary monarchy which uniquely combines a parliamentary democracy with direct democratic rights of the people. Following an invitation from U.S. President Biden, the Liechtenstein prime minister participated in the 2023 Summit for Democracy. Despite having abolished its own small army in 1868, Liechtenstein survived the turmoil of both World Wars without being occupied. Today, it is still a non-aligned country with no military or security alliances, but clearly Western-oriented. Its immediate neighbours Switzerland and Austria enjoy the status of internationally recognised permanent neutrality.

According to its 2019 foreign policy report, bilateral cooperation with the U.S. is a priority for the Liechtenstein government. Given its history of facilitating tax evasion, fighting financial crimes is an important area of cooperation and has translated into a mutual legal assistance treaty (2002), a tax information exchange agreement (2008) and a foreign account tax compliance act (2014). In 2024 the U.S. and Liechtenstein established a Strategic and Economic Partnership Dialogue, committing to regular meetings at senior official level and closer exchanges on topics of bilateral and global interest. In the context of growing geopolitical tensions, a close partnership with the U.S. has gained strategic value for Liechtenstein. U.S. security engagement in Europe is very much appreciated, especially with a view to Russia's war of aggression against Ukraine. Liechtenstein aligns with the EU's restrictive measures against Russia.

Cooperation also takes place in international organisations, within which both countries share membership such as the Organisation for Security and Cooperation in Europe (OSCE), the UN and the World Trade Organisation (WTO). Liechtenstein advocates for a rules-based, liberal international order and for human rights, democracy and the rule of law as the foundation of international security. Respect for such values is indispensable for a small state. In 2022, Liechtenstein successfully led an initiative which mandates a standing UN General Assembly debate in the wake of any Security Council veto by one or more of the five permanent members. This initiative was supported by the U.S. As a small, non-aligned country, Liechtenstein is usually seen, and sometimes called upon, as an honest broker. Since 2014 it has also been a Permanent Observer to the Organisation of American States, and in 2024 joined the International Monetary Fund (IMF).

Public Perception

As in other European societies, the cultural influence of the U.S. in Liechtenstein is considerable. English is taught at school and the public perception across political parties and the media towards the U.S. is generally positive. The ideological distance between the political parties is in fact small. The two major parties are in the political centre, while three smaller groupings diverge slightly to the left or right. There is no record of open anti-Americanism in the population, albeit during the 2024 referendum campaign on accession to the International Monetary Fund (IMF) some opponents warned of U.S. dominance.

Liechtenstein is a Western country and its relations with the U.S. have *per se* no impact on those with the EU. The second Trump presidency will not significantly affect Liechtenstein's political relations with the U.S., but cooperation in multilateral fora is likely to be more challenging and exports could face new U.S. tariffs.

Recommendations

Firstly, the protectionist turn in U.S. trade policy over recent years and its rivalry with China is also putting pressure on the EU/EEA. The EU should seek closer transatlantic cooperation in the EU-U.S. Trade and Technology Council and in the World Trade Organisation (WTO). Thanks to existing free trade agreements, outsourcing to Mexico could become more attractive for European companies should the U.S. business climate deteriorate. However, the U.S.-Mexico-Canada Agreement is subject to renegotiation in 2026. The EU also needs to clarify its own trade strategy *vis-à-vis* China. 'De-risking' implies moving in the direction of 'local for local', producing in China for the Chinese market.

Secondly, the EU should uphold and strengthen multilateralism and universal values. Respect for international law and open markets is vital for small countries, which lack the resources for effective military and economic defence.

Thirdly, Russia should not be rewarded for its blatant violation of Ukraine's sovereignty and territorial integrity by forcing Ukraine to accept an unfavourable deal.

Finally, the EU needs to improve its strategic autonomy while working against a weakening of U.S. interest in European security as a result of its 'pivot' to the Indo-Pacific and a more likely confrontation with China.

Sieglinde Gstöhl is Professor and Director of the Department of EU International Relations and Diplomacy Studies at the College of Europe in Bruges, Belgium. Previous positions have been held at the Institute of Social Sciences, Humboldt University Berlin, Germany, and the Liechtenstein-Institut in Bendern, Liechtenstein. She was also a Fellow at the Center for International Affairs at Harvard University, Cambridge/MA, U.S., and a member of the Research Advisory Boards of the German Institute for International and Security Affairs (SWP) in Berlin and of the Liechtenstein-Institut. She is an alumna of the Graduate Institute of International and Development Studies in Geneva and the University of St. Gallen, Switzerland.

The College of Europe, established in Bruges (Belgium) in 1949, is the oldest postgraduate institute of European studies. It offers Master-level study programmes in Bruges, Natolin (Warsaw, Poland, since 1992) and Tirana (Albania, since 2024) with different specialisations in EU affairs. Students live and study together on campus in a multinational environment, where they are taught by both academics and practitioners.

Moldova-U.S. Partnership: Towards a More Ambitious and Strategic Engagement

Iulian Groza and Mihai Mogildea

The U.S. has been one of Moldova's most important partners over the last three decades. This bilateral relationship is primarily focused on strengthening democracy and the rule of law, as well as Moldova's economic and social development in line with the EU accession process. In light of today's turbulent regional environment, brought about largely by Russia's brutal war against Ukraine, Washington's role in consolidating Moldova's security resilience has become critical and prominent for its internal stability.

Enhanced Political and Security Cooperation

Political cooperation between the U.S. and Moldova is anchored in the U.S.-Moldova Strategic Dialogue, established in 2013. This platform includes various joint working groups focused on bilateral commitments in areas such as: good governance and the rule of law, economic development and energy security, general national security, public diplomacy and civil society. After a five-year hiatus due to the democratic backsliding of Moldova's political leadership, the Strategic Dialogue was reinstated in 2022. Since then, three annual dialogue meetings have taken place in Chișinău and Washington.

I. Groza (✉) · M. Mogildea
Institute for European Policies and Reforms, Chișinău, Moldova
e-mail: iulian.groza@ipre.md

M. Mogildea
e-mail: mihai.mogildea@ipre.md

The current government in Chișinău has committed to upgrade its partnership with U.S. In the last three years, Secretary of State, Antony Blinken, paid two visits to Chisinau in order to highlight the U.S. support and assistance for Moldova. Similarly, the Moldovan administration has established stronger ties with their counterparts through a series of official visits, such as President Maia Sandu's visit to Washington, D.C. in December 2022 and her meeting with President Biden in Warsaw in February 2023.

The U.S. is the largest single-country donor to Moldova, with around USD 2.5 billion having been donated since 1992. After Russia's full-scale invasion of Ukraine in February 2022, the U.S. provided Moldova with more than USD 774 million in terms of economic, security, defence and humanitarian assistance. These funds helped the Moldovan authorities not only to respond to the economic, social and energy repercussions of the war in Ukraine, but also to enhance its military and security infrastructure.

In the context of Russia's war against Ukraine, the U.S. has expanded assistance for Moldova in the field of defence. In the last two years (2002–24) approximately USD 75 million were allocated to Moldova within the Foreign Military Financing to endorse its defence capabilities. Furthermore, the Moldovan army is engaged in regular military exercises conducted with U.S. and NATO support, providing continual training and transfer of best practices to the Moldovan armed forces. The U.S. is also offering technical and advisory support to the Ministry of Defence, aimed at advancing the army's modernisation and reform.

The U.S. Role in Advancing Moldova's EU Accession

Washington has a significant role in paving Moldova's EU accession path. With the large financial and technical assistance offered by the U.S., in 2021 Moldova initiated the vetting process of judges and prosecutors, a key reform for meeting the accession criteria to join the EU. Similarly, the U.S. provided assistance for various capacity-building projects in the justice sector, including tools not only to advance the courts' performance and efficiency, but also to ease citizens' access to justice. Other activities concern the promotion of good governance, fair and free elections and respect for human rights, fields in which Moldova has registered progress over recent years.

One strategic step made by Moldova with U.S. backing was the cutting of Moldova's energy dependency on Russia. In April 2024, for the first time, Moldova bought U.S. LNG from Alexandroupolis terminal in Greece. Diversification of import sources helped the Moldovan government to become immune to malign actions orchestrated by Russia in the last few years.

Donald Trump's victory in the U.S. presidential election may bring new uncertainty to Washington's relations with Europe, challenging transatlantic unity. Nevertheless, the bipartisan U.S. support for Moldova, reaffirmed through recent Congressional resolutions, backed by both Democrats and Republicans, provides a strong foundation for continued assistance and reinforces the U.S. commitment to

Moldova's democratic and European path. The U.S. is a strong and firm advocate of Moldova's European ambitions and complements its efforts with the EU to safeguard Chișinău's interests. One example in this sense is the regime of sanctions imposed in the last years against a number of fugitive Moldovan kleptocrats, who are involved in subversive activities aimed at provoking destabilisation and security incidents on Moldovan territory. Transatlantic dialogue on Moldova's dossier has the potential to limit the influence of hybrid threats and speed up the reform process. However, any shift in U.S. policy towards Russia and Ukraine could have significant implications for the entire continent of Europe's stability and security.

Public Perception About the U.S. in Moldova

According to a recent poll released by the Institute for European Policies and Reforms and the sociological company CBS-AXA, the U.S. is perceived as the third most important development partner for Moldova, following the EU and Russia. These perceptions are clearly misleading, influenced by disinformation about Russia's role and support for Moldova, along with fake news regarding U.S. priorities in the country. Meanwhile, Moldovan citizens consider the U.S. to be the fifth most relevant trade partner, after the EU, Ukraine, Russia and Turkey. However, trade figures from 2023 showed that the U.S. ranked 11th in terms of exports and 15th in terms of imports to Moldova.

Overall, the U.S. role in the modernisation of Moldova is appreciated positively by the mass media and society in general. However, weak societal resilience to propaganda and previous wide exposure to Russian media space have created wrong interpretations about the goals and importance of the U.S.-Moldova partnership within some groups of society, especially the Russian-speaking minorities. However, these attitudes and misperceptions are progressively in the course of change.

Recommendations

With the election of Donald Trump as U.S. President and the re-election of Maia Sandu as President of the Republic of Moldova, who has committed to achieving EU membership for Moldova by 2030, it is crucial for both administrations to strengthen their strategic partnership.

To achieve this, it is essential to enhance the efficiency of Moldova's administration to expedite justice reforms and anti-corruption efforts, especially in the face of Russian hybrid warfare tactics, such as using proxies, illegally funding political activities and circumventing international sanctions. Furthermore, the U.S. should expand its financial and technical assistance to Moldova's defence sector. Although better equipped than three years ago, the Moldovan army remains fragile and unprepared to respond to any short-term military threat from Russia. Priority should be given to securing airspace and acquiring air defence systems, along with training and preparing Moldovan military personnel in this area. While benefiting from U.S. support, Moldova should also become a more active contributor to regional security in the Black Sea region, particularly in the post-war reconstruction of Ukraine.

Lastly, the U.S. and Moldova must strengthen their economic and energy partnership, aiming to increase U.S. direct investment in Moldova and boost trade exchanges between the two countries. Both sides should explore additional acquisitions of U.S. natural gas through the Southeast European route, as this would contribute to Moldova's energy resilience.

The bipartisan commitment reinforces the U.S. stance on supporting Moldova's European path and countering regional destabilisation efforts. As a small European country progressing towards EU accession and not currently aspiring to join NATO, Moldova presents an opportunity for both the U.S. and EU to increase resilience in Eastern Europe, transforming Moldova into a robust stronghold for stability. Such continued U.S. support will be especially critical as Moldova approaches its 2025 parliamentary elections, where Russian interference is likely to intensify with the intent of derailing Moldova's European trajectory and inciting instability, insecurity, and chaos. This would not only undermine Moldova's progress but could also destabilise the broader region, posing risks to both the EU and Ukraine.

Iulian Groza is Executive Director of the Institute for European Policies and Reforms (IPRE). He is a former Deputy Foreign Minister of the Republic of Moldova in charge for European integration and international law. Iulian is an expert in international relations, European affairs and good governance, with a particular focus on EaP countries, EU, transatlantic cooperation and Russia.

Mihai Mogildea is Deputy Director of the Institute for European Policies and Reforms (IPRE). He previously conducted research at several institutions, such as Collegium Civitas (Warsaw), Leibniz Institute for Studies in Eastern and South-Eastern Europe (Regensburg) and Slovak Foreign Policy Association (Bratislava). Mihai's research interests are focused on the study of foreign policy and security developments in the Eastern European region.

The Institute for European Policies and Reforms (IPRE) is one of the leading think tanks in Moldova, promoting European integration, sustainable development, good governance and the rule of law. IPRE has a proven track-record of monitoring and evaluation of the Eastern Partnership policy, implementation and facilitation of multi-stakeholder policy dialogue, policy development and advocacy activities at the local, national and European levels related to Moldova's EU accession process.

NATO's Reality to Montenegro; It Marks Real Progress

Danijela Jaćimović and Dženana Đurković

Today's history of relations between Montenegro and the U.S. is best illustrated by the country's move from NATO bombing target to NATO member. The U.S. holds the Montenegrin government accountable for achieving its stated goals of Montenegro's full EU membership, active and credible membership in the NATO alliance, improving good neighbourly relations and strengthening Montenegro's role in multilateral organisations. Montenegro is investing especially in its commitment to the development and continual improvement of its bilateral relations with the U.S.

History of Relations: NATO—to Be or Not to Be

The break-up of the Socialist Federal Republic of Yugoslavia divided public opinion about the U.S., especially regarding NATO's intervention during the Kosovo War in 1999. NATO carried out bombing attacks against the Federal Republic of Yugoslavia, which by that time consisted only of Serbia and Montenegro. For one section of society, it was an illegal act of hegemony and aggression, coupled with the fact that it did not have UN Security Council approval; for the other section, it stopped the civil war and set the basis for a new beginning. Since Montenegro opposed Serbia's foreign policy, NATO did not target key Montenegrin transport and industrial infrastructure. Moreover, the intervention was significantly shorter

D. Jaćimović (✉) · D. Đurković
University of Montenegro, Podgorica, Montenegro
e-mail: danijelaj@ucg.ac.me

D. Đurković
e-mail: dzenana.dj@ucg.ac.me

than it was in Serbia. However, the lack of precision in certain attacks led to the death of civilians and the destruction of non-military objects.

Montenegro declared its independence in 2006 and turned to the West, starting the process of joining the EU in 2012 and then joining NATO in 2017. Montenegro's economic relations with the U.S. have remained negligible and the dominant form of cooperation is still political.

However, the governments of Montenegro and the U.S. enjoy excellent relations characterised by long-term friendship and partnership, reflected through well-developed bilateral and multilateral cooperation, which is additionally strengthened by the alliance within NATO. Montenegro wants to continue to strengthen this friendship, developing and continually improving bilateral relations and ties with the U.S., one of its most important foreign allies, based on these well-established, solid foundations.

The U.S. believes that a democratic Montenegro firmly rooted in the Euro-Atlantic community as a reliable NATO ally and an impending EU member will lead to a more prosperous and secure future for all its citizens and the broader region. The current administration of the Democratic Party's foreign policy fully supports Montenegro's EU accession and further Euro-Atlantic integration, significantly diminishing the EU's political influence within the region.

Pride and Prejudice

Most political parties in Montenegro tend to see Euro-Atlantic integration as holding the promise of Montenegrin independence and peace in the Western Balkans. They consider the country's strategic position on the coastline of the Adriatic Sea as a precondition for becoming relevant in the geopolitical playground. Conversely, right-wing politicians perceive the U.S. as the main enemy of democracy. They accuse the ambassadors of the so-called Quintet (UK, Germany, France and Italy, led by the U.S.), of interference with the electoral will of the citizens by choosing who can form the government.

For NATO supporters in Montenegro, being a member brings a sense of belonging, safety and relief, so important for a small country that simply wants to settle down and live quietly. It is a precious opportunity to think about the general welfare and not to bother with unattainable dreams or dangerous threats. According to the NATO Secretary General's Annual Report for 2023, a total of 46% of Montenegrin citizens support NATO membership, while 44% would vote for the exit of Montenegro from the Alliance, albeit with the Ukrainian war the level of support for NATO is constantly increasing.

However, for opponents of NATO, being a member brings with it suspicious and unwanted feelings of inferiority, all masked under the veil of obedience. Why follow the rules set by Washington without the right to object? Furthermore, could it be paying for the past, of commitment to Russia, that is haunting for Montenegrin NATO critics? After all, a pro-Russian sentiment is part of the collective spirit of the country's society, whether it is the ideal of freedom, the Orthodox faith, or socialism. Both sides of this divide have their media for support and engagement, ever-encouraging the polarisation of society. Meanwhile, it is being shown that the tone of each media outlet depends on its funding; the dominant doctrine is never to question deeply the occasional hubris of the political elite, but silently to choose the side you follow.

The Second Trump Term Could Speed Everything Up

Trump's presidency could influence Montenegro in two key ways: directly through bilateral relations with the U.S. and indirectly through relations with the EU. In 2017, President Trump signed the Protocol for Montenegro's accession to NATO and during that time both U.S. Vice President Mike Pence and Secretary of State Mike Pompeo made their first visits to Podgorica. This demonstrated the administration's respect and regard for Montenegro, something that the new Republican government is unlikely to overlook—an acknowledgement that Montenegro should value.

In the current presidential campaign, Christos Marafatsos, Vice Chairman of the National Diversity Coalition for President Trump, told Voice of America that Trump's foreign policy in the Western Balkans would prioritise trade partnerships, economic opportunities and strategic economic agreements. Strengthening economic ties could help bridge the socio-economic gap and open doors for the Balkans toward European integration, potentially accelerating Montenegro's path toward the EU.

The second dimension involves the EU's approach to the region in this new reality. A constructive outcome could see the EU pushing for deeper integration, potentially hastening Montenegro's alignment with EU standards. This is one possible direction, but there are others.

What Can Be Done? Some Recommendations

During Trump's first term, U.S. policy toward the Western Balkans saw little change. Similarly, there was no major shift under President Joe Biden, suggesting that Trump's administration may continue the long-standing U.S. approach to the region, supporting European and transatlantic integration.

To sum up, Montenegro should always invest in its commitment to the development and continual improvement of bilateral relations with the U.S., as the preservation of peace and the strengthening of democracy is important for any further progress toward membership of the EU. Working together could lead to the achievement of important aims, such as improving the rule of law, fighting corruption, bolstering civil society, improving media professionalisation, exposing disinformation, countering malign influences, protecting minority rights and furthering defence cooperation.

Such an approach could develop the strengthening and development of Euro-Atlantic integration, as well as enhancing the prosperity of all citizens, particularly as Russia's war against Ukraine is a grim reminder that NATO Allies must all be diligent in defending the continent's freedom.

Danijela Jaćimović is Professor at the Faculty of Economics of the University of Montenegro and a member of the TEPSA Board. Her fields of interest include international relations and European integration.

Dženana Đurković is Teaching Associate at the Faculty of Economics of the University of Montenegro. Her fields of interest include international economics and monetary economics.

The University of Montenegro is a public higher education institution and the oldest in Montenegro. The Faculty of Economics, as one of the most important educational and research institutions in the country, is also a member of TEPSA.

North Macedonia—U.S. Relations: Dominated by Politics and Diplomacy

Irena Rajchinovska Pandeva

North Macedonia and the U.S. uphold joint cooperative relations in a vast spectrum of topics concerning political, social, economic, cultural, military and educational issues. For the past 30 years, the two countries have established and maintained good bilateral relations. The narrative includes strategic partnership and dialogue as well as shared and joint dedication to values promoted by alignment and participation in the same international organisations, including UN, OSCE, NATO, IMF, World Bank and WTO.

From the outset, the U.S. has demonstrated strong support for North Macedonia's aspirations. These include full integration into Euro-Atlantic institutions, as well as commitment to assist the country in facing numerous challenges as a newly established democracy, particularly vital support to the consolidation of its multiethnic society. Taking into consideration its assistance and support to North Macedonia during critically important and pivotal times in its history, the U.S. has undeniably gained the status of a key external actor in the Macedonian political arena.

Good Bilateral Relations

The U.S. first recognised North Macedonia in February 1994 under the country's provisional name of the Former Yugoslav Republic of Macedonia and announced its intent to establish full diplomatic relations. However, it had been only in

I. Rajchinovska Pandeva (✉)
Iustinianus Primus Law Faculty, Ss. Cyril and Methodius University in Skopje, Skopje, North Macedonia
e-mail: i.rajchinovskapandeva@pf.ukim.edu.mk

December 1993 that the U.S. opened a Liaison Office in Skopje, followed by an elevation of U.S. Legation to Embassy Status three years later with the presentation of credentials of the first U.S. Ambassador Christopher R. Hill in July 1996.

U.S. recognition of the country under its constitutional name at the time, Republic of Macedonia, was announced in 2004. Despite the decade of delay, this was nevertheless highly appreciated and welcomed. It was perceived as the final confirmation of Macedonian statehood and in line with its aspirations for full Euro-Atlantic integration.

In 2008 after years of struggles for the country's international recognition which affected the start of EU accession and NATO membership, failure of the 2008 NATO summit was tempered thanks to strong support from the U.S. government, with the signing of a Declaration of Strategic Partnership and Cooperation between the U.S. and the Republic of Macedonia. This Declaration opened the path for expansion and deepening of already close ties between the two countries based upon common goals, interests and values. Both countries expressed a desire to enhance their strategic relationship by employing intensified consultation and cooperation in security, people-to-people links and commerce.

The U.S., EU and various European countries are the major Western external actors with proven and recognised position in the Macedonian political milieu. Their influence was decisive during a number of historic events. These include: the 2001 conflict and reaching the Ohrid Framework Agreement; resolution of the 2016 political crisis followed by the Przino agreement; signing of the Treaty on Good Neighbourly relations with Bulgaria in 2017; the Prespa Agreement with Greece in 2018 to resolve the name dispute; and the accession of North Macedonia to NATO as the Alliance's 30th member in 2020.

Economic Relations

Since Macedonian independence in 1991, U.S. assistance to North Macedonia for the first three decades amounted to USD 891 million, including most significantly support for the country's accession path to the EU, democratic consolidation, economic growth and implementation of reforms. Assistance in the past few years has been focused on civil society and political processes, law enforcement, anti-corruption, the rule of law and good governance, as well as energy and education. Emergency assistance has also been provided to help, for instance, in mitigating the impact of the COVID-19 pandemic.

A huge portion of this assistance—USD 561 million, according to the U.S. Embassy in Skopje—was dedicated to democratic processes and good governance. Most specifically this came as support for judiciary independence, a process which is still ongoing and to date only partially successful despite its critical nature due to the poor state of the country's justice system.

An extended level of collaboration between both countries also exists in the area of education and culture, through various academic, professional and cultural exchange programmes involving academia, youth and other relevant segments of North Macedonian society. Some programmes involve the development and fostering of cultural and other ties between the countries, as well as an American contribution to the process of preservation and promotion of Macedonian cultural heritage.

According to the UN Comtrade database on international trade in 2023, North Macedonia exports to the U.S. were USD 53.66 million, whilst Macedonian imports from the U.S. were USD 267 million. Principal products of exports from North Macedonia to the U.S. included vehicles other than railway, tramway, electrical, electronic equipment as well as tobacco and tobacco substitutes.

Political Relations

The EU and NATO have been projected as strategic priorities and goals by consecutive Macedonian governments for more than three decades since the Republic gained its independence. Any support and assistance to achieve these strategic aspirations is more than valuable for a small country such as North Macedonia. American backing has been stable and critical from the outset, playing a key role: in the country's 1995 participation in the Partnership for Peace initiative; at the 1999 Washington summit when it became a NATO candidate; and in 2020 when the Republic of North Macedonia became a full-fledged member. On a bilateral level, close political and diplomatic ties were enhanced after 2001, a year that coincided with two events which reshaped or affected first and foremost the domestic environments in both countries—the 2001 conflict in North Macedonia and the Global War on Terrorism after the 11 September attacks in the U.S.

U.S. support was and still is crucial for North Macedonia's EU accession process. The U.S. continually emphasises the importance of advancing the EU accession process for North Macedonia, supporting its constructive involvement in regional stability and security initiatives, its OSCE Chairmanship in 2023 and primarily the national reform processes prompted by Euro integration. Furthermore, the U.S. regularly cites North Macedonia as being a valuable partner to both NATO and the EU in terms of facing and fighting threats to security, stability as well as other challenges on the continent and worldwide.

A 2023 poll shows that 24.2% of Macedonians rank U.S. contributions to the democratic development of North Macedonia as the most valuable in contrast to responses on American support for the country's economic development. A 2022 poll showed significant public support for the U.S., ranking it as second friendliest nation towards North Macedonia, with 18% support for the U.S. as economic and 29% support as security partner.

Recommendations

Enhancing strategic cooperation between the two countries is hugely important for North Macedonia during the upcoming period, given its stalled progress to EU accession. This is especially important since the offering of a powerful foreign hand in crucially important chapters of North Macedonian history, is certainly needed.

The U.S. has provided continual and expanded assistance to the country in facing its most difficult problems related to good governance, fighting corruption, energy diversification and independence, strengthening of media freedom, the NGO sector and other issues. However, it should now consider extending the strategic dialogue to previously initiated topics that aim to contribute to the commonly expected improvement of cooperation. These include participating in the U.S. Customs and Border Protection's Global Entry Program, broadening and deepening bilateral economic and commercial cooperation, reducing trade and investment barriers and collaborating with the U.S. International Development Finance Corporation.

Furthermore, according to the current Integrated Country Strategy of the U.S., North Macedonia is listed as a strategic opportunity for U.S. engagement in the West Balkans region. One of the Strategy's mission goals is to leverage the U.S.-North Macedonia partnership so as to promote stability in this region, in addition to the pronounced dedication of both countries to advance shared priorities on security and prosperity bilaterally, within the European continent and globally. Subsequently, the U.S. should further its political and diplomatic support to North Macedonia *vis-à-vis* present obstacles to its full integration into the Euro-Atlantic community. If progress on the Macedonian path to EU integration is not ensured in the near future, it may result in a total shift of popular support to external factors, resulting in an inevitable turn towards other non-Western partners. Hence, U.S. assistance in North Macedonia's accession to the EU should be boosted and viable in order to accomplish the country's strategic priorities and goals set at the dawn of its independence, bearing in mind that excellent cooperation with the U.S. cannot and should not be considered as substitute for North Macedonia's EU integration.

In essence, the U.S. policy towards North Macedonia during the second Trump presidency cannot be envisaged without the regional context including existing relations and problems in the Western Balkans. Some regional leaders have maintained close relations with the Trump team; however, how the Trump administration will approach the Russia-Ukraine war, what effect it will have on regional security and how prepared is the EU to manage future challenges, from security to economy, will be imperative.

Irena Rajchinovska Pandeva, Prof. Dr. Sci., is Full Professor in Political Science at the Iustinianus Primus Law Faculty, Ss. Cyril and Methodius University in Skopje, North Macedonia. She served as Vice Dean for Science and International Cooperation from 2016 to 2024. Currently she is Head of the Institute for political science, media and communications at the Faculty and member of its Executive Board. From 2020 until 2023 she was a member of the TEPSA Board.

The Iustinianus Primus Law Faculty is the oldest higher education institution in the country offering programmes in law, political science and media. It is part of the Ss. Cyril and Methodius University in Skopje.

Norway and Transatlantic Relations: From Predictability to Uncertainty

Pernille Rieker

The relationship between Norway and the U.S. has deep historical roots. This strong transatlantic bond has resulted in economic cooperation, investments and strategic collaboration. However, today's geopolitical landscape is shifting. The U.S. is reorienting itself towards the Pacific region, creating uncertainty around future security guarantees for Europe and Norway. At the same time, Norway is closely linked to the EU through the EEA agreement and there is an increasing need to balance transatlantic relations with closer cooperation within Europe.

The State of U.S.-Norway Relations

The relationship between Norway and the U.S. is deeply rooted in history, shaped by immigration, cultural ties and shared values. In the late nineteenth and early twentieth centuries, many Norwegians emigrated to the U.S., particularly to the Midwest, creating strong bonds between the two nations. During the Second World War, Norway's government-in-exile received support from the U.S., further strengthening political ties. After the war, Norway became a founding member of NATO, cementing its relationship with the U.S. during the Cold War and beyond. Overall, the relationship between Norway and the U.S. was characterised by reciprocal dependencies in economic, political and security areas. Norway has benefited from security provided by the U.S. through NATO, while the U.S. has benefited

P. Rieker (✉)
ARENA, Center for European Studies, Norwegian Institute of International Affairs, University of Oslo, Oslo, Norway
e-mail: pernille.rieker@arena.uio.no

from Norway's strategic position in the Arctic. During the Cold War, the bilateral relationship between Norway and the U.S. was particularly strong and often referred to as "an alliance in the alliance". Economically, the U.S. is also a significant trading partner and investor in Norway, while Norway's sovereign wealth fund has substantial investments in the U.S. The question is whether these close ties will remain so in a new geopolitical context where the U.S. is gradually reorienting itself away from Europe and towards the South Pacific.

Political relations between Norway and the U.S. have traditionally been characterised by a high degree of alignment on many global issues, underpinned by shared democratic values and strategic interests. Norway has consistently supported U.S.-led initiatives in international fora such as the UN and NATO. Norway's security relationship with the U.S. has been a cornerstone of its defence policy, primarily through its membership of NATO. So far, the U.S. has played a crucial role in European security, which has been especially important for Norway given its geographical proximity to Russia and strategic position in the Arctic. The election of Joe Biden brought a renewed focus on transatlantic relations, with an emphasis on strengthening NATO and addressing new security challenges such as cyber threats and climate change. For Norway, Biden's commitment to NATO and multilateralism was reassuring, particularly after the level of uncertainty that characterised the first Trump administration's approach to the alliance.

Economic relations between Norway and the U.S. are robust, focusing on trade, investments and energy cooperation. In 2023, the U.S. was Norway's third-largest export market, with exports valued at approximately USD 8.5 billion. Major exports from Norway to the U.S. include petroleum products, machinery, seafood and aluminium. The U.S. exported goods worth USD 5.7 billion to Norway, mainly in machinery, aircraft and agricultural products. FDI is another crucial aspect of economic ties. The U.S. is one of the largest sources of FDI in Norway, especially in the oil and gas sector, technology and manufacturing. Similarly, Norway has invested significantly in the U.S., particularly through its sovereign wealth fund. Currently, this fund has invested approximately NOK 1.5 trillion (around USD 150 billion) in the U.S. stock and bond markets. This accounts for about 40% of the fund's global equity investments, making the U.S. its largest single market.

U.S. cultural influence on Norwegian society is also significant, particularly in music, film, technology and fashion. English, heavily influenced by American media, is widely spoken in Norway. American culture is also present in education and the workplace, with many Norwegians studying or working for U.S. companies. While there are some concerns that American culture might overshadow Norwegian culture, the overall impact is seen as positive.

The Public Perception of the U.S. in Norway

The combination of this close relationship and Norwegian non-membership in the EU has also resulted in a greater coverage of U.S. politics in Norwegian media than European politics. In general, there is a consensus on the importance of strong ties with the U.S., first and foremost for security reasons. Until recently, Norwegian media has maintained a relatively balanced tone toward the U.S. However, perceptions of the U.S. have varied somewhat across the political spectrum with left-wing parties being more critical of American foreign policies, particularly military interventions, advocating for a more independent Norwegian foreign policy. Right-wing parties have generally been more supportive of close ties with the U.S., emphasising the NATO alliance's importance.

During the first Trump administration, coverage was more critical, particularly on climate, immigration and international diplomacy. The Biden administration has received more positive coverage, especially on climate policy and multilateralism. Since Trump has returned to the White House, and given the radical shift in US foreign policy that his administration introduced from the very beginning, the public perception has become increasingly critical and there seem to be the case across the political spectrum.

Implications for Norway's Relations to the EU

As a highly integrated non-member through the EEA agreement and a range of other agreements, Norway closely aligns with most EU policies. Yet, it has so far retained a degree of independence in its foreign policy, including the U.S. relationship. While Norwegian foreign and security policy tends to be more Atlantic oriented, uncertainty around the future of American security guarantees has made Norwegian policymakers more eager to foster a closer cooperation with the EU and key European allies. This type of hedging is likely to be reinforced due to the radical shift in U.S. foreign policy we have witnessed only two months (at the time of writing) into the Trump administrations second term. U.S strategic interests are no longer the same and it is uncertain whether the U.S. will continue to be as heavily engaged in Europe as it has been for decades. These recent changes are likely to affect Norway's relations both with the US and the EU. Norway will probably try to leverage its traditional close ties with both the U.S. and the EU to promote the strengthening of transatlantic cooperation, particularly in security and energy. Norway's expertise in the Arctic and its role as a major energy producer can also be valuable in shaping EU policies. But it remains to be seen if this will be sufficient.

Recommendation

The EU and Norway should do their best to try to uphold their cooperation and alliance with the U.S. as European security will be dependent on this for the foreseeable future. Norway can play a key role in supporting Ukraine much more than it has done so far, it can also promote sustainable energy policies, closely collaborating with both the U.S. and the EU in this area. However, while it remains essential to maintain strong ties with the U.S., the EU and European non-members,

Norway must also prepare for a less Europe-friendly American foreign policy under a second Trump presidency. Such a change will require the building of a stronger and more autonomous EU in most areas, which will require a further strengthening of Norway's integration into EU structures.

Pernille Rieker is Director at ARENA, Center for European Studies at the University of Oslo and Research Professor (part-time) at NUPI. Her research interests are European integration and European foreign and security policies, including France and the Nordic countries. ARENA Centre for European Studies is a multidisciplinary research centre at the University of Oslo, studying the direction, dynamics and sustainability of the evolving European political order. ARENA has conducted research on political, economic, legal and social integration, transformation and cooperation in Europe since 1994.

The Norwegian Institute of International Affairs (NUPI) is one of Norway's leading research institutes, focusing on international relations, security policy and global political economy.

Serbian-American Relations: Navigating Historical Alliances, Open Conflicts and Strategic Partnerships

Sava Mitrović and Milena Mihajlović Denić

Despite historical alliances, negative perceptions of the U.S. persist due to its role in the 1990s wars and biased media coverage. Nonetheless, Serbia's government views the U.S. as one of its four key foreign policy partners, especially for security and EU accession support.

Reviving Relations After Years of Sanctions and International Isolation: How Important is the U.S. For Serbia?

Since the establishment of diplomatic relations between the U.S. and Serbia in 1881–1882, Serbian-American relations have gone through various phases, reaching a historical zenith during the First World War and a historical nadir during the NATO military campaign against Serbia in 1999. Despite being allies in two World Wars and having solid relations throughout the twentieth century, the scare of NATO bombing and the perceived U.S. anti-Serbian foreign policy during the Yugoslav wars in the 1990s still burden relations between the two nations. Nevertheless, after democratic changes in Serbia in 2000, Serbia-U.S. relations entered a phase of growth, characterised by a warming of political relations and a flourishing of economic ties. During that period, there was a significant increase in the influx of American FDI in Serbia. A number of prominent American companies, including global giants such as U.S. Steel, Philip Morris and British American

S. Mitrović (✉) · M. Mihajlović Denić
European Policy Centre (CEP), Belgrade, Serbia
e-mail: sava.mitrovic@cep.org.rs

M. Mihajlović Denić
e-mail: milena.mihajlovic@cep.org.rs

Tobacco, began operations in Serbia, establishing the U.S. as the largest foreign investor in the early years after democratic changes.

However, in the last decade, American FDI and trade relations with Serbia have been substantially overshadowed by the EU and China. As Serbia's National Bank data show, FDI from the U.S. in 2023 amounted to EUR 58.1 million, accounting for less than 1.3% of Serbia's total FDI inflow. Looking at a decade-long perspective, American FDI in Serbia reached its highest point in 2019 with EUR 185.7 million, representing 4.9% of the total FDI in Serbia. However, it still lags far behind EU investments, which have consistently been above EUR 1 billion, and Chinese investments, which have grown to nearly EUR 1.4 billion in both 2022 and 2023. When it comes to Serbian-U.S. trade relations, the total trade volume in 2023 has exceeded USD 1.1. billion, with a small deficit on the Serbian side. In the past five years, Serbian exports to the U.S. have grown slightly from USD 303 million in 2019 (1.5%) to USD 557 million in 2023 (1.8%), while imports from the U.S. have varied between USD 440 and 725 million (maximum 2% of total Serbian imports). However, the U.S. is much less prominent than Serbia's major trade partners, primarily the EU, with a total trade volume exceeding USD 42 billion, or China, from which Serbia imports goods worth nearly USD 5 billion.

In terms of political relations, the U.S. has been considered one of the four pillars of Serbia's multi-vector foreign policy, alongside the EU, Russia and China. Yet, unlike the association agreement signed with the EU and the strategic partnerships established with Russia and China, there is no similar formalisation of bilateral relations with the U.S. Although all of Serbia's governments after 2000 have labelled the U.S. as one of the key strategic partners, political relations have often been under strain due to major disagreements regarding the status of Kosovo. Following five years of revitalisation (2000–2005), relations have again started to deteriorate following Pristina's unilateral declaration of independence in 2008 and the immediate recognition and crucial support from the U.S. for Kosovo's further international affirmation. Nowadays, Washington supports EU-facilitated Dialogue on normalisation between Belgrade and Pristina. In that regard, U.S. officials have shown understanding for Belgrade's positions by highlighting the necessity of establishing the Association of Serb Majority Municipalities in Kosovo and criticising Pristina's unilateral actions that inflame tensions in the region. However, Serbia's continued reliance on Russian support in the UN Security Council concerning Kosovo's status and its consequent hesitation to align with U.S./EU sanctions against Russia illustrates the complexity of the Kosovo issue, which greatly complicates Serbia's EU accession process and its bilateral relations with the U.S.

The U.S. Through the Eyes of Serbian Citizens: Friend or Foe?

Public perception of the U.S. in Serbia is still weighed down by the 1999 NATO intervention and the role the U.S. played in Kosovo's secession. This perception is largely shaped by predominantly anti-American narratives in Serbian tabloids and

TV stations with national frequencies. A study on media reporting by the Centre for Research, Transparency and Accountability has revealed that, in the context of the war in Ukraine, TVs with national frequencies reported negatively about the U.S. in 36% of cases, with only 2% of reports being positive. The U.S., along with the EU, are portrayed in the media as proponents of pressure and actors aiming to impose their will on Serbia, while tabloids spread false or misleading information in order to depict the U.S., the EU, and NATO negatively.

In light of anti-Western reporting and widespread propaganda promoting Russian supremacy, it is not surprising that public opinion reflects these narratives. Specifically, when asked whom Serbia should rely on the most in international relations, only 2.6% of Serbian citizens indicated the U.S., compared to 44% who view Russia as the most important ally. Moreover, as many as 39% of Serbian citizens consider the U.S. to be an enemy of Serbia, while only 16% perceive it as a friend. However, although Russia and China are seen as more important partners, a significant majority of Serbian people also recognise the importance of cooperating with both the EU and the U.S. for Serbia's national interests (62.5% and 57.5%, respectively), thus aligning with the country's four-pillar foreign policy.

Military Neutrality Coupled with a Security Partnership

Despite opting for military neutrality, Serbia has developed very significant cooperation with NATO and the U.S. on security and defence matters. Since 2007, Serbia has been part of the NATO Partnership for Peace programme, subsequently concluding two Individual Partnership Action Plans as the highest mechanism of NATO's cooperation with non-member states. The long-standing partnership between the Serbian army and the Ohio National Guard stands out as one of the most notable aspects of U.S.-Serbia bilateral cooperation. Furthermore, despite the official moratorium on international military exercises, the Serbian army's continuation of hosting the traditional tactical exercise 'Platinum Wolf', co-organised with the U.S. European Command, underscores the significance of defence cooperation with the U.S. Finally, considering the role of NATO-led Kosovo Force in ensuring security for the Serbian community and cultural heritage sites in Kosovo, the importance of cooperation with the U.S. and NATO becomes even more crucial. The fact that Serbia provided Ukraine with nearly USD 1 billion worth of armaments highlights its role in the Euro-Atlantic security architecture, resulting in decreased pressure on Serbia's government to join the sanctions against Russia.

Does the Road to Brussels Lead Through Washington?

In most cases, the broadening of U.S.-Serbia relations is not seen as problematic for Serbia's EU accession process due to a widespread belief that the U.S. could be a key political ally in this endeavour. This stance is based on the fact that none of the former socialist countries joined the EU without previously establishing a strategic partnership with the U.S. by entering NATO. However, following the U.S. positions even when they go against the EU's CFSP, which Serbia needs to align with as a candidate country, can have a negative impact on Serbia's EU integration path. This was particularly the case when Serbia's president signed the Washington Agreement in 2020, although it included commitments that were not aligned with the CFSP, such as moving its embassy from Tel Aviv to Jerusalem. Yet, it should be noted that this Agreement was signed with the moderation of former U.S. President Trump, prone to making moves without coordination and consultation with EU partners. In this context, Trump's victory in the 2024 U.S. elections could bring about new tensions and discrepancies between the U.S. and EU priorities, which could potentially put Serbia in a difficult position to choose between these two major international actors.

Recommendations

In terms of the Belgrade-Pristina normalisation process, the EU needs to speak with one voice and clearly communicate its positions. Ensuring that all Member States adhere to jointly agreed positions remains crucial for the Dialogue to succeed. On the one hand, although the U.S.' role in this process is important, the success of this initiative will greatly depend on the level of coordination and alignment between the EU and U.S. positions. On the other hand, it is important for EU Member States to enhance defence cooperation among themselves and strengthen the EU's military capabilities to reduce dependence and achieve strategic autonomy *vis-à-vis* the U.S. This would help the EU formulate its autonomous position in relation to external powers, which are particularly active in Serbia and the Western Balkan region. In that regard, when addressing the malignant influence of non-EU actors in Serbia, the European Commission should not restrain from publicly 'naming and shaming' projects involving U.S. companies that deviate from EU standards and practice—such as the Morava highway constructed by American Bechtel, exempted from the Law on Public Procurement.

Sava Mitrović works as Researcher at the Faculty of Political Science, University of Belgrade, being engaged as External Associate at the European Policy Centre (CEP), Belgrade. In his role at CEP, he provides expert support across two programme areas—Good Governance & Our Europe—through which he has been actively involved in monitoring the implementation of EU-related reforms in the Western Balkan region. He has played an important role in developing and advocating for the Model of Staged Accession to the EU. In addition, he is currently engaged as Consultant at Serbia's Ministry of European Integration, overseeing the implementation of the Reform Agenda as part of Serbia's EU accession process.

Milena Mihajlović Denić is Founder and Programme Director at the European Policy Centre (CEP), a leading think tank based in Belgrade. A specialist in public administration reform and European affairs, she served as Special Adviser to Serbia's Deputy Prime Minister in 2014–2015. She co-authored the Template for a Staged Accession to the EU, a key proposal for EU enlargement reform. Milena holds a BA in European Studies and International Relations from the American University in Bulgaria and an MA from the College of Europe.

European Policy Centre *(Centar za evropske politike—CEP)* is a non-governmental, non-profit, independent think tank based in Belgrade. Founded in 2011, CEP's team shares a vision of improving the policymaking environment in Serbia by rendering it more evidence-based, open and inclusive and substantially EU-accession-driven. From 2018, CEP has been the best-ranked think tank in the Western Balkans and among the top ten in Central and Eastern Europe, according to Global Go To Think Tank Index reports.

Switzerland: Sister Republics and Their Squabbles

Frank Schimmelfennig

Swiss-U.S. relations are shaped by common values and dense transnational interconnections. At the same time, Switzerland's position as a neutral state and major financial marketplace brings about regular quarrels—also in the context of the Russo-Ukrainian war.

Shared Values, Good Offices and Deep Economic Ties

Switzerland and the U.S. look back on a long history of friendly relations. Their shared commitment to republicanism, liberalism and federalism—going back to the early nineteenth century—has earned them the title of 'sister republics'. The constitution of the modern Swiss federation of 1848 borrowed heavily from the U.S. model; in 1850, both countries concluded a Treaty on Friendship and Commerce, which is still in force today. Switzerland also has a tradition of providing good offices to the U.S. in cases of conflict. For a long time, Switzerland represented U.S. interests in Cuba and has done so in Iran since 1980. Economic relations run deep. The U.S. is Switzerland's second-largest trading partner (after Germany) and the main destination of Swiss exports. With around CHF 300 billion (or 22.5% of total investments), the U.S. is also by far the main recipient of Swiss FDIs, making Switzerland the seventh largest investor in the U.S. Moreover, the U.S. is the most important country of origin for FDI in Switzerland.

F. Schimmelfennig (✉)
Centre for Comparative and International Studies, ETH Zurich and University of Zurich, Zurich, Switzerland
e-mail: frank.schimmelfennig@eup.gess.ethz.ch

Neutrality, Banking Secrecy and the Russian War Against Ukraine

At the same time, Switzerland's status as a neutral country and its importance as a global financial centre have led to recurring disputes with the U.S. Since the U.S.' ascendance to world power status, American administrations have put pressure on Switzerland to fall into line. Under threat of U.S. economic sanctions, Switzerland agreed to restrict trade with the Warsaw Pact countries during the Cold War. Thereafter, U.S. pressure has been focused on Switzerland's financial services and banking secrecy. During the mid-1990s, the issue of 'dormant assets' from Holocaust victims came to a head. In 2008, the Swiss bank UBS came under scrutiny for helping U.S. citizens with tax evasion. The affair ended not only with a record fine for UBS, but also with an agreement to disclose the names of customers to the U.S. tax authorities. Subsequently, in 2013 Switzerland signed the Foreign Account Tax Compliance Act, which obliges all Swiss banks to cooperate with the U.S. Internal Revenue Service. It is mainly due to U.S. pressure that Swiss banking secrecy has effectively ended for foreigners.

These issues have come up again after Russia's invasion of Ukraine. In 2023, the U.S. ambassador openly criticised Switzerland's Ukraine policy in a newspaper interview and official letter, calling upon Swiss authorities to freeze additional assets of Russian oligarchs, join the G7 task force to coordinate sanctions and liberalise the export of arms and ammunition. He even raised the whole question of Swiss neutrality. These squabbles and pressures of course affect public opinion. In 2023, only 51% of Swiss respondents trusted the U.S. That even this level of trust was up by 23% in comparison with 2019 also shows the massive effect of the government change from Trump to Biden.

Rethinking Neutrality?

As in earlier dispute episodes, representatives of the U.S. government voice concerns and criticisms that are widely shared among Western partners. In addition, U.S. threats of sanctions have often had a stronger effect on Switzerland than the efforts of European neighbours—as in the case of banking secrecy. So far, the Swiss reaction to the most recent U.S. criticism has followed earlier patterns of denial, indignation, as well as references to the Swiss constitution and laws. Hence, there have been no policy reversals. Switzerland has not joined the sanctions task force or changed its arms export policies. Yet, the domestic debate on the redefinition of Swiss neutrality and security policy is in full swing.

In June 2024, the security policy committee of the National Council (the lower house of the Swiss Parliament) recommended lowering restrictions on the re-export of Swiss arms. In August 2024, an expert committee appointed by Viola Amherd, the Swiss minister of defence, not only urged the re-export ban to be scrapped, but also recommended deepening cooperation with NATO and the EU with the aim of developing a "common defence capacity". Such steps are highly contested from both the right (the Swiss People's Party) and the left, though, and thus are far from being assured success. According to the 'Security 2024' study, Swiss public opinion is evenly divided on further rapprochement with NATO and on taking sides in international conflicts—nevertheless 91% (down from 97%) remain in favour of Swiss neutrality.

The outcome of the U.S. elections is likely to have uneven effects on Switzerland. Under the second Trump administration, the pressures on Swiss neutrality and policy towards the war in Ukraine might ease—after all, Switzerland enjoyed relatively smooth relations with the U.S. during the previous Trump presidency. At the same time, Switzerland is unlikely to be exempt from U.S. protectionism, especially because the Swiss export surplus has increased in recent years. By contrast, public opinion on the U.S. will probably become massively more negative again.

Recommendations

The EU and Switzerland should consider and facilitate further Swiss participation in EU security and defence policy beyond the steps that have already been taken in the context of PESCO. The Swiss Parliament should also move on deciding to ease the current restrictions on arms exports. In this case, the EU should further try to include Switzerland in its efforts to build an integrated defence market and joint capacity for defence production. Switzerland should further deepen its cooperation with NATO within the limits of formal neutrality. Finally, the EU and Switzerland should join forces in countering a potential increase in American protectionism. The speedy conclusion of current negotiations on future EU-Swiss relations would be helpful to support these aims.

Frank Schimmelfennig is Professor of European Politics at ETH Zurich. He is also a member of the Swiss National Research Council, Associate of the Robert Schuman Centre for Advanced Studies at the European University Institute and Chairman of the Scientific Board of Institut für Europäische Politik Berlin. His research focuses on the theory and development of European integration.

The Centre for Comparative and International Studies (CIS) is a joint research centre of political scientists at the ETH Zurich and the University of Zurich, offering a Master's programme (MACIS). CIS is a TEPSA member.

U.S.-Turkey Relations and the EU: Managing Cooperation in an Era of Strategic Autonomy

Megan Gisclon

As both Turkey and the EU have sought to assert their own policies of strategic autonomy in recent years, U.S.-Turkey as well as EU-Turkey relations have become increasingly transactional.

Past and Present Relations

U.S.-Turkey relations are historically grounded in both bilateral and multilateral security cooperation, based on the post-war U.S. strategy to stabilise Europe. Although the two countries had developed solid political and economic relations after the Republic of Turkey's founding, bilateral cooperation became more institutionalised during the Cold War as Turkey entered NATO in 1952. Despite differences on many political issues over the past century, the U.S. has played an active role in promoting military, agricultural and educational cooperation between the two states and societies. Today, though, relations have faced many challenges due to monumental shifts in both U.S. and Turkish foreign policy as well as the liberal international order.

According to the U.S. Trade Representative's office, bilateral trade reached USD 42 billion in 2022, with Turkey recording a USD 3.1 billion trade surplus. U.S. FDI in Turkey totalled USD 5.8 billion that same year. The U.S. was Turkey's third largest export partner and fifth largest import partner during the first three months of 2024, according to the Turkish Statistical Institute.

M. Gisclon (✉)
Istanbul Policy Center, Istanbul, Turkey
e-mail: megan.gisclon@sabanciuniv.edu

© The Author(s), under exclusive license to Springer Nature Switzerland AG 2025
M. Kaeding et al. (eds.), *The United States and the Future of Europe*,
https://doi.org/10.1007/978-3-031-83350-2_39

Over 2,000 U.S. companies operate in Turkey, according to the Turkish Ministry of Foreign Affairs. Despite calls for a global boycott of certain U.S. brands and businesses, which was wildly popular among Turkey's Muslim-majority population, following the Israel-Hamas war that broke out on 7 October 2023, American companies continue to be prominent economic establishments throughout the country, especially in large cities such as Istanbul.

Educational exchange remains an important fixture of cultural relations. The U.S. Department of State reports that over 8,600 students from Turkey were enrolled at U.S. academic institutions during the 2022/23 school year, with 200 taking part in the Fulbright programme. Many prominent figures, including former Turkish prime ministers, writers, scholars and journalists, have either studied or worked in the U.S.

Public Perception of Relations

Distrust in the U.S., as well as the West as a whole, is widespread across all political parties and factions of society in Turkey. Survey results from Kadir Has' Turkey Trends report in 2021 show that 56.1% of participants consider the U.S. a threat, while only 15.7% consider the U.S. a friend. In Kadir's Has' 2022 survey on Turkish Foreign Policy, which assesses perceptions of Turkey's relations with the U.S. and breaks down this data according to political party, a significant portion of participants (23.8%–33.7%) who identify with one of Turkey's main political parties views the U.S. as an unreliable partner.

Reporting on the U.S. remains largely negative, resulting especially from U.S. support for Israel in the wake of the Israel-Hamas war. Additionally, diverging security priorities between the U.S. and Turkey in recent years have led to frequent negative headlines. It is common to see headlines referring to U.S. conspiracies to undermine Turkey. These have been particularly popular since the U.S. decision to partner with the Syrian Democratic Forces in Syria and the failed coup attempt on 15 July 2016. Such perceptions are unlikely to change in the near future.

Security Relations

The U.S.-Turkey relationship is centred on the countries' membership in NATO, which has become increasingly important since Russia's full-scale invasion of Ukraine. While the two allies have both provided significant support to Ukraine, Turkey's relationship with Russia, including its earlier purchase of the Russian-made S-400 surface-to-air missile system in 2018 and its continuing energy dependence on Moscow, has been a major cause for concern in the U.S. To alleviate this, Turkey has tried to leverage its strategic position as a bridge and mediator between the West and Russia. Turkey's role in the UN's Black Sea Grain Initiative and in a recent hostage exchange between Washington and Moscow have been applauded by many U.S. officials and given some hope for renewed relations between Ankara and Washington. However, Turkey's support for Hamas and its (so far) unsuccessful mediation efforts in the Israel-Hamas war, threaten to erode Turkey's mediator role. Any new U.S. administration is likely to attempt to keep Turkey close, albeit not too close, as differences persist in security roles.

Policy Implications for the EU

The U.S. has been an active supporter of Turkey-EU relations since Turkey launched its candidacy over two decades ago. However, since Ankara's interactions with both the EU and U.S. have become increasingly transactional as Turkey's membership prospects have dimmed, so have EU and U.S. policies toward Turkey also become increasingly transactional. One needs to look no further than the EU-Turkey Refugee Deal or the recent sale of F-16s to Ankara in exchange for approval of Sweden's NATO membership. The EU's transactional relationship with Turkey and Ankara's diminished membership prospects are unlikely to change under any U.S. administration, as we have seen under successive U.S. presidents since the 2010s. While a Donald Trump presidency will facilitate closer leader-to-leader relations between Trump and Erdoğan, institutional cooperation is unlikely to improve without major geopolitical developments.

Recommendations

Because both Turkey and Europe have sought to decouple from the U.S. security umbrella in recent years to pursue their own policies of strategic autonomy, Ankara and the EU should facilitate closer defence cooperation to diversify their weapons stocks away from their dependence on the U.S. As Turkey has put in considerable investment and national pride into developing its own defence industry, further EU investment in the Turkish defence sector would strengthen European autonomy. Furthermore, as European weapons manufacturers have taken steps to increase output since the war in Ukraine, Turkey and the EU should work together to avoid duplication of supply. As Turkish armed drones have become an international success story, European manufacturers should consider purchasing additional drones from Turkey rather than seeking to develop their own models, for example.

Turkey and the EU should also increase cooperation on maritime security, both within a bilateral and multilateral (NATO) framework. As attacks on trade, energy supplies and critical infrastructure have greatly increased in recent years, Turkey and the EU should seek to resolve issues between Turkey and Member States and increase maritime security around their territorial waters. This would be of great benefit to U.S. security and trade interests in both Europe and the Middle East. As the U.S. has taken a greater interest in the Black Sea since the war in Ukraine, cooperation between Ankara and the two EU Black Sea littoral states (Romania and Bulgaria) would benefit all parties, especially within the NATO framework.

Megan Gisclon is the managing editor and researcher at Istanbul Policy Center, where she conducts research on transatlantic security, NATO and U.S.-Turkey relations.

Istanbul Policy Center (IPC) is a global policy research institution that specialises in key social and political issues ranging from democratisation to climate change, transatlantic relations to conflict resolution and mediation. Since 2001, IPC has provided decision-makers, opinion leaders and other major stakeholders with objective analyses and innovative policy recommendations.

The Price and Weight of the Washington-Kyiv Strategic Partnership

Yuriy Yakymenko and Mykhailo Pashkov

Not only the future of Ukraine, but also the prospects of European political and security architecture hinge on U.S. policy. The relationship between Washington and Kyiv is crucial, not just bilaterally, but also in the context of the U.S.-EU relationship and on a broader scale. With this in mind, the U.S.-Ukraine partnership carries tremendous geopolitical weight and significance.

From Chicken Kiev Speech to the Charter on Strategic Partnership

In the early 1990s, Ukraine was seen as a 'distant star' for the U.S., often viewed within the Soviet/Russian framework. It is no coincidence that in August 1991 President George H.W. Bush delivered his famous 'Chicken Kiev' speech, in which he warned Ukrainians against 'suicidal nationalism' and tried to persuade them to remain part of the 'renewed' confederation of former Soviet republics.

At the time, Ukraine was a conglomerate of internal problems and conflicts, with Russia consistently attempting to pull the country back into its orbit. Consequently, Kyiv sought guarantees of independence and territorial integrity from the U.S., as well as its support in establishing democratic political institutions and economic assistance, especially in the early difficult years of independence.

Y. Yakymenko (✉) · M. Pashkov
Razumkov Centre, Kyiv, Ukraine
e-mail: yakymenko@razumkov.org.ua

M. Pashkov
e-mail: pashkov@razumkov.org.ua

Washington appreciated Ukraine's intention to build a European-style state and become a centre of democracy in the former Soviet Union. At the same time, a key priority for the U.S. was to convince Ukraine to give up its nuclear weapons, as the fear of uncontrolled arms proliferation was then very strong. In 1994, Washington and Moscow persuaded Kyiv to sign the Budapest Memorandum. Ukraine surrendered its status as a nuclear power and the world's third largest nuclear arsenal but received no real security guarantees in return.

Ukraine tried to fill the resulting security vacuum by forging cooperation with NATO, while seeking good neighbourly relations with Russia, which seemed to be in line with U.S. wishes. However, rapprochement between Ukraine and NATO did not sit well with Russia, which actively interfered in Ukrainian domestic politics to bring openly pro-Russian politicians to power.

Confrontation between pro-Western and pro-Russian forces in Ukraine culminated in the 2004 presidential elections, known as the Orange Revolution. Victory for the democratic, pro-Western candidate Viktor Yushchenko, made possible by massive peaceful protests against election fraud, contributed to Ukraine's popularity in the U.S. and intensified Washington-Kyiv cooperation.

Over time, U.S.-Ukraine relations evolved to reach a strategic level. In December 2008, the countries signed the Charter on Strategic Partnership, which at that time was truly unique in the system of Ukraine's contractual relations with the world. Ukraine's current Foreign Policy Strategy (August 2021) further emphasises the priority and strategic nature of Ukraine's relations with the U.S. The U.S.-Ukraine Commission on Strategic Partnership is now in place. However, while building relations with Ukraine, American governments have not stopped 'looking back' at Russia, as evidenced by Washington's traditionally restrained reaction to Ukraine's NATO membership aspirations, as well as its surprisingly weak response to Russia's annexation of Crimea and the onset of hybrid aggression in 2014.

The U.S. has consistently supported Ukraine in building democratic institutions. Washington's support for the development of civil society, political culture and civic engagement, as well as cooperation in education and culture, has been significant. Although Kyiv is hardly America's priority economic partner (in 2021, trade between the partners was only about USD 5 billion), hundreds of U.S. companies, some world-renowned, operate in Ukraine.

In the context of Russia's 2022 full-scale invasion, U.S.-Ukraine relations have reached a record high. In particular, the two countries' presidents met in June and July of that year; a long-term security agreement was signed between Ukraine and the U.S., while U.S. Congress and government delegations regularly visit Ukraine. It is understandable that at a time of war, political and diplomatic dialogue is mostly focused on security and defence.

Ukrainian Society: A Look Across the Ocean

In the pre-war years, Ukrainians had reserved attitudes towards the U.S. The Razumkov Centre's studies show that from 2000 to 2014 only 2% to 6% of respondents considered relations with the U.S. as a priority. This was primarily due to the inertia of post-Soviet stereotypes, the multi-vector nature of foreign policy and pro-Russian sentiments in large parts of society.

However, Russian aggression has radically altered Ukrainians' moods and preferences, including those towards the U.S. In March 2024, as many as 80% of Ukrainians expressed sympathy towards the U.S., and 78% had a positive attitude towards President Biden. Additionally, an overwhelming 84% of citizens support Ukraine's accession to the EU, indicating a dominant pro-Western orientation in Ukrainian society. It is not surprising that anti-American sentiments are generally absent among Ukraine's leading political forces, NGOs and media.

At the same time, there is widespread criticism of American restrictions on the use of its weapons, delays in arms delivery and Washington's sensitivity to the Kremlin's 'nuclear blackmail'. Ukrainians are also concerned about the possible consequences of the U.S. presidential election.

The American Component of European Security in the Context of Global Trends

Russia's aggression against Ukraine has changed the logic of further development not only in Europe, but also globally. Security issues have become a priority for the EU's foreign policy, affecting its further expansion and transformation.

The Ukraine war reflects a wider trend of dangerous polarisation within the international community along a democracy-authoritarianism axis. Authoritarian regimes, such as Russia, China and North Korea, are increasingly consolidating and cooperating politically and militarily. The BRICS bloc is also growing in influence and adopting a non-Western orientation. There are good reasons to predict that any confrontation between the alliance of democratic states and the camp of authoritarian countries will become a global mainstream issue sooner rather than later.

In this context, Donald Trump's coming to power in the U.S. will have widespread implications for the geopolitical landscape, particularly in relation to the EU and Ukraine. His landslide victory in the presidential race and the Republicans' gaining control of the U.S. Senate is a significant political and psychological factor and, de facto, *carte blanche* for the American leader domestically and internationally.

Brussels is likely to face challenges, such as: the newly elected U.S. president's tough protectionist policy that could harm the EU's export-oriented economy; demands for increased defence spending; a shift in U.S. focus from Europe to the Indo-Pacific region; and a possible revision of the U.S. role in the Euro-Atlantic partnership system. Moreover, the EU will need to adapt to Washington's foreign policy, which prioritises American interests as understood by Trump, and agreements, including those with authoritarian regimes, over values and principles that are fundamental to the EU. Furthermore, the EU will have to reckon with the personal contacts between the Republican leader and the leaders of individual European countries. In particular, the chronic 'Orbán problem' for the EU will become geopolitical, rapidly increasing the relevance of strategic autonomy and security self-sufficiency for Europe.

While there are both threats and opportunities in Donald Trump's policy towards Ukraine, it is important for Kyiv to maintain U.S. military and financial assistance and Washington's leading role in accumulating international solidarity and support for Ukraine, as well as to overcome previous difficulties in the relationship between Trump and Ukrainian President Volodymyr Zelenskyy.

Kyiv and Brussels have two main priorities: increasing personal contacts with Trump and his entourage to influence directly or indirectly the materialisation of his election promises into a concrete plan to end the war in Ukraine; and promoting a set of preventive political, financial and economic initiatives that would interest the U.S. leader. In this sense, the president of the European Commission made the first step by proposing to increase the supply of American LNG to the EU.

For Ukraine, Donald Trump's presidency is primarily associated with a complex and ambiguous compromise plan to end the war, the parameters, ways of implementation and consequences of which are currently unclear. It is predicted that after attempting a 'compromise settlement', the U.S. will realise that it is possible to talk to the aggressor only from a position of strength.

One way or another, a difficult stage of political and economic diplomacy looms ahead, where the Ukraine war is essentially a piece of the puzzle in a more global confrontation between democracy and authoritarianism. In this context, the unity and determination of the democratic world will be decisive.

The Overseas Factor of Ukraine's European Integration

For Ukraine, the U.S. involvement in European security is a factor of survival, national statehood and realisation of its strategic goal of joining the EU. Washington and Brussels have been major contributors of military and financial assistance to Ukraine during the war. They have also helped to consolidate international political and diplomatic support and solidarity with Ukraine, ensure coordinated arms supplies and lead the sanctions front against the aggressor. Continuing such cooperation is vital for Ukraine.

The warring Ukraine has reached the final stage of its European integration. In realistic terms, after completing necessary technical procedures, the first negotiating cluster on fundamentals is expected to open in early 2025 during Poland's Council of the EU presidency. Obviously, this negotiation marathon involves strengthening and developing military, reinforcing financial and economic partnerships and fostering cooperation with the U.S., the EU and other allies.

Recommendations

In the current context, therefore, the following steps and activities by the EU seem appropriate.

Firstly, develop an operational action plan to address potential post-election transformations in U.S. policy, providing for a set of preventive political, security and economic measures. To achieve this, the EU should utilise existing strategies such as the Strategic Compass and the European Defence Industrial Strategy to initiate the development of a European Defence Doctrine and the concept of EU strategic autonomy.

Secondly, intensify the process of EU enlargement, providing for the participation of candidate countries as observers with an advisory vote in the work of EU institutions and ensure increased participation of candidate countries in EU structural funds and programmes.

Finally, within the European Commission, formulate a set of organisational, legal, political, diplomatic, financial and economic activities aiming to prevent and thwart the actions of individual EU Member States that undermine the EU, by contradicting its common policies as well as principles and norms.

Yuriy Yakymenko Ph.D., is President of the Razumkov Centre (Kyiv, Ukraine). Before joining the Razumkov Centre, he worked for the administration of the president of Ukraine as political analyst from 1995 to 2002, Head of Division for liaison with political parties and public organisation, Deputy Head of the Main Department of Political Analysis and Forecast. He studied political science at Taras Shevchenko National University of Kyiv, obtained a MA degree in Political Theory at the University of Manchester (1994) and holds a Ph.D. in Political Science.

Mykhailo Pashkov Ph.D., has been Co-director of Foreign Relations and International Security Programmes at the Razumkov Centre since 2010. He graduated from the Smolensk Pedagogical Institute (1979); Moscow Youth Institute, Faculty of Journalism (1986); Kyiv Institute of Political Science and Social Management (1991). He is a political scientist with vast experience and particular expertise on Russia-Ukraine politics, NATO, European and Euro-Atlantic integration. Before joining the Razumkov Centre he worked at the National Academy of Sciences of Ukraine and served as diplomat at the Embassy of Ukraine in the Russian Federation and as chief consultant at the Analytical Service of the National Security and Defence Council.

The Razumkov Centre is a non-governmental think tank founded in 1994, uniting experts in the fields of economy, energy, law, political sciences, international relations, military security, land relations, sociology history and philosophy. The Centre is also a member of TEPSA.

Will the UK Choose America or Europe?

Brendan Donnelly

As part of its rapprochement with the EU, the new UK government hopes to reinforce its collaboration with the EU on defence matters. This may involve an unwelcome choice between America and Europe.

The Special Relationship

Since the Second World War, the relationship between the UK and the U.S. has played a central role in the British political elite's worldview. There has been some hostility from the extreme left of British politics to the American link and some distaste for American cultural exports from Conservative traditionalists. However, in general the 'Special Relationship' has been seen as a welcome keystone of the UK's post-war geopolitical identity, particularly as far as security and defence policy was concerned.

There are both objective and subjective reasons for this attitude. Military and intelligence co-ordination between the UK and U.S. remains strong even today. The U.S. is the UK's most important single trading partner (17.1% of UK trade), although far behind the UK's economic exchanges with the EU as a whole (between 40 and 50%). On a more emotional level, the 'Special Relationship' is a reminder of what is still the dominant event of modern British history, namely its victory in the Second World War.

Throughout the latter half of the twentieth century, successive American governments were broadly supportive of British membership in the EU, seeing in the

B. Donnelly (✉)
Federal Trust, London, England
e-mail: brendan.donnelly@fedtrust.co.uk

UK a potential ally in what it recognised as an increasingly influential actor on the world stage. This changed though at the beginning of the twenty-first century and in a way that reflected the growing polarisation of American domestic politics.

The administration of Republican George W. Bush was temperamentally suspicious of supranational organisations, which saw them as challengers to American pre-eminence after the end of the Cold War. He was not unhappy to see the EU divided at the time of the Second Iraq War, with the UK taking the U.S. side, while France and Germany refused to join the American-led coalition. The Democratic President Barack Obama by contrast prided himself on his internationalist credentials and attempted (perhaps counterproductively) during the Brexit referendum in 2016 to encourage a vote to remain within the EU.

America and Brexit

There was an important American sub-text to the Brexit debate in 2016. A small but influential strand of Brexiter thinking advocated leaving the EU, in order to make the British economy more like that of the U.S. Nigel Farage publicised his supposed close personal ties to Donald Trump. It was widely argued by the Leave side in the referendum that more favourable trading relations with the U.S. would be achievable for a UK emancipated from the EU.

The last eight years have shown the hollowness of the preceding arguments. The great majority of the British citizens do not want the country's economic and social arrangements to resemble those of the U.S. Farage's supposed personal relationship with Trump has been discredited and no bilateral trade agreement between the UK and the U.S. is remotely in prospect. The economic promises of Brexit are widely recognised to have been illusions. Yet 2024 witnessed in the UK an unexpected and forceful reappearance of these three ghosts from its recent past: Farage, Trump and Brexit.

UK/EU/U.S.: Starmer's Eternal Triangle

Keir Starmer came to power in July 2024 with two ill-assorted elements to his European policy. He was emphatic that the UK would not rejoin the EU under his premiership, or even participate in the EU's Single Market and Customs Union. Under pressure from Farage's Reform Party, he even went so far on the eve of the election as to claim that the UK would not rejoin the EU "in his lifetime". However, he insisted that such 'red lines' were not incompatible with a "reset" of relations between the UK and the EU, based on shared interests and cordial good-neighbourliness. His intention was to "make Brexit work."

Starmer and his colleagues have invested particular hopes for this "reset" in the prospect of closer defence collaboration with the EU. They believe that the UK, as one of Europe's stronger military powers, will be a credible partner for the EU in this field. They are also attracted by the predominantly inter-governmental nature of the EU's defence structures. Collaboration between the EU and UK during the Ukraine war has set a hopeful precedent for enhanced defence co-operation in future.

However, defence collaboration between the UK and its former partners in the EU will not be without its challenges and principal among them will be the American/NATO dimension. America and NATO have traditionally been the major pillars around which the UK has oriented its defence strategy and procurement. While it was a member of the EU it regularly acted as a brake on the EU's developing a defence identity that might be seen as threatening NATO or American leadership in European defence.

If the EU does now advance further in its proclaimed goal of greater defence integration, the UK may find itself forced to choose between its long-standing unwillingness to countenance a European security architecture not based on NATO and its desire to maintain at least some ties with the EU it has left. This choice will be particularly stark under the second Trump presidency. Trump is not a popular figure in the UK, but he has influential supporters such as Farage and many Conservative MPs. It is easy to imagine Starmer, reluctantly, coming to the conclusion that any "reset" of relations with the EU in the defence field must be sacrificed to the need for pleasing a re-elected Trump, whose hostility towards the EU is visceral and well-known.

Recommendations

Two consequences of Brexit are that the UK can no longer significantly contribute to the debate within the EU on such crucial topics as EU/USA relations; furthermore, its own range of policy options is constrained by being outside the EU. In its own interest, the UK should use whatever influence it can muster to encourage a more cohesive EU approach to defence and security issues. However, its voice will not be influential and it may well prioritise its (partly self-interested) loyalty to the U.S. as an alternative pole of attraction. How stable the U.S. pole of attraction will remain and how attractive the EU may become as a security actor are questions to which only time will provide an answer.

Brendan Donnelly is Director of the Federal Trust for Education and Research in London, a founder member of the TEPSA network. He is a former Member of the EP and British diplomat, who has written and commented widely on EU/UK relations, particularly since Brexit.

The Federal Trust is a think tank that studies the interactions between regional, national, European and global levels of government. Founded in 1945 on the initiative of Sir William Beveridge, it has long made a powerful contribution to the study of federalism and federal systems. It has always had a particular interest in the EU and Britain's place therein.

The Future of Transatlantic Relations

The future of transatlantic relations is not exclusively or even primarily a matter of what Donald Trump decides to do during his second term as President. Trump's policy choices will be important, but the context matters more. The transatlantic partners built the global economy in their own image and to suit their own interests. They relied on liberal democratic institutions to underpin popular legitimacy. They forged a delicate balance between nuclear deterrence and conventional defence, in weaving everything together using a complex of international organisations within which they held privileged positions both in establishing and enforcing international law. Now these elements are all problematic. The transatlantic partners are struggling to maintain their competitiveness in the global economy they created. Citizens on both sides of the Atlantic are using democratic institutions to express their dissatisfaction with politics and even to question the legitimacy of democratic arrangements both at home and abroad. As a result, Western governments are turning against existing multilateral institutions even as non-Western governments focus their attention on alternative arrangements, that they themselves have created. All this is happening at a time when new technologies are blurring the boundaries between violent and non-violent conflict, while at the same time upending the effectiveness of traditional conventional armaments and so destabilising the relationship between deterrence and defence.

Policy-makers on both sides of the Atlantic would have to deal with these issues no matter who was elected U.S. president. They will also have to deal with the impact of climate change and with the corresponding need to shift energy production away from reliance on hydrocarbons and internal combustion engines. It is those policy choices on both sides of the Atlantic—and not the Trump administration, per se—that will create challenges within the transatlantic relationship. The most important challenge will be to find some way to coordinate both to ensure that the policies adopted have their desired effect, using the combined economic and political weight of the transatlantic partners to influence the choices made by non-Western governments. There is little prospect that such coordination will lead to a reprisal of transatlantic global leadership on the scale or magnitude witnessed during Cold War or early post-Cold War periods. However, coordination across the Atlantic has a better chance of influencing policies elsewhere than a lack of transatlantic coordination, or worse, transatlantic conflict. In turn, that influence may improve the chances of success for efforts to reengineer the global economy, strengthen democracy, provide security, restore multilateral cooperation and mitigate and adapt to climate change.

The Consequences of Globalisation

The creation of an international economic system centred on the North Atlantic and its evolution into a globalised world economy was in many ways a huge success. It nurtured Western European prosperity in a way that fostered peace on the European continent and even laid the foundations for the end of the Cold War as well as the (partial) reconciliation between Western and Eastern Europe. It facilitated a gradual transition from American hegemony to something more closely resembling transatlantic partnership and shared global leadership. It also helped to integrate other parts of the world into complex patterns of distributed manufacturing and varied economic relationships that helped spread prosperity more broadly. This arrangement benefited the transatlantic partners disproportionately, but it also made it possible for governments in non-Western countries to lift billions of people out of poverty and to foster the development of their economies. These were all intended consequences.

The development of a global economy based on the transatlantic model also had unintended or unwanted consequences. It tended to skew the distribution of adjustment costs onto the lowest productivity workers, first in agriculture, then in services and manufacturing, with the result that income and wealth inequalities increased both in Europe and in North America. The development of a global economy also pushed firms to rely on common market infrastructures for payments, banking, insurance, foreign exchange, telecommunications and data storage as well as transport. This created effective oligopolies, particularly in those areas where connectivity leads to an increase in scale economies and, as a consequence, opportunities for predatory pricing. The global economy then pushed increasing amounts of manufacturing activity into national economies where governments used non-market practices such as subsidies or tax advantages to achieve global market dominance in key industries (including those infrastructures mentioned early—think of cloud computing).

These unintended and unwanted consequences of the globalised world economy cannot be addressed through market instruments. They can be addressed only through redistribution, regulation and subsidies or other non-market incentives. That explains why the administration of Joe Biden placed so much emphasis on what it called a 'foreign policy for the middle class'. It is why the first European Commission headed by Ursula von der Leyen stressed the importance of 'strategic autonomy'. Furthermore, it is what former Italian Prime Minster Mario Draghi means when he talks about the need to restore European 'competitiveness'.

Even before Donald Trump was re-elected as President of the U.S., Europeans were complaining about the subsidies provided by the Biden administration's IRA. Americans were cautioning against the uses of European strategic autonomy, while policy-makers on both sides of the Atlantic were agreed that de-risking, friend-shoring and other non-market arrangements were necessary to re-engineer the global economy in the interests of the transatlantic partners.

Democracy and Its Discontents

This transatlantic convergence on the need to reorganise the global economy says more about domestic politics than international relations. Governments on both sides of the Atlantic have long been aware of the fact that governments elsewhere are using subsidies and other non-market instruments to foster their domestic industries. That was the expected price for integrating new parts of the world into American- or European-led global value chains. This was more than offset by the structural advantages retained by firms in the U.S. and Europe as first movers, standard setters and, more often than not, owners and operators of the market infrastructures—the ports, finance, currency, telecommunications and so on—that are necessary to access the global economy.

The disproportionate burdens placed on low-skilled workers and the rising perception of income and wealth inequality changed the political calculus. The emergence of figures such as Donald Trump are more symptom than cause in that sense, and he was hardly the first. Jean-Marie Le Pen, Henry Ross Perot and Silvio Berlusconi played similar roles in the late 1980s and early-to-mid 1990s in the U.S. and Europe, as did Jörg Haider and Pim Fortuyn in the late 1990s and early 2000s. Such figures mobilised support around discontent, often bringing in voters who had been long disaffected by democratic politics and then swelling their ranks with those who felt they had been left out of the growth and prosperity that the advocates of the global economy promised. This mobilisation strategy was anti-elite more than it was anti-globalisation and yet many of the charges levelled against elites rested on their connection to large firms and their advocacy for free trade, open borders and easier migration.

The challenge to democracy came from the style of this as much as from the content. These anti-elite politicians may have emerged from established political traditions, as with Le Pen and Haider on the far right for instance, but they deployed communication strategies to connect with voters well beyond their traditional constituencies. In doing so, they openly challenged the norms of democratic politics and the legitimacy of democratic institutions. They also challenged the use of non-majoritarian institutions to administer economic policy, like politically independent central banks, but also including supranational or multilateral organisations such as the European Commission and the WTO. Such challenges had an appeal across the political spectrum insofar as they implicated Western democracy in efforts to remove important economic decisions from the reach of democratic politics. The failure of the TTIP dramatically illustrated the strength of popular frustration. That agreement was supposed to harvest low-hanging fruit in terms of growth and employment for both sides of the Atlantic; instead, it foundered on an unexpected—and unexpectedly broad—wave of popular discontent (even before Donald Trump first came to office).

Whose Rules-Based Multilateral System?

The failure of TTIP was only one of several large multilateral trade agreements to break down in the twenty-first century. The Doha Round of Trade and Development Talks within the WTO was an even bigger disappointment, if only because it was a larger and more ambitious effort to bring order and inclusiveness to the global economy. Abandonment of the Trans-Pacific Partnership by both major candidates in the 2016 U.S. Presidential contest was another disappointment for the advocates of globalisation. What such failures revealed was the wide degree to which governments and peoples across the globe disputed the legitimacy of the rules-based multilateral system as it has evolved since the Second World War. It also revealed the extent to which globalisation had frustrated key constituencies within Western democracies with the functioning of multilateral institutions while at the same time empowering non-Western governments to create their own arrangements.

The Chinese government took the lead in pushing for new institutions to finance the development of new global infrastructures, while at the same time insulating itself and other governments from the influence of Western sanctions or other instruments of economic statecraft. The Chinese also became more active in the use of existing multilateral arrangements to challenge trade policies made in the U.S. and Europe, to redesign global standards and to reorganise relations among non-Western governments outside the framework created by the transatlantic partners. In doing so, the Chinese benefitted from access to energy resources from Russia and the Middle East, natural resources from Africa, trading partners in Latin America and their own 'regional comprehensive economic partnership' across East and Southeast Asia. The strength of these relationships made it possible for the Chinese government to push back against American efforts to thwart the creation of an Asian Infrastructure Investment Bank, to challenge American dominance in the WTO and to build out the BRICS group from an acronym for private investors seeking to identify emerging market economies into a forum for bringing non-Western governments into conversation.

This evolution explains why successive U.S. administrations have begun to undermine the functioning of the WTO's dispute resolution mechanism, which they no longer believe reflects U.S. interests. It also explains why the EU has difficulty repeating its support for 'effective' multilateralism: not all multilateral arrangements are equally effective at promoting European interests and it is unclear how much freedom the EU has to pick and choose between them, particularly when the U.S. already chosen. The EU has pivoted to the pursuit of 'open strategic autonomy' as a way of insisting that it will seek to follow European interests.

As the U.S. and China move in different directions, though, it is more likely that European political leaders will have to choose one side or the other than that they can forge some kind of independent or compromise path.

The Transformation of Collective Security

The Russian government's full-scale invasion of Ukraine seemed to simplify the choice. The Atlantic partnership has always been primarily about security. Economic integration was originally a set of instruments to push back against the threat of Soviet communism. That economic arrangement may have evolved into a wider global economy, but that evolution did not eliminate the transatlantic security imperative either for Europe or for the U.S. Once that security was threatened, the transatlantic partnership quickly revealed its solidarity.

Russia's war in Ukraine has also provided a sharp reminder of Atlantic security's two dimensions, one based on nuclear deterrence and the other based on conventional defence. Deterrence has played an important role on both sides of the conflict, preventing the Western allies from provoking Russia unnecessarily while at the same time keeping Russia from escalating. Meanwhile, all parties have learned harsh lessons about the changing nature of conventional defence and the high cost of a prolonged military campaign. The human toll on both sides is staggering and the personal social costs will last for decades. The success of Ukraine in holding back Russia's unprovoked aggression is also impressive. The Ukrainian government's ability to prevent Russia from accessing the Black Sea without even possessing a navy suggests a rapid depreciation of existing military assets—ships, airports, planes, weapon and fuel depots—in the face of new low-cost drones guided by readily available and relatively easily adaptable technologies.

This plucky resilience is inspiring and yet it also delivers a cautionary message. Governments on both sides of the Atlantic have struggled to ramp up their production and procurement of conventional weapons; they have also struggled to adapt existing strategies for procurement, equipment and deployment to the rapidly changing paradigm for conventional defence. Looking ahead, the Ukraine war has raised questions about the division of labour across the Atlantic. The question is not just whether governments on either side should pay more for security, but also whether the U.S. should focus on its role as nuclear deterrent while the Europeans assume responsibility for their conventional defence—which is a formula popular among members of the incoming Trump administration.

This is not the first time the Atlantic partners have engaged in this kind of burden-sharing debate. Each of the previous episodes were accompanied by a deep sense of insecurity that Europeans would not be able to defend themselves with conventional weapons and that the U.S. would lose credibility as a nuclear deterrent. The security debate that stretches from 'massive retaliation' to 'flexible response' in late 1950s and early 1960s offers the most dramatic illustration of this dynamic, but the 'double-track' period in the late 1970s and early 1980s and the 'double-zero' debate in the late 1980s were also important moments of stress in the Atlantic partnership. The fact that these 'allusions' will be unfamiliar to most readers should raise a deep note of concern. There is much that we have forgotten about the dynamics underpinning the transatlantic partnership's security imperative that we are about to rediscover – and that raises the real prospect of divisions across the Atlantic.

Climate Change and the New Logic of Interdependence

Now is not a good time for division. Discussion about the consequences of globalisation, democratic contestation, international organisation and Western solidarity is only the backdrop against which the transatlantic partners will need to redouble efforts to mitigate and adapt to climate change. Success in that project will depend on an ability to coordinate efforts across the Atlantic. It will also depend on the ability of the transatlantic partners to work together with non-Western governments. Crucially, it will depend upon the Atlantic partners' ability to agree on a formula for burden-sharing with the rest of the world. The election of Donald Trump as U.S. President will complicate those efforts. So will elections in Europe. However, failure is not an option that either side of the Atlantic can afford—for effective climate action, for Ukraine, for world order, or for democratic politics.

The European Commission's support for production of this publication does not constitute an endorsement of the contents, which reflect the views only of the authors. Moreover, the Commission cannot be held responsible for any use which may be made of the information contained herein.

Erik Jones is Director of the Robert Schuman Centre for Advanced Studies and Non-resident Scholar at Carnegie Europe. He has published several books and edited or co-edited more than 30 books and special issues of journals on topics related to European politics and political economy. His commentary has appeared in major newspapers and magazines including the Financial Times, the New York Times and Foreign Affairs.

The Robert Schuman Centre for Advanced Studies is an inter-disciplinary research centre at the heart of the European University Institute (EUI) in Florence. It was established in 1992 to complement the four disciplinary departments that make up the EUI with the vocation of being involved in both basic and policy research, collaborating with other centres of excellence in Europe.

Co-funded by
the European Union

GPSR Compliance

The European Union's (EU) General Product Safety Regulation (GPSR) is a set of rules that requires consumer products to be safe and our obligations to ensure this.

If you have any concerns about our products, you can contact us on

ProductSafety@springernature.com

In case Publisher is established outside the EU, the EU authorized representative is:

Springer Nature Customer Service Center GmbH
Europaplatz 3
69115 Heidelberg, Germany

www.ingramcontent.com/pod-product-compliance
Lightning Source LLC
LaVergne TN
LVHW010340260326
834688LV00036B/799